MEDIACOLOGY

Studies in the
Postmodern Theory of Education

Joe L. Kincheloe and Shirley R. Steinberg
General Editors

Vol. 343

PETER LANG
New York • Washington, D.C./Baltimore • Bern
Frankfurt am Main • Berlin • Brussels • Vienna • Oxford

Antonio López

MEDIACOLOGY

A Multicultural Approach to Media Literacy in the Twenty-first Century

PETER LANG
New York • Washington, D.C./Baltimore • Bern
Frankfurt am Main • Berlin • Brussels • Vienna • Oxford

Library of Congress Cataloging-in-Publication Data

López, Antonio.
Mediacology: a multicultural approach to media literacy
in the twenty-first century / Antonio López.
p. cm. — (Counterpoints; v. 343)
Includes bibliographical references.
1. Media literacy. 2. Mass media—Study and teaching.
3. Mass media and technology. 4. Human ecology. I. Title.
P96.M4L67   302.23–dc22   2008003299
ISBN 978-0-8204-9707-5
ISSN 1058-1634

Bibliographic information published by **Die Deutsche Bibliothek**.
Die Deutsche Bibliothek lists this publication in the "Deutsche
Nationalbibliografie"; detailed bibliographic data is available
on the Internet at http://dnb.ddb.de/.

Cover image by Antonio López

The paper in this book meets the guidelines for permanence and durability
of the Committee on Production Guidelines for Book Longevity
of the Council of Library Resources.

© 2008 Antonio López
Peter Lang Publishing, Inc., New York
29 Broadway, 18th floor, New York, NY 10006
www.peterlang.com

Printed in the United States of America

This book is dedicated to the Hopi people and Verde Valley School.

Without them I would not have known the alternative path.

And to Cristina and Kika for being the light.

Contents

A User's Guide to Mediacology

To cultivate one's soul is then the quest that will back up the skills of the eyes, the ears, the hands and the body with the synthetic power of the mind and ultimately will cast aside the cages of separateness. Separateness is a peculiar invention of man and it is a menace to his position within the evolving universe. Small or large, the individual work is a contribution toward or an inquiry on the body of the species. The responsibility is personal and awesome and the punishment is as intrinsic to the performance as much as are the rewards. Each of us is a universal man or woman because we all are of the universe. To neglect this is purely to neglect oneself, a neglect that kills.

Paolo Soleri, *The Bridge Between Matter & Spirit Is Matter Becoming Spirit*

The principal theme of this book is that current media literacy pedagogy is stuck in the nineteenth century. Most current media education practices view media from a print literate perspective and dualism of the Cartesian thought. Print has a specific history that evolved from alphabetic literacy and has a particular way of biasing the world. People of the Western intellectual tradition see their own media as teleological, meaning it comes from an evolutionary trajectory of inevitability. One of these intellectual legacies is to view reality as inherently false; the other is to believe we are autonomous beings disconnected from the environment. These attitudes and the remarkable technology of the alphabet were refined and codified by the Greeks. It's astonishing that in an era of globalization when we could learn so much from other cultures, we have so internalized these beliefs we rarely look beyond them.

In my life I have been fortunate enough to experience an alternative epistemology. As both a student and teacher in Native American communities, what I have learned is that if you tune into the natural rhythms of life and nature, life then becomes very real. Part of the problem is that the Western intellectual tradition is always going against the grain and is preoccupied with theological questions that we call philosophy. Long before the rise of academia, Buddha, the creator of the first known mindfulness approach, was well aware of this problem and refused to answer philosophical questions because he viewed them as leading to more misery. Buddha was concerned with alleviating suffering, so he centered his teachings on the practical. In a sense you could say this is also true of my approach. I have suffered greatly from probing the deep philosophical problems of the West, yet I have never come closer to any kind of resolution, just as modern science has not made humans more peaceful. Moreover, as someone deeply concerned about education and the powerful impact of media on youth, I have become more and more dissatisfied with various books about the problem with media and their attendant activist approaches because all they do is make me fearful and feel disempowered. It's a tough pill to swallow when every critical discussion you read deepens the sense that your only lot in life is to be brainwashed by the system. And the remedy is no better. The position of most media critics is just to be critical. Frankly, I'm tired of being enraged by the people who should be my allies.

My personal breakthrough came as a result of deploying what cognition expert Edward de Bono calls "water logic." In his study of the brain, Bono identified a faulty thought process that is endangering humanity and the planet. He calls it "rock logic." This is the intellectual legacy of the West: identifying with a rigid structure and logic based on true or false, right and wrong that keeps us spinning in circles like the center of a Tibetan mandala in which a cock, pig and snake chase each other round and round because of their rigid adherence to stubborn mental attitudes. The brain, according to Bono, does not function in a linear fashion such as the old image of an operator sitting at the helm of a phone switchboard—a perception based on the belief in a soul. Rather, the brain works on the principle of self-organization and patterning. There is no operator at the control panel, but rather there is a holistic, nonlinear, holographic process at play. Not surprisingly, theories about the universe and biology are coming to the same conclusion.

In terms of how this applies to media education, consider the analogy of euclidean geometry. It works perfectly well when applied to flat surfaces but fails when applied to spheres (as in parallel lines never connect on a plane, but do so on a sphere). So though euclidean geometry is perfectly logical and reasonable in one universe, it completely fails in another. In a sense it is like different game worlds. Pac-Man would surely die quickly in World of Warcraft and vice versa. It's necessary to understand the operating principles of the game spaces we occupy so as to be effective strategists and players. Consequently, producing disempowered students who replicate the assumptions of the power structure as a result of our pedagogy serves nobody. It fails the underlying goal of education, which is to teach how to learn, not what to think. To paraphrase a famous biblical passage, rather than produce miracles we must teach people how to fish. The question remains, will they be better at fishing in Flatland, or in the spherical realm of new media?

The problem with conventional media education is that it focuses on effects/causes instead of design. The former approach is like allopathic cancer therapy: remove the tumor and poison the body with as many toxins as possible. The latter is akin to acupuncture: work with the body's design to strengthen its system so it can heal itself. The approach I advocate is a combination of media literacy and ecology, something I call mediacology: a holistic path to media education that is closer to acupuncture, and can be likened to the difference between organic and permaculture gardening versus industrial farming.

Admittedly I'm a bit of an outsider; my approach to media and education comes from a punk rock, do-it-yourself approach, with a tinge of polemics. I don't hold any degrees in education, but my PhD in punk rock has taught me to be more than a witness and to do it myself, that is, become a self-educated practitioner. With glue, scissors and tape in hand, as an old school zine publisher, I take Mark P.'s infamous punk challenge to heart: "This is a chord. This is another. This is a third. *Now form a band.*" So consider this my postmodern-pagan, garage band attack on the epistemology of the West. In my three-chord theory pursuit (I acknowledge that I favor particular "chords," such as Marshall McLuhan, Neil Postman, and Fritjof Capra), I've ended up in one of those Borges libraries that never ends, using the hypertext of print architecture to jump from one footnote to another. I ask in advance that you forgive my Gen X sensibility to cut-and-paste and DJ my way through this process. No doubt some gaps will exist, and my beats didn't quite match between cuts, but I did my best to take my intuition and flesh it out with critical and theoretical concepts that can help clarify my process—some by academics, a lot by visionaries from outside the academy. If there is one thing I did learn in my undergrad epistemology seminar, universities tightly guard their thinking and, as the saying goes, paradigms change one funeral at a time.

I'm well aware of the irony that my principal criticism of media literacy is that it uses a print literacy model and that I am writing a book to explain why this is a problem. Despite my criticism, I remain one of the biggest fans of books, obsessively collecting them and spending my retirement funds to maintain an ever-growing library (too bad books don't pay rent!). Even more ironic, I feel compelled to quote books as a way of legitimizing my argument. As you will see, one of my chief concerns is how we justify ideas based on whether or not they are reified; and one of the primary ways concepts get "thingified" is by putting them in books. Since I am arguing that media literacy in the twenty-first century requires a circular approach because digital media fits closer to this model than does print, how does one proceed given the linear nature of a book? I've chosen to break my arguments into discrete chunks, or meditations, if you will, that flow in a particular pattern like water down a drainage basin. But along the way there are some twists and turns, snags and rocks. In some cases the flow goes backward. But rest assured, in the appendix there are some practical tools that can be applied in the classroom.

Activist approaches often call for the heroic individual to liberate society from corporate tyranny, yet they rarely challenge traditional pedagogy. They create an "us" versus "them" view of media, inadvertently allowing their position to be framed by the dominant culture. "Opposition" and "resistance" are ennobling labels, but I suggest that it is better to be a "proposition"; it is certainly more proactive and less angry. As an evolving media educator, I've learned that demonizing media is not an effective way to engage youth. Media interact with their world and rather than rip apart that reality, it's better to show them how to engage it mindfully. Let them discover how to be learners and explorers of their environment and habitat. Finally, a popular media activist slogan, "reclaim the media," is a defeatist view that we no longer have media; that is certainly not the case, especially coming from independent media producers. Moreover, media are not something possessed any more than language is something owned. Such sweeping hostility against corporate media systems reflects older, combative views of media that seemed true under conditions of modernity when individuals believed they had clearly defined positions in relationship to mass media, governments, and corporations. But our moment of postmodernity blurs those boundaries: consumers are also producers of media. So why do we still design our activist and educational strategies as if these boundaries exist? This is not to deny a very real problem of corporate consolidation of mass media, but I propose more of a strategy akin to the Japanese martial art of aikido, in which you let the weight of your opponent become self-defeating while you build a base founded on cognition, community, networks, and education.

The continued anger and fear generated by media activists can be a kind of mental violence, so I think it's worthwhile to recall what the Dalai Lama said about violent resistance to the occupation of Tibet. He remarked that the mind can justify any sort of bloodshed, but the heart would never go along with it. To pursue violence is to go to war with oneself. Thus he concludes, "They have taken everything away from us, I won't let them take away my mind." I'm aware that the defenders of rock logic can be vicious predators who will guard their thought system until death. Just look at the current slate of wars being waged in the name of belief and it is easy to see why a more flexible prototype of human needs cultivation. It is my hope that this book can at least be one stream that enters the flow of a greater understanding of how best to harmonize with the principles of nature, media, and education, and that it helps avoid the very thing that the late-great science fiction writer Philip K. Dick (1991, p.134) warned us against: "To fight the Empire is to be infected by its derangement. This is a paradox: whoever defeats a segment of the Empire becomes the Empire; it proliferates like a virus, imposing its form on its enemies. Thereby it becomes its enemies."

Acknowledgments

I would like to thank many of the people who contributed to this project, both directly and indirectly. I first want to acknowledge my high school, Verde Valley School, which was responsible for planting the primary seed of this book. It was because of the school's annual field trip program that I had an opportunity to live in Hopiland. It goes without saying that the graciousness of the Banyacya family during my stay at Hopi, and Thomas in particular, also set the tone for the ideas that would eventually become this book. My experience at the Turtle Island Bioregional Gathering in Tepoztlan, Mexico in 1996 and my later dialogues with Frances Harwood (RIP) at the Ecoversity were essential to exposing me to the concepts of permaculture and bioregionalism. I thank the Bioneers for deepening my understanding of ecology. Thankfulness for all the Native American communities that have hosted me and taught me so much. Without that experience none of the words in the book would have been possible.

Many of the ideas in this book are an extension of my chapter in the *Learning Race and Ethnicity* book from the MacArthur Foundation's Digital Learning in the 21st Century book series. I thank Henry Jenkins for critiquing the early form of the work, Anna Everett for including me in the series and for helping shape the initial piece, and the other authors who gave feedback (Ambar Basu, Graham D. Bodie, Dara N. Byrne, Jessie Daniels, Mohan J. Dutta, Raiford Guins, Guisela Latorre, Chela Sandoval, Tyrone D. Taborn, Douglas Thomas). Mark Ericson and Whitney Laughlin also gave me invaluable advice in the early stages of the draft.

The New Mexico Media Literacy Project, whose methodology I learned during one of its annual catalyst trainings, initially inspired the worksheets in the appendix. The ideas in "Reading Aesthetics" were inspired by the work of media educator and artist, T.Foley. Carrie McLaren of *Stay Free!* deserves credit for the plant survey idea mentioned in chapter three.

Thanks to Derrick de Kerckhove for letting me use the graphic for "Figure 3" on page 35.

A million thanks to Shirley Steinberg who invited me to write this book. And gratitude to the fine folks at Peter Lang, in particular Chris Myers and Sophie Appel, for guiding me through the editorial process.

Of course, the collective and distributed intelligence of the media literacy movement contributed to the various ideas of this project. Keep up the good fight!

I'd also like to mention Paul Ryan and Paolo Carpignano at the New School for inspiring the development of many thoughts used in this text.

If it were not for the value my family placed on education, I wouldn't be doing this in the first place, so a shout out to my grandparents who pioneered education back in the day, and to my parents for supporting me and creating an educational environment.

Mitakuye oyasin!

Media Permaculture

You are a part of the earth, and the earth is a part of you. You did not weave the web of life, you are merely a strand in it. Whatever you do to the web, you do to yourself.

Chief Seattle

Failure to understand the organic character of electric technology is evident in our continuing concern with the dangers of mechanizing the world. Rather, we are in great danger of wiping out our entire investment in the preelectric technology of the literate and mechanical kind by means of an indiscriminate use of electrical energy.

Marshall McLuhan, *Understanding Media*

Though most media literacy practitioners are probably not conscious of this, I now believe the goal of media education is to help people find a sense of place, butressing the argument that the Western pathology is the consequence of individuals having no stable center. The process of the capitalist enclosure to uproot people from the land, to dislocate their center, and to reconfigure their consciousness into an abstraction is just the latest symptom of a much more ancient design flaw in our particular model of civilization. As Naomi Klein (2007) argues in her tome, *The Shock Doctrine*, the way for people to recover from displacement and shock is to know where they are, to be oriented. Trouble is, if you are sleepwalking, how is that possible? The visual evidence of our collective fugue abounds. Increasingly, hotels that are way stations for the international business traveler have created palatial beds with ridiculous pyramids of pillows and comforters that serve as props for larger televisions with expanding content delivery networks. Americans appear to wander in a trance state, with our daily dress more and more resembling pajamas. News programs are framed by advertising for psychoactive medications for maladies such as "Social Anxiety Disorder," as in alienation, but we're now too screwed up to even be alienated. On the surface this reality progressively resembles a frightening dystopia, and my sense is that most media literacy educators I have come into contact with are trying to provide an orientation device to ground people who are lost in this decentered reality of somnambulant mediation.

Curiously, more than a hundred years ago there was an institutionally created pathology called "mad traveler's fugue," in which people overcome by a possessed state found themselves in new, unknown locations when their lucidity returned. Ian Hacking's (1998) study of this strange phenomenon has a lot of parallels with the work of media scholars who examined the shifts of consciousness taking place in the nineteenth century. He uses an "ecological niche" metaphor to explain the rise and fall of the diagnosis of the fugue pathology in Europe. Hacking says that two conditions in particular make the ground fertile for the concept: travel and disassociation caused by trauma. Mary Ann Doane and Jonathan Crary have both addressed these elements in their study of nineteenth-century media. Both agree that modernity was a kind of shock to society, one key element being the speed by which people could travel, mainly by train. Crary discusses the problem of attention. Industrialization required workers to focus on repetitive, focused tasks, yet new urbanization, mass media, and travel created a kaleidoscope of sensory experience that required a mental kind of multitasking. The requirements of the division of labor came into conflict with new sensory input, thereby causing a state that is not unlike schizophrenia. It's no wonder that Freud's concept of an unconscious would arrive around the same time: there needed to be a way to explain dueling realities and modes of perception.

Hacking also discusses the "double consciousness" diagnosis that predated the concept of schizophrenia. "Doubling," in relation to Doane, was a by-product of recorded media. It may seem trivial to us now because we are accustomed to it, but the ability to record time with photography, film, and wax cylinders was a conceptual shock. Some early reactions to the new technology were to apply a "spiritualist" approach: records and photographs were believed to capture spirits. The concept of electricity and telegraphy, which separated communication from geography (that is a message could be delivered instantaneously rather than by horse, human, or train), was also believed to have supernatural components. Doane's novel study of early cinema also makes the argument that technological catastrophe had become a social anxiety, symbolized by train wrecks and maintained today through our fixation on plane accidents (which are minor social problems in comparison to

AIDS and smoking). New media of that era was a way of containing "time" and "contingency," and hence "catastrophe," all elements that were fast escaping social control and the mental order that had defined European civilization since the Greeks. The lost time of the fugue and its relationship to travel has an eerie resemblance to these other anxieties. Travel coupled with new media meant that time was being "lost," and that there was a kind of mental and social disorder resulting from the rupture. Though the fugue diagnosis did not take off in the United States, it may have manifested in other forms, such as the alien abduction phenomena that later came about as a delayed response to the social anxiety of time and space disruptions, or in their antecedent embodied by Indian abduction novels. The shock of modernity and emerging electrically powered media certainly contributed to the ecological niche that made fugues vogue in Europe, and now we are confronted with a similar kind of disturbance with new digital media challenging our conceptions of reality.

Obviously the psychoactive drugs marketed these days are not the solution. But what about media literacy? The problem has become that many of the tactics and strategies of media education are also caught up in the ecological niche of the Western intellectual mindset; so though the tools of media literacy are supposed to center us in some kind of objective reality where truth is clear and corporations suck, the techniques may in fact reinforce the same reality construction they purport to fight. Unfortunately, we may have become victims of our own metaphors. By focusing on media as a kind of "conduit" that transports information objects, we are failing to grasp how deeply our perception influences the manner by which we frame information, communication, and the world. The danger is that media literacy threatens to become just a vogue pedagogy grasping for a way to diagnose the mass malaise of our current civilization's trajectory. What is necessary is to turn our own deconstruction tactics on themselves in order to design a better pedagogy—one that enables us to gain an authentic sense of place and to transform the alienating thought process that has led to the creation of the mediated world that most of us rail against.

The solution requires going outside our discipline. Media Studies is an amalgam anyway, combining such areas as sociology, economics, communications, history, psychology, and gender and culture studies. What has not happened up to this point is running media education through the filter of ecological design. Yes, there is such a thing as media ecology, which views communication systems as environments, but this movement is not necessarily ecological in the sense that we conventionally think about "ecology." Media ecologists draw on the literal concept of "ecology," which at its core is a system of systems, to examine how communications technology impacts human perception. According to Postman (http://www.media-ecology.org/media_ecology/), who coined the phrase: "Media ecology looks into the matter of how media of communication affect human perception, understanding, feeling, and value; and how our interaction with media facilitates or impedes our chances of survival." Although sustainability is implied by the insertion of the word "survival," the core concepts of sustainability from environmental activism are not included in the definition. For people who study media—academics and advertisers alike—"ecology" has become one of those one-size-fits-all terms that can encompass many ideas (for example, MySpace and Facebook are called "ecologies" by marketers). Other catch phrases like "viral media" and "memes" fit in with popular biological descriptions of media, yet when you examine how these concepts are actually utilized, they rarely reflect true ecological principles.

My goal is to move toward some ethical position in which sustainability is a core value of our pedagogy. Thus, there is an innate conceit in my argument that ecology as a value means deep ecology: the promotion of a systems paradigm that is emotionally and spiritually connected within the Web of Life. If this sounds flaky, it's too late. The network economy is making sure we're linked whether we like it or not; we just need to extend the form to our thinking and broaden it to all living systems. In media studies we pay lip service to connectivity all the time when we talk of the Internet and the electronic "global village," yet do we use the correct tools to actually achieve a perspective that is based on connectivity with things beyond the realm of synthetic communications? Visionary architect Soleri (1973, p. 29) puts the matter this way:

> The validity of information is not so much measured by weight, time or space extension, but by the threads it offers for connections within the condition of man. If information offers these connections, I call it environmental information, if it is incapable of them, I call it synthetic information. The psychosomatic structure of man himself defines these two kinds of information: The synthetic or abstract, on the one hand, and the environmental or "ecological," on the other. The synthetic tends to be the monopoly of the brain and is stored in its archives, whereas the environmental acts pervasively and is experienced.

By finding "threads" to that which is truly underlying the human condition, our work then becomes of a profound service to the world.

The necessary change in our pedagogy is quite simple, but incredibly profound. To quote graphic designer Bruce Mau (2004, p. 11), our work is not "about the world of design; it's about the design of the world." In a nutshell this encompasses the tension between an old world approach to media literacy versus one that is ecological, because most education efforts focus on the world of designed *products*, meaning advertising or commercial media, but not the *design* of the system itself; by design I don't mean an analysis of the economic power structure of multinational media corporations or the ideology of liberal capitalism, which are what I consider to be symptoms of deeper issues. Here I want to consider what environmental educator David Orr (1994) calls "ecological design arts," which he defines as a "set of perceptual and analytical abilities: ecological wisdom, and practical wherewithal essential to making things that 'fit' in a world of trees, microbes, rivers, animals, bugs, and small children. In other words, ecological design is the careful meshing of human purposes with the larger patterns and flows of the natural world and the study of those patterns and flows to inform human purposes" (p.104). Orr proposes that we need "biologic": "When human artifacts and systems are well designed, they are in harmony with the larger patterns in which they are embedded" (p.105).

In this context it is important to consider Wendell Berry's (2005, pp. 33-4) concept of "designing for pattern," which argues that design solutions should not create more problems, but on the contrary, should solve other problems as well:

> A bad solution is bad, then, because it acts destructively upon the larger patterns in which it is contained. It acts destructively upon those patterns, most likely, because it is formed in ignorance or disregard of them. A bad solution solves for a single purpose or goal.... A good solution is good because it is in harmony with those larger patterns— and this harmony will, I think, be found to have the nature of analogy. A bad solution acts within the larger pattern the way a disease or addiction acts within the body. A good solution acts within the larger pattern the way a healthy organ acts within the body. But it must at once be understood that a healthy organ does not —as the mechanistic or industrial mind would say—"give" health to the body, is not exploited for the body's health, but is a part of its health. The health of organ and organism is the same, just as the health of organism and ecosystem is the same. And these structures of organ, organism, and ecosystem—as John Todd has so ably understood—belong to a series of analogical integrities that begins with the organelle and ends with the biosphere.

A good example of this principle in action is the Center for Ecoliteracy's School Lunch Initiative (see Briggs, 2005). The center set out to design an ecological program that could maximize as many solutions as possible. When the Berkeley-based organization completed its investigation, it discovered that one of the major issues facing northern California was the disintegration of family farms, which appeared to be the source of many social problems. They concluded that an organic foods program in area public schools would not only create a market for family farms, but it would also improve the life of students and their ability to learn. It turns out that students who eat nutritious food learn better, are happier, and are less demoralized. The organization also found that after the pilot program was implemented at Berkeley High School, the cafeteria workers were happier because instead of microwaving prepackaged foods that were no better than TV dinners, the meals they now prepared improved student morale, and that made the workers feel good. This is an example of a well-designed ecological solution because it solved for pattern by supporting families, schools, students, and workers, all the while promoting ecological farming practices. As a result of the program's success, several schools around the United States are adopting its model.

Though on the surface this project may seem unrelated to media, we can say that in many respects it is related. For one thing, media influence many of our beliefs surrounding food, nutrition, and farming. Moreover, the project's pedagogy has design principles embedded into it that enable participants to see the relationships between various activities. The chief lesson for media educators is that conventional media literacy practices should not look at mass media without building a community-based solution as well. Community-based media supports local needs because it is designed for shared communication, storytelling, and community building. Most importantly, one of the most powerful tools for social change is to reclaim the moral authority of authenticity, which is best done at the local level: the "... power of the institutions of economic and political domination depends on their ability to perpetuate a falsified and inauthentic cultural trance based on beliefs and values at odds with reality. Break the trance, replace the values of an inauthentic culture with the values of an authentic culture grounded in a love of life rather than a love of money, and people will realign their life energy and bring forth the life-serving institutions of a new era. The key is to change the stories by which we define ourselves" (Korten, 2006, p.18). This doesn't mean trying to compete with corporate media at their game; but it does mean leveraging the game when possible, or flowing around or through it. For example, rather than fund a project to put a public service announcement on television (which is what many grants are designed to fund), the alternative is to build a local infrastructure or to create media that are distributed and shared locally through events that include food and sharing via local libraries and film festivals or virtually through online social networks. Other examples include community radio "barn raisings" where volunteers come together to build and train locals to create community stations. But most importantly, *how* we think is just as significant as broadcasting *what* we think.

Finally, rather than fix *causes*, the Center for Ecoliteracy designed a solution. The difference is subtle but intrinsic: in media education and activism, we largely focus on analyzing effects with the intention to find causes, as in uncritical war reporting is the result of the corporate consolidation of media. But in response do we have a design solution? Often media critics are just critical, considering their ultimate goal to be "independent," and by virtue of independence they have created a solution. The strategy of the so-called media reform movement, aside from changing laws and regulatory policies, has at its core the goal of more independent media. A design response is to work toward "interdependence," because the concept of independence reinforces nineteenth-century notions of mechanistic and dualistic reality filters that have led to the industrialization of media in the first place. This is not to deny the need for independent media and regulation of corporate media—that goes without saying—but the movement's pedagogy needs to be reframed with the intention of designing an interdependent understanding of the world. Rather than promote an epistemology inhabited by autonomous subjects consuming autonomous information objects, the new paradigm signifies that we are all connected and that we exist in an environment of systems, including those outside the realm we normally conceive of as "media."

Orr (1994, p.106) suggests that "poor design results from poorly equipped minds":

> Good design can only be done by people who understand harmony, patterns, and systems. Good design requires a breadth of view that leads people to ask how human artifacts and purposes 'fit' within the immediate locality and within the region. Industrial cleverness, however, is mostly evident in the minutiae of things, not in their totality or in their overall harmony. Moreover, good design uses nature as a standard and so requires ecological intelligence, by which I mean a broad and intimate familiarity with how nature works. For all of the recent interest in environment and ecology, this kind of knowledge, which is a product of both local experience and stable culture, is fast disappearing.

Looking at nature for workable patterns might seem utterly impossible given the general prejudice that media represent all things false, but that attitude prevents us from designing sustainable media education solutions. Some leading ecology activists think electronic media are so dangerous that teaching people how to read them just makes them more interesting and therefore should be avoided. This is a non-solution and is reminiscent of the tendency to focus on effects/causes—a type of duality that dominates our pedagogy—without considering design. Again, Orr (p. 108) argues that, "Design focuses on the structure of problems as opposed to their coefficients." As K.O. Berge (1989, p.12) notes, "Technology, data, information, media all become more approachable if we can see them as parts of a living organism— not as the cold, heartless products of hardware. A Gaian [Earth centric] view of the Information Age may help us deal with the current phenomenon by reducing our fears of technology— fears that are abundant and, I believe, symptomatic of failure to come up with a workable model for understanding the new systems we're bringing into being." Finally, we are far from this stage, but ultimately in our media literacy practices, we can work to detoxify media— not just from our minds, but the physical world as well, because information technology has a very concrete toxic by-product, be it from the waste and dumping of old computer systems or the discarding of televisions or CRT monitors in developing nations where poor people salvage them for precious metals under very dangerous conditions (Parks, 2004, pp. 48-54).

One of the first steps toward harmonizing our pedagogy with the principles of ecology is to understand how the difference between modes of reality construction and learning pertain to the left and right brains, two hemispheric modes of consciousness I call GridThink and HoloGrok. In short, print literacy is a type of GridThink that dominates the current education model, which is largely based on left-brain functions that are rational, abstract, and linear. New media primarily requires right-brain processing that is spherical, musical, multi-sensory, and nonlinear. I call this mentality HoloGrok because it is something that is more easily "grasped" than taught. "Holo," from "holograph," is at the root of the word "holistic," and "grok" is a nod to Robert Heinlein's classic science-fiction tale, *Stranger in a Strange Land*. In it the main protagonist, a human raised by Martians, has a completely different set of perceptual tools than his fellow Earthlings. His ability to comprehend instantaneously, "grok" in Martian, was an important buzzword of the Dionysian culture of the 1960s that symbolized a major breakdown of the GridThink mentality. In terms of education, I believe the GridThink frame of mind is about teaching us *what* to learn, whereas the HoloGrok approach is about teaching *how* to learn. And because our standard educational model approaches the world from the GridThink perspective, it's as if we are driving forward by using the rearview mirror (to borrow a McLuhan metaphor).

If the structural design of our media can be simplified to their essential quality, then a good place to start is with the concept of paradigms. As Thomas S. Kuhn (1996) famously argues, paradigms frame:

- What is to be examined and studied
- The types of questions asked
- The formation of the questions
- How to interpret the answers

Though it would be difficult to say definitively that there is a "media literacy" paradigm, because media literacy practitioners are quite diverse, some core assumptions of the media literacy movement can be deduced by looking at how "media basics" are defined by various influential organizations. What becomes apparent is that many media literacy practitioners are operating with a mass media model that emerged during the period of modernity (roughly the 100-year period from the mid-1800s to the mid-1900s) and is viewed with a mentality that emerged from the printing press. The cost of mass media production has required the business model of advertising to deliver audiences to big business. Most of us agree that this has been a fundamental fault in our media system, and given the necessity of shifting into a new paradigm of sustainability, we need to develop new models of production and consumption. Scholarship has also noted that the rise in mass media coincided with the rise of the "public sphere." This entailed a new constituency of a leisure and educated class (mostly white males) who share public forms of communication supplied by the rise of mass media, first in the form of newspapers, then radio, film, and finally television. In each case, with some exceptions of course, the model existed as a one-to-many distribution network. A single media company (in competition with others on a similar scale) would broadcast or print its informed voice assembled by educated professionals (under hierarchal, factory-like production modes learned in trade schools) to a large audience that shared the same mode of language and communication. The ability to "talk back" was historically limited to letters to the editor, or paid advertisements, or by creating a small, adversary press.

Though books took power away from kings and Popes, they also made us silent, isolated readers who abstract the world according to the form of print. A great visualization of this occurs in the last scene of François Truffaut's *Fahrenheit 451*. In order to evade the wrath of the totalitarian thought police, the print-loving rebels choose to memorize one book each in order to save humanity's literary heritage. In the end we see a group of disconnected people wandering through the forest reciting books to themselves without interacting with each other. The "book people" look decidedly unhappy. Print also biases our perception to see the world as concrete and divisible into discrete pieces. Consider how the page is laid out with its neat columns and letters breaking every sound into bits of information; or someone who articulates opinions is a "columnist" as if she or he is a pillar holding up a particular architecture of thought.

The basic principles of most media literacy organizations have internalized the mass media model. A common approach to this media model has been created by the Canadian organization, Media Awareness Network, which developed a set of core media analysis concepts that have been replicated many times over in variation by other media literacy organizations:

1. All media are constructions.
2. The media construct reality.
3. Audiences negotiate meaning in media.
4. Media have commercial implications.
5. Media contain ideological and value messages.

(http://www.media-awareness.ca/english/index.cfm)

The Center for Media Literacy deviates slightly:

1. All media messages are constructed.
2. Media messages are constructed using a creative language with its own rules.
3. Different people experience the same messages differently.
4. Media have embedded values and points of view.
5. Media messages are constructed to gain profit and/or power.

(http://www.medialit.org/)

There is an inherent assumption made by both these lists that messages are being delivered via a one-to-many platform. This leads to an analytical approach that I call the "Read-Text" model (see Figure 1). Typically it means deconstructing a media artifact by "reading" and responding in some analytical fashion with a set of questions modeled on the Five-W rule of journalism (Who, What, Where, When, Why). This is a variation on the common generic definition of media literacy, which is the capability "to access, analyze, evaluate, produce and communicate a variety of media texts and forms." The work of this approach heavily emphasizes critiquing television and print, and treats both media as the same rather than as different forms. Using Kuhn's criteria, this means:

- What is observed and scrutinized are autonomous objects produced by mass media corporations, commonly referred to as Big Media;
- The kinds of questions that are asked in relation to this subject are the five W's;
- How these questions are to be structured is to ask the individual to analyze *what* something means;

- The results of the analysis should create an independent-minded individual who can make informed choices as an information consumer.

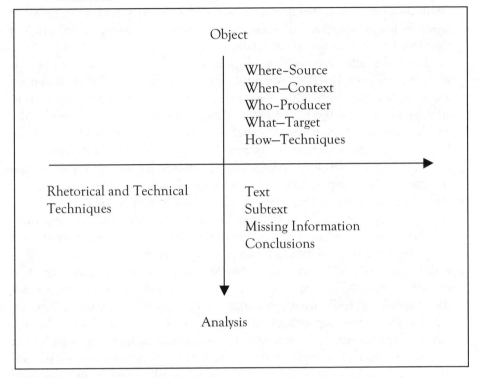

Figure 1: Read-Text Deconstruction Grid

The mass media approach breaks down substantially when applied to Henry Jenkins's (2006) model of *Convergence Culture*, which argues that new media practices are characterized by the following:

- collective intelligence;
- affective economics;
- transmedia storytelling; and
- participatory culture.

Some key points of this transformation include consumer-as-producer ("prosumer"), open source code, creative commons, barter economics, a decentralized media infrastructure, networked knowledge communities, and the change from traditional labor to knowledge work. This doesn't mean the end of "Big Media" and their impact on people's beliefs, but what is transpiring is a radical reconfiguration that even the advertising business is having difficulty modeling when it uses nostalgic terms like "old world" and "traditional" media to describe how things used to be, meaning the good ol' days. Media production and media users are becoming far more sophisticated than the media literacy model can bear.

Just as euclidean geometry works perfectly well on a flat surface but fails when applied to spheres, these traditional core principles function fine if we are only working with the mass media construct. However, applied to convergence media, the model breaks down very quickly because one of the key changes in our networked economy right now is the emergence of the "prosumer," a creature that is audience, consumer and producer. Under the conditions of so-called knowledge work, consumers increasingly are producing the content for corporations. For example, Google is dependent on user input, as is MySpace and the various other user-generated social network sites. But it's not just on these grounds that I find objectionable the assumptions of the core principles: again they replicate the same GridThink paradigm that got us in this mess in the first place by promoting clearly defined reality realms, with the media world being "false" in contrast to something that is "real." I empathize with the general sentiment of the core principles, because I think the complaint is really against manufactured communications versus organic, self-organized communications that arise from vibrant, living human relationships. Given this awareness we can point out how corporate media translate self-organized media (such as folk culture) into imitative packages. The most obvious example is Disney, which basically pirated folk tales from the public domain and made them into copyrighted property assets. This process is repeated in other realms when the intellectual commons of Native American medicinal knowledge is converted into patented pharmaceuticals.

With the following adjustments, I think it is possible to achieve a more holistic understanding of media. To reiterate, it is best to avoid absolutes. I think it is useful to incorporate Gregory Bateson's (2000) concept of the "budget of flexibility." His analogy is the person who walks a tightrope and whose balance bar gets continually shortened when biological diversity is reduced; in our case, when we become inflexible with our thinking we threaten to fall off our intellectual tightrope. So please consider these guidelines as a long balance bar as opposed to rules. This kind of maneuverability gives us ample space to make adjustments as the environment warrants.

1. "All media/messages are constructions" changes to "Media messages are reconstructions of other media that comprise mediaspheric niches."

As the work of Jay David Bolter and Richard Grusin (1999) has demonstrated very effectively, media "remediate"; that is, they build on older communication methods, codes, signals, and techniques: "As a digital network, cyberspace remediates the electric communications networks of the past 150 years, the telegraph and the telephone; as virtual reality, it remediates the visual space of painting, film, and television; and as a social space, it remediates such historical places as cities and parks and such nonplaces as theme parks and shopping malls. Like other contemporary mediated spaces, cyberspace refashions and extends earlier media, which are themselves embedded in material and social environments" (Bolter and Grusin, p. 183). This is contrary to the view that new media forms obliterate older ones (though they go to war with each other as I argue in the case of GridThink going to war against HoloGrok in chapter one). Consider the Roman Empire's strategy for empire building: incorporate the cultures and beliefs of the conquered territories. Thus, media don't construct—they reconstruct the known into new configurations. Furthermore, one of the key principles of ecological sustainability is "nested systems." Put simply, a tributary is a nested system of a larger river's watershed complex. I call these nested systems "mediaspheric niches," which is explained in more detail in chapter two of the same name, but can be described here as a complex of codes and communication techniques.

2. "The media construct reality" changes to "Media reconstruct and emulate reality and/or belief systems."

Media favor and reconstruct biased ways of perceiving the world. Media do not invent or generate reality, but merely extend and amplify previously existing perceptual predispositions. It is true that media can overemphasize and disrupt those tendencies that are considered more "natural," but they do not invent anything from scratch. You do not live in a simulation, although it's worth considering the original concept of simulacra which is to distort something to make it look more real, such as slightly curving Greek pillars so that they appear straight instead of bending as light normally does in our eyes. In this case we can say that media deploy illusory techniques.

3. "Audiences negotiate meaning in media" changes to "Audiences and individuals negotiate meaning in media."

Fair enough. I would say that meaning is negotiated in groups *and* as individuals. The term "audience" is ambiguous and amorphous and disempowering to the individual reader because it assumes that he or she only has a group opinion or point of view. This may or may not be true. We have to leave room for variation and diversity. It is worth noting here that demographics, the study of people by marketers, does not make a community, nor can it account for zeitgeist, something that usually comes about via discovery, accident, or cross patterning. Communication is a complex relationship between producer and audience. Rarely is there a unidirectional (or syringe model) trajectory of any message. Society's values are both reflected and directed by media. This does not mean there is an equal power relationship between producers and consumers of media, but feedback does factor into the relationship between producer and audience.

4. "Media have commercial implications" changes to "Sombunall media have commercial implications and sombunall are done for pleasure."

Here the rephrasing by Center for Media Literacy is more enlightened than the Media Awareness Network's statement that media "have embedded values and points of view." If you suggest that "sombunall"—"some but not all," a term created by philosopher trickster Robert Anton Wilson (1986)—media have commercial implications, it's inclusive of alternative media that are open source and made and distributed freely. "Sombunall" media are folk or fan culture, such as Harry Potter-fan fiction or *Star Trek* and *Star Wars* fan movies.

5. "Media contain ideological and value messages" changes to "Media are a map."

This depends on how one defines ideology. Ideology in the Marxist sense means that media contain invisible relations embodied in the commodity fetish. I would take it to a deeper level to say that media contain brain hemispheric tendencies that can favor modes of perception. As for the CML statement that media are constructed to gain profit and/or power, this is flat-out misdirected and is really a reflection of the concept's own bias that media are only produced in the mass media model. I believe this is by far one of the most misleading and wrongheaded arguments that media literacy advocates can make. Just as art produced by ancient cultures informs us of their values and perceptions, media have a similar capacity to inform us of the belief systems of their producers. "Media as maps" allow us to understand the territory of values and beliefs related to the cultural, spiritual, and/or economic system that creates media. Additionally, TV is not a box that contains information objects; it is a *structure*. Commercial media should be viewed in the context of power, economics, and the inherent value in the belief in technology, including electricity.

In summary, my central core principles are:

1. Media messages are reconstructions of other media that comprise mediaspheric niches.
2. Media reconstruct and emulate reality.
3. Audiences and individuals negotiate meaning in media.
4. Sombunall media have commercial implications, and sombunall media are done for pleasure.
5. Media are a map.

In keeping with the principles of critical media pedagogy that is intended to also challenge the assumptions of hegemonic power, I would like to include these additional concepts:

6. Media Are Composed of a System of Symbols

Symbols are signs of cultural meaning that enable us to understand media messages. Brands, logos, and text convey messages that are interpreted according to individual belief systems, education, conditioning, and domestication.

7. Commercial Media Put a Familiar Face on Abstract Legal Entities

Media translate abstract legal entities, such as corporations, into symbolic worlds. We begin to identify models, actors, and spokespeople as real people within the symbolic world of media-generated realities. People such as the Verizon man or Shakira are characters in a story told by the media.

8. The Symbolic World of Advertising is the Dream Life of Corporations

Rarely does advertising represent the aspirations and desires of real people, but rather it projects desires and ideals of body types, attitudes, and beliefs upon artificial entities (such as corporations represented by brands). Because our system of mass media is driven by the commercial imperative to entice product sales, "brands" and products become the most highly prized components of media messages. They have the power to grant love, happiness, and esteem. Their lack is nearly always portrayed as a cause of misery. Human relations are almost always secondary to products.

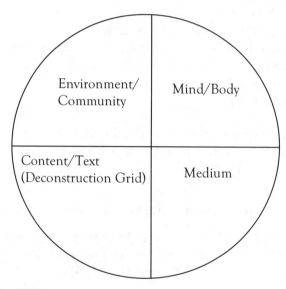

Figure 2: Media Wheel

I now want to draw on a very useful sustainability concept, permaculture. Coined by ecologists Bill Mollison and David Holmgren, "permaculture" is "'Consciously designed landscapes which mimic the patterns and relationships found in nature, while yielding an abundance of food, fiber and energy for provision of local needs.' People, their buildings and the ways they organize themselves are central to permaculture. Thus the permaculture vision of permanent (sustainable) agriculture has evolved to one of permanent (sustainable) culture" (Holmgren, 2002, p. xix). As a farming and gardening technique, permaculture leverages the strength of the local ecology so that it can maximize available resources. So in the desert, for example, you design a system that can sustain itself within the natural capacity of the environment, which means minimizing water usage. In this case, grass lawns are most definitely not appropriate, but desert meadowlands are. But as Holmgren's definition indicates, the idea is not just agricultural; it's cultural because as a design solution it goes beyond being a technique for gardening and instead is a principle for organizing society (see Table 1).

Table 1. Cultural systems

Mode	Gridthink: Independent–Industrial Culture	Hologrok: Interdependent - Permaculture
Organization	Centralized	Distributed network
Energy Base	Non-renewable	Renewable
Material Flows	Linear	Cyclical
Scale	Large	Small
Movement	Fast	Slow
Feedback	Positive	Negative
Focus	Center	Edge
Activity	Episodic change	Rhythmic stability
Thinking	Reductionist	Holistic
Gender	Male	Female
Nature	Biophobia	Biophelia
Byproduct	Waste	Compost
Mediacology	Mass Media	Networked Media
Communications	Selling	Stories
Information flow	Push	Pull
Core emotion	Fear	Love
Resources	Scarcity	Sufficiency
Ownership	Intellectual Property	Creative Commons
Perception	The "Real"	Open Reality
Analysis	Object/Thing	Relationship/Event
Representation	Illusion	Magic

Note: Rows 1-11 are from Holmgren (p. xxvii).

If permaculture is a design solution for the biosphere, then "mediacology" is a design solution for the "semiosphere"—the "synchronistic semiotic space which fills the borders of culture" (Lotman, 2001, p.3). Mediacology achieves these permaculture principles by applying cybernetic thinking and paradigm mapping. Cybernetics takes the view that our information environment is inherently a feedback system. As such, mediacology uses natural models based on systems thinking to map and reconfigure media education pedagogy by applying a circular inquiry process called the "Media Wheel" (see "DIY Mediacology" and Figure 2). It is my sense that media literacy represents a "sick" pedagogy, so mediacology is meant to "remediate," using both senses of the term. On the one hand remediation means mending troubled ecological niches, and on the other the media theory concept that newer media forms incorporate older media forms with the contradictory purpose of having immediacy and opacity. Mediacology "remediates" (fixes) the industrial model of mass media literacy and its print literate perspective, and it also remediates (incorporates) alternative epistemologies to become more fluid.

As a design solution, mediacology promotes sustainable human cultural and economic practices in its approach to content by revealing patterns of thinking that underlie the forms of media systems. Intrinsic to this approach is a multicultural view that recognizes perceptual and semiological border worlds called "mediaspheric niches." These zones are the mediacological equivalent of bioregions, which are ecologies defined by watersheds. As such, mediacology is an approach that can be flexible according to particular community needs, just as sustainable agriculture needs to be practiced according to the particular characteristics of a bioregion. To extend the cultivation metaphor, synthetic communication produced by corporate mainstream media can be likened to industrial agricultural, whereas community media is akin to organic farming and permaculture. This means integrating the local with the global, thereby "glocalizing" our practices.

At some point the culture at the foundation of Western civilization decided that the internal world is separate from the outer world, something broadly known as duality. This concept of separation, in my view, has not served us well, and ultimately is at the crux of our self-destructive path because the prevailing power structure doesn't value community or nature, but focuses rather on individualism and codified greed. This is a really dangerous thought process, a maladapted cultural trait that requires serious reevaluation. Why is it so popular? Why does it keep replicating itself to the point that it will destroy everything in its environment, thereby inhibiting its very own survival? It's as if a parasitic thought process is about to kill its host. This is a test of the evolutionary idea of cultural transmission. If we have a propensity to assimilate and learn behavior that enhances our chance for biological survival, surely it will happen. But somehow I don't take this as a given. Will the process of natural selection once and for all reject the concept of civilization?

According to most media activists from both the Left and the Right, our historical moment is one of pure tragedy. But it's also possible to see the situation as an opening, as in the New Age trope that the Chinese word for crisis means danger and opportunity. We cannot simply survive by attacking the system, but we need to go as deeply as possible to comprehend the values it emanates and to design a solution. Doing so is to change the fundamental operating system of our ideological global technomedia system from a mentality of "separation" to one of "connection," not in just in the rhetoric of the global village but in action and deeds. It is my view that the fundamental root of our environmental crisis (as manifested in climate change) is a belief that our actions have no consequences because we as individuals live in mental isolation from the world outside our bodies and hence the broader biosphere. When we believe on a fundamental level that harming someone else or damaging the environment also changes our internal condition, then our behaviors will change. It is not so cynical to say that until people understand they are fouling their nest that they will stop polluting and toxifying their bodies and minds; but humans have a quality of self-interest, so let that be a leverage point. There is a benefit to that mindset, which is survival. The challenge is whether or not our strategies are based on competition or cooperation. Is individual prosperity necessarily in conflict with the communal? Such a dichotomy has dominated the Industrial Age "isms," and it has become so normalized that it is an invisible ideology, one so pervasive that simply pointing a finger at it is to be labeled a heretic.

In a globally connected world, a sense of place is cultivated simultaneously with our ecological niches and also through the extension of our senses on a global scale. We are at a unique point in time when we can actually look at the universe while pointing the cameras back at ourselves. Some day you may actually see yourself while viewing Google maps and wonder, how did I get here/there? Thus, I concur with Derrick de Kerckhove's (1997, p. 217) argument that the reproduced image of planet Earth has made us into a new species:

> Thanks to this photograph, I am the Earth and so is everybody else. This is a new psychological experience with immense implications. The best revenge against psychotechnologies that would turn us into extensions of themselves is to include them with our personal psychology. A new human is in the making.

By utilizing the concepts introduced in this book, it is my hope that the new human is properly equipped to survive that which seems impossible.

CHAPTER ONE

War of the (Mediated) Worlds

The point is that very few people believe what anthropology teaches: that indigenous, small-scale traditional societies are not earlier (or degenerate) versions of our own. They are rather differing solutions to historical circumstances and environmental particulars that testify to the breadth of human intellectual creativity and its capacity for symbolization.

Eric Michaels, *Bad Aboriginal Art: Tradition, Media, and Technological Horizons*

Human history did not follow a straight line, as if everything pointed towards civilized societies as humanity's ultimate goal. On the contrary, at each bifurcation alternative stable states were possible, and once actualized, they coexisted and interacted with one another.

Manuel De Landa, *A Thousand Years of Nonlinear History*

It has been said that paradigms die one funeral at a time. The European epistemology I grew up studying didn't necessarily die within my own practice; instead it was composted during my years of teaching video production, writing and media literacy at a Native American boarding school. Additionally, while working in various Native American communities throughout the United States, I also became a student of Native American culture. In a sense, working on the Rez gave me that proverbial Zen-like "beginner's mind" necessary to lift me out of the media literacy reality bubble that was troubling me. As a non-Native American, this does not make me an expert of Native American culture, but my experience does provide a rich context for understanding greater patterns at play in the world. To begin with, I have been rethinking what sociologist C. Wright Mills (1963, pp. 405-6) once wrote: "Those who rule the management of symbols, rule the world." Is symbol management all that is necessary to conquer minds and people? Is control just a management issue? For many Native Americans, symbols are ciphers of power, a type of symbolic "medicine." I first understood this at age 15 when I had the rare opportunity to live as a "bahana" (white person) in Hopiland, the small reservation in northern Arizona in a region that Native Americans have called home for thousands of years. My host was Thomas Banyacya, a man appointed by Hopi leaders to convey the tribe's spiritual teachings to the outside world. Fittingly, Banyacya, who died in 1999, had an audience with the Pope and addressed the United Nations General Assembly in 1992. What he shared with me during that stay more than 25 years ago remains with me today, informing my approach to digital media literacy.

While staying in the village of New Oraibi (now called Kykotsmovi), a community that split in 1906 because of tribal divisions created by U.S. government and white cultural influence, Banyacya told me about the Hopis' first encounter with the Spaniards in 1540. The Hopis intuitively read the conquerors' intentions by interpreting their overarching visual symbol, the crucifix. The Hopis were interested in the mental reflection of the symbol's shape: a grid formed by intersecting, angular lines. As such, they correctly assessed the Europeans' intellectual agility and ingenuity, but what troubled them was a missing element in the European's symbolism—an element that the Hopis possessed. By contrast, the Hopis' tribal symbol, a cross enclosed by a circle, contains a holistic concept of life, such as the medicine wheel common among North American tribes that represents the cardinal directions and a complete view of humanity: emotional, spiritual, mental, and physical. The Hopis understood that whatever the Europeans intended to achieve, it would not be sustainable. Because of a faulty thought process (or operating system in modern parlance), logic and reason without holism were doomed to fail; from the Hopis' vantage point, it's hard to argue against how this interpretation has played out. For example, the most important coal operation in the region, an energy production complex forming the basis of the United States' southwestern power grid, is housed on Hopi and Diné land. But many regional tribal members lack access to electricity (some by choice), and coal is transported from the mines by slurrying: in this case, the pumping of crushed coal mixed with rare and fresh drinking water that the area's inhabitants need for survival. That our society would sacrifice our environment to power the bright neon lights and video screens of Las Vegas or sports stadiums of Phoenix says much about the current matrix between media, technology and ecology.

As an educator promoting digital media literacy, what interests me about the story of the cross and circle is the genius and perceptibility that the Hopis had regarding the cultural uses of symbols; they drew on their metaphysical understanding of symbolism to perceive the practical application of differing paradigms. They were creative media deconstructionists before such a term came into existence 400 years later, and like most other Native American tribes in North America, they still maintain a savvy, critically engaged relationship with the dominant power structure and its media system. The Hopis understood our guiding symbols to be cosmological maps, and as such, they present to us a powerful lesson in comprehending socially constructed communication systems and their long-term impact on community and the environment. They force us to question technology's inevitability and to remain constantly skeptical of its application, including the mindset that accompanies emerging technological systems. As Hopi artist, filmmaker, and educator Victor Masayesva Jr. (2006) said, "We are knowledgeable about obsessing on technology at the expense of life and living. We have experienced the impacts of technology beginning with control of water in our desert environment and the unequal powers created by such technologies … personally, I have continued to reinforce the message that the Internet is only a rumor and until the context is clear we will always be cautious about the messenger."

In terms of understanding the differing mentalities of the circle and the cross, Native American scholar Donald L. Fixico (2003, p. 15) believes: "The wars fought between Indians and the whites were more than just over land—they were wars of the minds. The American mainstream thinks in a linear fashion, which is very different from the circular fashion of traditionalists. These two are at odds when both are not realized, as by one not knowing the other one." In other words, it's a war between GridThink and HoloGrok. In sociological jargon, what we are dealing with are different subjectivities—ways of perceiving and being in the world. Thus, we can extend this discussion to a broader understanding of communication systems as mental environments, or as "media ecologies," for "the five-hundred-year relationship between America's indigenous people and Europeans and their descendents may easily be described as an unending chain of rhetorical situations" (Stromberg 2006, p. 5). Relating this concept of media ecology to a generalized view of the impact of technology and media to our interaction with the world, media scholar Neil Postman (1993, p. 16) remarks:

> new technologies compete with old ones—for time, attention for money, for prestige, but mostly for dominance of world-view. This competition is implicit once we acknowledge that a medium contains an ideological bias. And it is a fierce competition, as only ideological competitions can be. It is not merely a matter of tool against tool—the alphabet attacking ideographic writing, the printing press attacking the illuminated manuscript, the photograph attacking the art of painting, television attacking the printed word. When media make war against each other, it is a case of world-views in collision.

Consequently, schools represent primary battlegrounds for worldviews in collision. As advocates of digital media education, it's important to be cognizant of alternate modes of engagement and to design programming that is appropriate and sensitive to these differences—not out of a tokenistic desire for multiculturalism, but out of a real engagement of difference that is positive and constructive. While examining the training program implicit within compulsory government education, Native Americans have observed the manner in which education is conventionally used as a tool for control and assimilation into the dominant society. From what I've learned by working in the public school system and at Native American schools, I take it as a given that government educational standards do not necessarily promote challenging the power grid's assumptions; rather, they encourage students to reinforce the economic and political structure of our society through educational standards. My beliefs are echoed by former teacher and education critic John Taylor Gatto (1992, p. 13) who observes: "School, as it was built, is an essential support system for a model of social engineering that condemns most people to be subordinate stones in a pyramid that narrows as it ascends to a terminal of control. School is an artifice that makes such a pyramidical social order seem inevitable, even though such a premise is a fundamental betrayal of the American Revolution."

While recognizing that there are plenty of excellent and well-meaning educators who do work in the system, it's important to recognize how Gatto's critique concurs with how Native American education policy played out ("Kill the Indian, Save the Man" summarizes the initial education strategy). This microcosm has implications for the broader social structure, for this discussion is ultimately also about how our society deals with education, technology, and racism with non-GridThink cultures. As a teacher serving Native American communities, I found it necessary to probe deeper into my own operating paradigm to fully understand what is required to nurture critically engaged youth so that they will not simply replicate the assumptions of our system, but also will engage in culturally and locally relevant pedagogy. Ultimately, I concluded that this is not just a Native American issue, but one facing our broader society—for what happens in Vegas doesn't just stay there, it infects the entire grid. The playing field of standardized education is a kind of cognitive reservation in which certain aspects of our consciousness are being systematically obliterated. But because we now primarily live in a world of electronically delivered symbols designed to replicate the power structure, it is necessary to develop an education strategy that is both practical and constructive in the sense of preserving cultural integrity and sustainability. In other words, we need an education strategy with a principle of harmony in its design. The opposite is the image of a broken medicine wheel, a potent symbol for the kind of despair many Native American youth are experiencing. I also put forward the concept that the inherited GridThink mental system is a shattered means of engaging the world. Our perceptual wheel is broken, and in terms of media education we need to deploy the Pottery Barn rule: we smashed it, now we own the problem and must fix it.

Ultimately my goal is not to encourage a war of media worlds, but to find peace between them. After all, the metaphor of the medicine wheel is not about a cross *or* circle, but rather the two working together in harmony. Bridging the circle and cross, thereby reuniting disparate modes of consciousness that have been split for thousands of years, may be achieved if we rethink what we normally assume to be true concerning the digital divide. Many people probably carry an image in their head that looks something like this: a white man sitting at a computer faces a caveman on the other side. The popular conception is that we increasingly live in a world of haves and have-nots, and those who don't or won't have access to information will not be able to participate in the world economy. This is a half-truth. I'm certain that as global economies become more integrated, access will be less of an issue, though it is certainly significant. After all, if electricity and media are the primary tools of the capitalist "enclosure" (along with war), it is most certain that larger populations will be wired together, for better or for worse. It probably will remain true that poorer regions will have slower Internet access, reiterating William Gibson's (2003) remark: "The future is already here – it's just not evenly distributed." Though I agree access is a significant issue, what's more important is a different kind of divide, one that looks like a brain with each hemisphere separated into a kind of lobotomized reality filter. With media systems and communications as technological extensions of the nervous system, I think even more pertinent than the divide of access is the divide between wisdom and rationality that is influenced by different parts of the brain.

As a Native American elder once said, "Any road can get you somewhere." The question is, where is the information highway taking us? Banyacya provided a map of these paths when he told the story of the cross and the circle. The cross represented not a religion, but a mentality that engineered a religion. Its angular shape has two straight euclidean lines, which are geometric constructs that do not exist in nature; they are a product of the alphabetic culture that has produced the entire materialist revolution in science and a host of attitudes that peaked with industrial mass media. The cross's logical trajectory is the world of printed books and Renaissance linear perspective in which space is objectively constructed with autonomous people whose skin and clothes separate their interior worlds from their outer worlds.

In this respect, cars provide the perfect metaphor for "separation." Auto (auto=self) ads repeat the perception that cars represent places of isolation, and hence freedom from the outside annoyances of the world; they are external skeletons and muscles systems separated from the world by steel skin. Driving a car in this reality shield has no environmental consequences; the whole point of the car is to guard one from the environment, which is viewed like a movie through the windshield. Additionally, cars, as extensions of our feet (remember Fred Flintstone?), move us through space beyond the natural capacity of the body. This is a logical progression of the alphabet and printing press, which abstracts thought so it can be contained within books. Books are portable private spaces, such as the car's interior, and are autonomous from their surroundings (or so we are led to believe). Meanwhile, as we learn to love and worship our cars as extensions of our bifurcated minds, we inadvertently become servomechanisms of the auto industry through our participation in the system by paying taxes that subsidize the cost of vehicles; and we pay for the military that helps provide fuel flows and material resources and helps keep the markets open. We are taxed in nonlinear ways, too: our bodies are subject to car pollution, which can cause asthma or other related health conditions, and the auto industry contributes to climate change through carbon emissions. From a medicological perspective, we could go on to discuss the impact of the petrol-chemical, plastics, and pesticides industries as they relate to a host of social issues.

Alternatively, traditional Hopis view the world from a more holistic stance and are concerned that GridThink lacks a circular perspective. In essence, the Hopis talk about integrating two sides of the brain, a conclusion they made not based on rational Western science, but by interacting with nature. They know GridThink is left brain and HoloGrok is right brain, as illustrated when they speak of two sides of the body. The left, which contains the heart, is wise and compassionate but awkward. The right side is clever, strong, and rational, and hence dangerous. The left brain controls the right side of the body, and the right brain controls the left side. Moreover, the Hopis were ingenious in their symbol interpretation by understanding that symbols are important ciphers because they posses "harmonic" qualities. Consider the difference between the image of a cross and our primary symbol for the Internet, a "web." The Web encapsulates the character of networks in which each strand is connected to the other. Next to a cross, such a symbol generates a vastly different set of ideas. And as we will see, the difference between a cross and web require vastly different sets of thinking and conceptualization tools.

The following summarizes the differences between the brain hemispheres and how they relate to the cross and circle:

Eye-Left Hemisphere	Ear-Right Hemisphere
Visual-Speech-Verbal	Tactile-Spatial-Musical-Acoustic
Logical, Mathematical	Holistic
Linear, Detailed	Artistic, Symbolic
Sequential	Simultaneous
Controlled	Emotional
Intellectual	Intuitive, Creative
Dominant	Minor, Quiet
Quantitative	Qualitative
Active	Receptive
Analytic	Synthetic, Gestalt
Reading, Writing, Naming	Facial Recognition
Sequential Ordering	Simultaneous Comprehension
Perception of Significant Order	Perception of Abstract Patterns
Complex Motor Sequences	Recognition of Complex Figures
	(McLuhan and Powers 1989, p. 54)

People who perceive reality primarily through left-brain mechanisms are GridThinkers. GridThink evolves from a steady progression of cuneiform writing created by Sumerians to document goods being traded, to the alphabet, to writing, to linear perspective, to the printing press and so on. As Marshall McLuhan and Bruce R. Powers (p. 45) explain,

> To summarize, visual space structure is an artifact of Western civilization created by Greek phonetic literacy. It is a space perceived by the eyes when separated or abstracted from all other senses. As a construct of the mind, it is continuous, which is to say that it is infinite, divisible, extensible, and featureless—what the early Greek geometers referred to as physis. It is also connected (abstract figures with fixed boundaries, linked logically and sequentially but having no physical ground), homogeneous (uniform and everywhere), and static (qualitatively unchangeable). It is like "mind's eye" or visual imagination which dominates the thinking of literate Western people, some of whom demand ocular proof for existence itself.

> Acoustic space structure is the natural space of nature-in-the raw inhabited by non-literate people. It is like the "mind's ear" or acoustic imagination that dominates the thinking of pre-literate and post-literate humans alike (rock video has as much acoustic power as a Watusi mating dance). It is both discontinuous and nonhomogeneous. Its resonant and interpenetrating processes are simultaneously related with centers everywhere and boundaries nowhere. Like music, as communications engineer Barrington Nevitt puts it, acoustic space requires neither proof nor explanation but is made manifest through its cultural content. Acoustic and visual space structures may seem to be incommensurable, like history and eternity, yet at the same time, as complementary, like art and science or biculturalism.

More and more, GridThink has refined space to something that can be measured and conquered (think about the dual meaning of "rule" or the adage that grids are empire's geometry), thus producing the various scientific revolutions of the Western world with a continuum stretching like a filament between Copernicus, Bacon, Newton and Descartes. From them we inherited a distilled reality as materially based and the idea that the mind is separated from the body and all around it:

> This paradigm comprises a number of ideas and values that differ sharply from those of the Middle Ages; values that have been associated with various streams of Western culture, among them the Scientific Revolution, the Enlightenment, and the Industrial Revolution. They include the belief in the scientific method as the only valid approach to knowledge; the view of the universe as a mechanical system composed of elementary material building blocks; the view in life of society as a competitive struggle for existence; and the belief in unlimited material progress to be achieved through economic and technological growth. During the past decades all these ideas and values have been found severely limited and in need of radical revision (Capra 1983, p. 30).

The problem with modernization, David Orr (1994, p. 133) argues, is that it

> represented dramatic changes in how we regard the natural world and our role in it. These changes are now so thoroughly ingrained in us that we can scarcely conceive of any other manner of thinking. But crossing this divide first required us to discard the belief that the world was alive and worthy of respect, if not fear. To dead matter, we owe no obligations. Second, it was necessary to distance ourselves from animals who were transformed by Cartesian alchemy into mere machines. Again, no obligations or pity are owed to machines. In both cases, use is limited only by usefulness. Third, it was necessary to quiet whatever remaining sympathy we had for nature in favor of 'hard' data that could be weighed, measured, counted, and counted on to make a profit. Fourth, we needed a reason to join power, cash, and knowledge in order to transform the world into more useful forms. Francis Bacon provided the logic, and the evolution of government-funded research did the rest. Fifth, we required a philosophy of improvement and found it in the ideology of perpetual economic growth, now the central mission of governments everywhere. Sixth, biophobia required the sophisticated cultivation of dissatisfaction, which could be converted into mass consumption. The advertising industry and the annual style changes were invented.

GridThinkers occupy space, but they don't share it. They own atomized pieces of it, broken down into smaller and smaller commodities to the point that now even DNA is being trademarked. By contrast, digital media is like acoustic space and is breaking down GridThink reality in a substantial way. If you look at how new media practices are shaping up, you will see they much more strongly represent the tendencies of the right brain, which is characterized by sound, artistic expression, symbolic thinking, and pattern recognition. People who emphasize, or are more in balance with the right brain, are HoloGrokers.

GridThink is a kind of duality that manifests in different ways; it is not bad on its own, just as euclidean geometry is useful for analyzing geometry on flat surfaces. But when it is overemphasized and out of balance with other modes of perception, we are collectively doomed for self-destruction. Thus, when Orr makes the distinction between cleverness and knowledge, I think it's what Banyacya was getting at when he talked about the difference between the cross and circle. As Orr (p. 30) writes:

> At the heart of our pedagogy and curriculum is a fateful confusion of cleverness with intelligence. Cleverness, as I understand it, tends to fragment things and to focus on the short run. The epitome of cleverness is the specialist whose intellect and person have been shaped by the demands of a single function, what Nietzsche once called an "inverted cripple." Ecological intelligence, on the other hand, requires a broader view of the world and a long-term perspective. Cleverness can be adequately computed by the Scholastic Aptitude Test and the Graduate Record Exam, but intelligence is not so easily measured. In time I think we will come to see that true intelligence tends to be integrative and often works slowly while one is mulling things over.

Sadly, the world is full of clever people who have not advanced us significantly in terms of developing a harmonious relationship with our surroundings. In the United States, the education system emphasizes the left-brain/GridThink model when a right-brain/HoloGrok one is more appropriate for new digital media practices. You could say the problem is not one of literacy as we traditionally think about it, but that in the twenty-first century we are in danger of becoming right-brain illiterate (de Kerckhove 1997). This is not to say one is exclusive of the other, but balance between the hemispheres is paramount when we discuss the digital divide; this gives global unity a whole other meaning if we are to think of our brains as being spherical and the world as containing different perceptual modes. It's almost as if the conceptual divide between the northern and southern hemispheres is also a holographic projection of the hemispheric differences between the brain halves. We need to harmonize elements between the hemispheres, something McLuhan and Powers (p. 4) called the "resonant interval":

> The resonant interval may be considered an invisible borderline between visual and acoustic space. We all know that a frontier, or borderline, is a space between two worlds, making a kind of double plot or parallelism, which evokes a sense of the crowd, or universality. Whenever two cultures, or two events or two ideas are set in proximity to one another, an interplay takes place, a sort of magical change. The more unlike the interface, the greater the tension of the interchange.

This resonant interval is a bit like an "edge" ecosystem, in which two ecologies, such as a meadow and a forest, come into contact. These border worlds are fertilely biodiverse zones in the same way that national boundaries offer immense human diversity. It may be that the discourse to emerge from the 1990s surrounding hybridity, postmodernism, border identity and cyborgs in some ways occupies the transitional zone of the resonant interval. Boundaries separate and unify, belonging to both realms. Understanding how these realms interact in the mediasphere is paramount for our understanding of media education.

GridThink, HoloGrok, and Literacy

The distinction in thought processes between circles and squares may seem absurd to the average GridThinker, but for people surfing the resonant interval on the margins of mainstream society, such differences are quite obvious. During the campus apartheid debates of the 1980s in which students were demanding that educational institutions divest from South Africa, many of us felt it was important to recall that the reservations system in the United States also represents a kind of domestic apartheid. As mentioned, there remains an ongoing struggle in the southwestern United States' Four Corners region where the Hopi and Diné are pitted against each other in an intertribal strife over land and natural resources triggered by a historical conflict; yet the struggle also is a consequence of mining and "foreign" intervention (meaning the U.S. government). In 1985 we invited Diné activist Tom Bedone to visit to Oberlin's campus and to build an octagon-shaped traditional hogan (Diné home) among the shanties that were constructed by students to protest apartheid. Upon arrival, he said he had an epiphany during his first-ever flight as he watched the landscape unfold beneath the airplane: "No wonder you white people are so messed up," he said. "You all live in squares!"

The design component of Bedone's mental and cultural environment is circular, which enabled the foregrounding of our "square" world. The opposite for us is true. And because our "square" mentality is invisible to us, we can now foreground circular consciousness. This might explain the great distrust of new digital media, as various religious communities are feeling assaulted by emerging ways of engaging reality that are nonlinear and go against the grain of the grand drama of civilization that we have come to know, believe, and grasp onto, no matter how much suffering that causes (consider the Iraq war a prime example of the dangers of clinging to outmoded forms of world engagement). This also is why so much has been said about images of Earth from space, which allow us to grasp the spherical character of our environment; the images foreground Earth in a way that is unique to the modern technological age. You can also see this perceptual shifting in car commercials. Automobiles are so ubiquitous that they are the "environment." Often car ads feature the latest model in a natural context because that is the only way it can stand out. If a car ad features a vehicle in an urban environment, you will notice that no other cars exist in its fabricated world. In the extreme Hummer ads depict cars as extraterrestrial vehicles traveling on our alien planet. When the struggle is between what will become the figure set against the ambient, Earth or cars, media education's primary goal is to enable students to gain a deeper connection to their home world.

The standard North American education model is the legacy of "duality," a distinctly Western mode of consciousness that views everything as isolated objects and separate from consciousness. Former physicist Fritjof Capra (1983, p. 40), who has devoted his life to understanding our current operating paradigms and social structure, sums up the problem:

> The emphasis on rational thought in our culture is epitomized in Descartes' celebrated statement "Cogito, ergo sum"—"I think, therefore I exist"—which forcefully encouraged Western individuals to equate their identity with their rational mind rather than with their whole organism ... Retreating into our minds, we have forgotten how to "think" with our bodies, how to use them as agents of knowing. In doing so we have also cut ourselves off from our natural environment and have forgotten how to commune and cooperate with its rich variety of living organisms.... The division between mind and matter led to a view of the universe as a mechanical system consisting of separate objects, which in turn were reduced to fundamental material building blocks whose properties and interactions were thought to completely determine all natural phenomena. This Cartesian view of nature was further extended to living organisms, which were regarded as machines constructed from separate parts ... It has led to the well-known fragmentation in our academic disciplines and government agencies and has served as a rationale for treating the natural environment as if it consisted of separate parts, to be exploited by different interest groups.

Consider the overriding view of Roman Catholic perception at the time of Conquest: A separation from God a fear of God and the belief that the body is innately sinful, with the worship of nature a demonic activity. The Spanish Inquisition accused natives from the South to North as pagans and devil worshippers, yet from an indigenous perspective, the opposite was true. To indigenous people, the Spanish and their alien thought forms were a kind of evil or witchcraft. In some respects, if we can step away from our normal schooling on the subject, the experience of Conquest was like being invaded from outer space. It was, in the words of a Peruvian survivor, "A world in reverse" (Wright 1992, p. 8). Then there's the Hopi concept—Koyanaskatsi—which means world out of balance. Poet Paula Gunn Allen offers this thought experiment: she asks students in her Native American literature class to reflect upon what would they write about if a nuclear war destroyed their civilization and killed their family. Or worse yet, there might be a nuclear war waged by alien invaders who are products of your own, as is the case of *Battlestar Galactica* when the human-created Cylons decide to kill their creators and nuke the human race. The technological mindset is capable of this behavior. Thankfully, some aspects of popular culture seek to alert us to this mentality.

I'd like to suggest that the encounter between Europeans and Native Americans can enable us to see differing perceptual domains in action, especially in the context of trying to implement print literacy. "Media ecologists," such as Walter Ong, Harold Innis, Marshall McLuhan and Neil Postman, were concerned with cultural modes of communication as tools that shape consciousness. They observed that there have been two broad expressions of civilization: cultures characterized by orality and those by literacy. These are not absolutes, and I want to be careful by saying that ultimately it's dangerous to make such broad generalities about cultures. In some respects, what anthropologist Jack Goody (1995 [1977], pp. 146-7) calls the "Grand Dichotomy" has in the past been a way for Westerners to avoid complexity and difference: "The pervasive dichotomy between primitive and advanced societies, provides for some the frontier between anthropology and sociology, for others the divide between them and us, between the bricoleur and the scientist, between the non-logical, the non-rational, as against the logical and the rational, while some even see the one as the field for symbolic interpretations of social action, the other as calling for the application of a utilitarian calculus, the calculus of practical reason as against 'culture'.... I have suggested that this dichotomous treatment is inadequate to deal with the complexity of human development. Moreover, we have seen that it proposes no reasons for the difference and no mechanisms for change. On the contrary, it accepts a typology that phrases what might possibly be acceptable as a polarized field in terms of a binary division." Nonetheless these differing communication strategies remain good maps for understanding how values and choices are expressed in our engagement of the world. Moreover, if you take a typical list of binaries, such as primitive versus advanced, I would most certainly flip it. I truly believe there is no rational argument that can be made that our modern technological cultures translate as "advanced," as in the quip Gandhi made to a reporter who asked India's spiritual and political leader what he thought of Western civilization. Gandhi replied, "I think it would be a good idea." Why do we differentiate a scientific society from a magical one?

What is to prevent us from calling our entire economic and media system a kind of magic, science be damned?

HoloGrok is not simply the opposite of GridThink. Orality can have elements of text folded back into itself, and text can have aspects of orality, but for the sake of pattern seeking, we can still paint with broad brushstrokes in order to situate ourselves in the spectrum of communication forms. An essential difference is that HoloGrok can contain GridThink, whereas the opposite is not true. This is because orality is "aural" and "acoustic," based on sound, which has an all-encompassing quality that moves through mass and space (consider how sound moves through walls) and is immediate. Print literacy utilizes a kind of visuality specific to the dissecting movements of the eye when reading an alphabet. This is different than "looking," which is a kind of viewing that takes in all information at once (such as a Web page instead of a book page). Print literacy has the attendant qualities of sight (such as not going through walls), and the character of abstracting consciousness. As Ong (1982, p. 72) writes,

> Sight isolates, sound incorporate. Whereas situates the observer outside what he views, at a distance, sound pours into the hearer. Vision dissects, as Merleau-Ponty has observed (1961). Vision comes to a human being from one direction at a time: to look at a room or a landscape, I must move my eyes around from one part to another. When I hear, however, I gather sound simultaneously from every direction at once: I am at the center of my auditory world, which envelopes me, establishing me at a kind of core of sensation and existence. This centering effect of sound is what high-fidelity sound reproduction exploits with intense sophistication. You can immerse yourself in hearing, in sound. There is no way to immerse yourself similarly in sight.

Orality does not mean primitive, nor indigenous, although it is true that land-based cultures that did not develop alphabets are largely oral. Ong suggested that we are now moving back in the direction of the oral, calling it "secondary orality," a topic that will be explored more closely later.

The encounter of intercultural or cross-cultural mediation and literacies that resulted from Spanish conquest and Native Americans reveals the significance of implementing the alphabetic software. The Spanish entered the so-called "New World" when the Gutenberg press was expanding print in Europe; and linear perspective technique mastered during the Italian Renaissance had enhanced the mental software of European conquerors to chart, map, and site weapons. "Writing marched together with weapons, microbes, and centralized political organization as a modern agent of conquest" (Diamond 1999, p. 215); moreover, "Writing empowered European societies by facilitating political administration and economic exchanges, motivating and guiding exploration and conquest, and making available a range of information and human experience extending into remote places and times" (Diamond 1999, p. 360).

While it is true that Aztecs possessed logogram writing, de Kerckhove's (1997) survey of world writing systems shows that the alphabet is the only horizontal one, and that is a direct consequence of its left-brain bias, whereas vertical writing is right-brained. According to de Kerckhove, "the structure of our language has put pressure on our brain to emphasize its sequential and 'time-ordered' processing abilities." He then adds (p. 28),

> Since literacy is generally acquired during our formative years, and since it affects the organization of language—our most integral information-processing system—there are good reasons to suspect that the alphabet also affects the organization of our thought. Language is the software that drives human psychology. Any technology that significantly affects language must also affect behavior at a physical, emotional and mental level. The alphabet is like a computer program, but more powerful, more precise, more versatile and more comprehensive than any software yet written. A program designed to run the most powerful instrument in existence: the human being. The alphabet found its way in the brain to specify the routines that would support the firmware of the literate brainframe. The alphabet created two complementary revolutions: one in the brain and the other in the world.

This will "frame" the way we see the world. Additionally, McLuhan (2002, p. 50) believed the alphabet is uniquely capable of cannibalizing other thought forms:

> ... any society possessing the alphabet can translate any adjacent cultures into its alphabetic mode. But this is a one-way process. No non-alphabetic culture can take over an alphabetic one; because the alphabet cannot be assimilated; it can only liquidate and reduce. However, in the electronic age we may have discovered the limits of the alphabetic technology. It need no longer seem strange that peoples like the Greeks and Romans, who had experienced the alphabet, should also have been driven in the direction of conquest and organization-at-a-distance... [Harold Innis] explained why print causes nationalism and not tribalism; and why print causes price systems and markets such as cannot exist without print. In short, Harold Innis was the first person to hit upon the process of change as implicit in the forms of media technology.

We take the alienness of reading and writing for granted, yet consider that we spend at least 12 years in school trying to master and understand its basic rules and structures (and in the United States most still cannot master this skill beyond a basic understanding). Rather than exist as completely natural, the complex technology of writing is actually, in the greater scheme of human history, a unique cultural experience; but it also happens to be very successful at replicating itself and promoting a particular mode of engaging the world. Reading and writing orient the direction of how we think about space and a host of other characteristics. Abstraction and having a "point of view" are strong characteristic of the alphabetic mentality. As Ong notes, "Writing separates the knower from the known and this sets up conditions for 'objectivity,' in the sense of personal disengagement or distancing" (p. 46); and "... it takes only a moderate degree of literacy to make tremendous differences in thought processes" (p. 50).

Try the following exercise. In Figure 3, which line goes up, and which one goes down? If you said the left side goes up, it is because you are conditioned

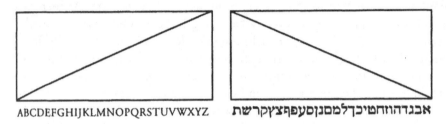

ABCDEFGHIJKLMNOPQRSTUVWXYZ   אבגדהוזחטיכךלמםנןסעפףצץקרשת

Figure 3

by print (since our eyes automatically move left to right). Now try this thought experiment: imagine the last time you took a bath. Did you see a picture of yourself, or did you feel yourself inside the hot water experiencing the relaxing sensation of the tub? If you saw a picture of yourself it is likely that you are conditioned by print culture, because people immersed in the reality of print have a tendency to objectify and to visually abstract their experience (see de Kerckhove). The one major exception to this, I presume, would be sex. This is only a guess, but if one were to perform the same memory exercise for the last time he or she made love, I bet that the memory would be of the body. Could it be that increasing sexualization of media content, especially for younger kids, is a response to an abstracted culture?

Native American scholar Fixico, who has extensively critiqued the linear quality of Western academics, writes, "Orality is the way of the American Indian mind" (p. 22). What does this mean? Fixico (p. 57) identifies circular perception at the core of orality:

The Circle of Life is the fundamental philosophy of traditional American Indians and it is integral to their belief system. It is also pertinent to many other cultures throughout the world in the annals of history. The "circle" symbolizes life itself. In this belief system of circularity, the circle encapsulates all of life. Like a Natural Democracy, all things are explained for those who share the same circular philosophy. All things are included in this circular system known to the native mind. Anything outside of the universe has not yet happened and its forthcoming existence becomes a part of the Circle of Life. Such new things are acknowledged and as more information about them occurs they become a part of the natural universe understood by the people.

At the basis of sustainability is the view that in a circular universe all is connected, all is related—hence the common Lakota prayer, Mitakuye Oyasin: "to all our relations," or the Mayan greeting, "in'lakesh," which means, "I am another yourself." In Internet parlance we could say, "to all our hyperlinked relations," or "I'm another your link."

The intention is not to emulate, imitate or force us to incorporate another's culture, but to recognize a meaningful design concept. As such, it's useful to see an example of how media can be viewed from a circular perspective. The following thought exercise for students of Buddhism is intended to highlight how a shift in perspective can completely change our relationship with our environment. In the exercise, novices are shown a piece of white paper and are asked to find clouds within it. A print-literate person would likely claim that the clouds are white and therefore are represented by the color of the paper, because GridThink always looks for things. But upon further probing, what students learn is that the clouds are actually in relationship with the paper. As the Buddhist monk Thich Nhat Hanh (1988, pp. 3-5) explains,

> If you are a poet, you will see clearly that there is a cloud floating in this sheet of paper. Without a cloud, there will be no rain; without rain, the trees cannot grow, and without trees, we cannot make paper. The cloud is essential for the paper to exist. If the cloud is not here, the sheet of paper cannot be here either... If you look into this sheet of paper even more deeply, we can see the sunshine in it. If the sunshine is not there, the tree cannot grow. In fact, nothing can grow. Even we cannot grow without sunshine. And so we know that the sunshine is also in this sheet of paper. The paper and the sunshine inter-are. And if we continue to look, we can see the logger who cut the tree and brought it to the mill to be transformed into paper. And we see the wheat. We know that the logger cannot exist without his daily bread, and therefore the wheat that became his bread is also in this sheet of paper. And the logger's father and mother are in it too... You cannot point out one thing that is not here—time, space, the earth, the rain, the minerals in the soil, the sunshine, the cloud, the river, the heat. Everything co-exists with this sheet of paper...As thin as this sheet of paper is, it contains everything in the universe in it.

We learn from the exercise that clouds are not a thing, but a process, a system. While it is true that the blank paper might look like clouds, making an image out of nothing is merely developing a mental construct of what we think should be there.

In terms of understanding media, one other lesson we can glean from this exercise is that media are more like water than solid objects. If we are to take the brain as a self-patterning system, then we began to understand that the way the mind constructs beliefs or ideas is more like a topology with various channels for perception. We have perceptual drainage basins that are shaped by experience, biology, evolution, language, and the complexity of life. Information is more akin to liquid in terms of how it flows and finds appropriate channels that permit it to travel, like water through a canyon.

The cloud metaphor also instructs us that clouds are unique, transitory formations in time and space. Not all water becomes clouds, and not all clouds make rain, but it remains true that in a biosphere, water cycles and flows. So the circle metaphor is totally appropriate, because, after all, the water planet deserves a water logic.

CHAPTER TWO

Mediaspheric Niches

In fact, the secret ambition of design is to become invisible, to be taken up into the culture, absorbed into the background. The highest order of success in design is to achieve ubiquity, to become banal.

Bruce Mau, *Massive Change*

T here is something curious about the human mind when two completely alien cultures can communicate with symbols that were previously unknown to each other. It's my sense that the Hopis were looking at the crucifix tautologically to expose its self-evident truth, which is that the Spanish pursuit of empire building was concordant with their spiritual outlook. Postman (1995, p. 174) reminds us, "A metaphor is not an ornament. It is an organ of perception." Thus, visual metaphors like the cross and circle can transcend their context, but can also be altered by it. There's always a dance. Yuri M. Lotman (2001, p. 103), who conceived the semiosphere, argues that, "A symbol's memory is always more ancient that [sic] the memory of its non-symbolic text-context." Throughout the Americas, there were crosses that represented many things, such as the four directions, the tree of life, or the point where the constellation ellipses crossed the Milky Way. Among the Maya, a four-pointed star commonly represented Venus. In Europe, there were multiple permutations of crosses and circles as well. As Frank Waters (1975, pp. 212-13) notes in his comparison between the religious practices of Puebloans, Hopis and Mexicans, the cross and circle were navigated with great sophistication:

> Underlying all these interpretations is a common meaning. From the earliest ages of man, the cross has been a universal symbol. If the extension of its four arms in opposite directions represents conflict and division, their point of intersection signifies reconciliation and unification. It is the meeting point of the conscious, the mystic center identical and unconscious creative principle of the universe. Immemorially it has been shown surrounded by a circle, as often has been the entire cross. Now to leave the circumference of the circle for the center, as Cirlot reminds us, is equivalent to moving from the exterior to the interior, from multiplicity to unity, from form to contemplation. And it is here on these crosses that the Chamulas and Zinacantecos carve circles and hang flowers. The cross then is a Tree of Life, for

life develops only from conflict and reconciliation of the opposites; the "doorway" of communication between men and gods; and between our unconscious and conscious selves. It was to its mystic center that Quetzalcoatl journeyed. And so it is in these multitudinous, stark crosses in the Chiapas highlands we see reconciled ancient and contemporary Indian belief.

The Hopis could see the cross in the new light because of the symbol's potent capability to transmit cultural information (Lotman, p. 104):

> ...symbols reveal their duality: on the one hand, by recurring throughout a culture's history a symbol shows its invariancy and its repeatability. A symbol stands out as something different from the textual space that surrounds it, like an emissary from other cultural epochs (or from other cultures), a reminder of the ancient (or eternal) foundations of that culture. On the other hand, a symbol actively correlates with its cultural context, transforms it and is transformed by it. Its invariancy is realized in variants. And the changes which the "eternal" meaning of the symbol undergoes in the given culture, highlight the changeability of the context.... What is important is that the semantic potentials of the symbol are always greater than any realization of them: the links which, with the help of its expression, a symbol establishes with a particular semiotic context, never exhaust all its semantic valency. This is the semantic reserve thanks to which a symbol can enter into unexpected relationships, altering its essence and deforming its textual context in unpredictable ways.... The cross, the circle, the pentagram have many more semantic potentials that [sic] Titian's painting *The flaying of Marsyas* because between expression and content of simple symbols lies a gulf of mutual unprojectability. The "simple" symbols are the ones that form the symbolic nucleus of a culture, and whether a culture as a whole is of a symbolizing or de-symbolizing tendency can be judged by the number of them.

The Hopis were "de-symbolizing" the cross by recognizing it as a symptom. The Spanish, on the other hand, symbolized (thereby thingifying) Native Americans as animals, pagans and devil worshippers. Obviously the Spanish conquerors misperceived Native Americans (but not all Spaniards; there were some exceptionally perceptive and intuitive Castilians who grokked Native American culture), whereas Native Americans grasped the Spanish mindset, and were on many occasions capable of ingenious maneuverability. For example, Rigoberta Menchú (1984) wrote that when the Quiché Maya of Guatemala absorbed Christianity, they substituted the Bible's pantheon with their own, so when they went to church they were still praying to the sun and Mother Earth. Much of their cultural knowledge remained secret because they knew that the Spanish were clever and would try to twist their heritage into a language of oppression. For instance, one of the most overtly symbolic practices of the Spanish conquers was to dismantle indigenous temples and pyramids for materials to build their new cities and churches, or to simply build right on top of them. The Mixtec ruins of Mitla in Oaxaca, Mexico, have a Roman Catholic Church constructed on top of a temple; yet I have seen firsthand indigenous healers perform cleansing rituals in front of that church's altar as if the structure were invisible. In the case of Mexico City's central plaza, the zocalo, the cathedral and plaza grounds are built with pyramid stones. Yet off in one corner is an open archeological site, and every day Aztec dancers blow their conch shells, burn copal and pound deer-skin drums while rhythmically paying homage to nature's elements. With Diego Rivera's fresco history of Mexico's underclass—indigenous and oppressed in the adjacent National Palace— it's not difficult to realize in the center of the world's largest metropolis how transient the notion of conquest really is. In the end, the Hopis, Quiche Quiché Maya, and Chamulas ingeniously perceived an end game, as in the pattern at play, and were able to surf it through a transgression of the conquering power's symbolic order. To Spain's detriment (recall it was the most powerful empire in the world whose currency was the international gold standard during the period of conquest), it would be the right-brained capacity of the local population that would ultimately outlast the strategies of GridThink control.

The folly of GridThink empire building can be summed up by the Aztec concept of "In Xochtil, In Cuicatl"— flor y canto— "flower and song." It suggests that empires come and go, but what remains is poetry. Aztec poets remind us that we are on loan to each other, and that poetry lives on regardless of who is in power. This concept also relates to technology, which dies and becomes obsolete; but works of art, no matter how old, *live* on (even the images of the Altamira cave are still used, far outliving their stone tool contemporaries). In this sense we could say that this is a case of when HoloGrok is far more sustainable than GridThink (and a powerful argument for supporting arts education is school). Like the difference between love and fear, a GridThink mindset does not contain the poetic imagination, but the HoloGrok mind can embrace within it both a rational and analytical understanding of power, but also much more. These historical dramas illustrate why comprehending design is a matter of life and death.

Symbols make up the semiosphere, the communications equivalent of the biosphere. Lotman argues that, like our global ecosystem, there are smaller semiospheres with strong centers (such as written language with grammatical rules, or anything that appears "neutral," i.e., invisible) called "metalanguages" whose peripheries contain negotiable norms (such as avant-garde art). Like McLuhan's concept of environment/anti-environment (see chapter six), it's possible to know the center and border regions of any semiosphere by looking at the difference between foreground and background in any given media sample (such as cars and the natural world in an ad). In 2000, I walked nearly 600 miles across Spain. At one point I entered a car, and the experience significantly altered my relationship with the environment. While trekking the acoustic landscape was the foreground, and I was the background. In the car, the landscape was the background, with my velocity becoming a kind of violent foreground. In terms of media, this relates to the difference between looking and seeing. Depending on how we focus our eyes, we "see" differently. The alphabetic mind isolates and sees objects; the acoustic mind "monitors" space, containing all within it. This is like the difference between a Renaissance painting and a Chinese landscape. In classical Western painting there is a clear delineation between the figure and background, the human usually being the "anti-environment" (the thing that sticks out), and "nature" being the invisible ambient "environment." In the Chinese landscape, there is an equal balance between negative and positive space, like the symbol for yin and yang. The foreground and background coexist. This translates in Japanese animation as well when shots are used to draw in ambience, whether there are pauses and cuts of rain puddles, or lingering shots on empty space, such as a street or landscape.

I'd like to think of the fringes of semiospheres as being like ecological niches with their edge systems:

> The notion of boundary is an ambivalent one: it both separates and unites. It is always the boundary of something and so belongs to both frontier cultures, to both contiguous semiospheres. The boundary is bilingual and polylingual. The boundary is a mechanism for translating texts of an alien semiotics into "our" language, it is the place where what is "external" is transformed into what is "internal", it is a filtering membrane which so transforms foreign texts that they become part of the semiosphere's internal semiotics while still retaining their own characteristics (Lotman, pp. 136-7).

The semisophere is heterogeneous and asymmetrical in the same way that media forms express different functions of the brain hemispheres. This is critical to remember because when media literacy activists focus on Big Media, there is a tendency to exaggerate the homogeneous aspects of technological communication (though I think it's valid to argue that multinational corporate media have a way of flattening culture and language in the same way that a large flood can eliminate nooks, crannies or odd surfaces). Just as Postman argued that media make war on each other, it is likely that many media activists are trying to push books back into the center of the metalanguage domain, thereby relegating electronic media to the background.

In terms of thinking of semiospheres as ecosystems, we can interject one other biological metaphor. The biologists Janine Benyus and Elisabet Sahtouris draw on a model of forest ecology to explain economics by arguing, "The earliest, colonizing, stage of forest-system development is dominated by fast-growing, aggressively competitive, and transient species that are eventually displaced by the emergence of the more patient, cooperative, settled, energy-efficient species that define the mature phase" (quoted in Korten, p.15). This is one description of emergence theory which argues that systems eventually stabilize and self-organize after chaotic phases. Lotman (p. 134) sees the same behavior in the semiosphere: "... in the centre of the cultural space, sections of the semiosphere aspiring to the level of self-description become rigidly organized and self-regulating." Niklas Luhmann (2000) argues that media self-generate their own reality through a set of assumptions that frame the world in a specific, self-reflexive manner. He draws on the concept of autopoiesis, which is based on a model developed in the 1970s by Chilean biologists Humberto Maturana and Francisco Varela. Influenced by cybernetics and systems thinking, they saw that cells were self-making systems, rather than a bunch of separate components (demonstrated by the simple fact that they can re-grow and heal after an injury). They reformulated the concept of cell structure through their theory of autopoiesis—literally "self-made"—and have argued that it could be applied to larger living systems.

Luhmann views society as one large organism with eight autopoeitic subsystems, mass media being one subset of them. Each of these subsystems self-organize, generating their own reality, so to speak, by filtering information through a binary process of whether it belongs "inside" or "outside" of itself. Specifically, the mass media subsystem categorizes according to whether something is "information" or "non-information," information being characterized by "newness." Luhmman draws on Gregory Bateson's definition of information: "any difference that makes a difference in some later event" (p. 18). So in terms of its self-reflective, reality defining properties, mass media constantly processes the world into its coding (schemas), drawing from the noise generated by butting against other subsystems: "What is happening... is autopoiesis—the reproduction of communication from the outcomes of communication" (p. 83).

What happens when nothing is new anymore, as in the postmodern conundrum that we are at the end of history and everything has been done before? What occurs is probably what is happening right now, which is the general media system composting (or remediating) old media. Just as postmodernism cannibalized all past forms of art, media, architectures and whatnot, the "newness" machine runs tirelessly in place just to stay relevant (more on this in chapter six). On the edge of this rat race engine I imagine the tiny sparks of an eternal fire crackling like city lights on the horizon, where all that gets filtered in and out of the membrane percolate and procreate to emerge in the center of the media zeitgeist.

We can certainly say that modern electronic media are in many ways like the hyperactive and competitive young forest. Perhaps with the social networks of Web 2.0, the dominance of the mash-up aesthetic (which is recursive because it relies on sampling and refashioning old media), and the collapse of traditional boundaries once occupied by fringe arts and fashion, the larger media system of the West is starting to mature and become self-organized in the same way as cities are. By comparing media to StarLogo (a chaos and emergence simulation software program), Steven Johnson (2001, pp. 219-20) describes the "emergence theory" model of new media:

> It begins with a perfectly ordered grid, like an aerial view of Kansas farmland: each network has its line-up in place, each radio station has its playlist. And then the convergence wave washes across that world and eliminates all the borders. Suddenly, every miniseries, every dance remix, every thriller, every music video ever made, is available from anywhere, anytime. The grid shatters into a million free-floating agents, roaming aimlessly across the landscape like those original slime mold cells. All chaos, no order. And then, slowly, clusters begin to form, shapes emerging out of the shapelessness. Some clusters grow into larger entities—perhaps the size of small cable networks and last for many years. Other clusters are more idiosyncratic, and fleeting. Some map onto the physical world ("inner-city residents"); some are built out of demographic categories ("senior citizens"); many appear based on patterns in our cultural tastes that we never knew existed, because we lacked the tools to perceive them ("Asian American Carroll O'Connor fans"). These new shapes will be like the aggregations of slime mold cells...; they will be like the towns blossoming across Europe eight hundred years ago; they will be like the neighborhoods of Paris or New York City. They will be like those other shapes because they will be generated by the same underlying processes: pattern-matching, negative feedback, ordered randomness, distributed intelligence. The only difference is the materials they are made of: swarm cells, sidewalks, zeros and ones.

This is where a permaculture perspective of the semiosphere, which aids our understanding of niche ecologies, can be supported by approaches to video game literacy. The concept of "semiotic domains" coined by James Paul Gee (2003) explains varying contexts of symbol management and mental systems. For Gee, a semiotic domain is "any set of practices that recruits one or more modalities (for example, oral or written language, images, equations, symbols, sounds, gestures, graphs, artifacts) to communicate distinctive types of meanings. Here are some examples of semiotic domains: cellular biology, porn literary criticism, first-person-shooter video games, high-fashion advertisements, Roman Catholic theology, modernist painting, midwifery, rap music, wine connoisseurship—through a nearly endless, motley, and ever changing list" (p.18). As is the case of the cross and circle, "All of these thing are signs (symbols, representations, whatever term you want to use) that 'stand for' (take on) different meanings in different situations, contexts, practices, cultures, and historical periods. For example, the image of a cross means Christ (or Christ's death) in the context of Christian social practices, and it means the four points of the compass (north, south, west, and east) in the context of other social practices (e.g., in some African religions)" (pp.17-18).

The concept of a semiotic domain is useful because when we talk of literacy we need to know that words, symbols or communication forms have meanings in different contexts, such as a kiva (an underground chamber where Hopis perform ceremonies) or a classroom in a public high school. Literacy from a traditional approach advocates a "general" knowledge that is appropriate for all situations (remember the ridiculous books that came out in the 1990s about cultural literacy?), usually guided by a bias toward print. I agree with Gee (p. 19) when he argues:

> In the modern world, print literacy is not enough. People need to be literate in a great variety of different semiotic domains. If these domains involve print, people often need the print bits, of course. However, the vast majority of domains involve semiotic (symbolic, representational) resources besides print and some don't involve print as a resource at all. Furthermore, and more important, people need to be able to learn to be literate in new semiotic domains throughout their lives. If our modem, global, high-tech, and science-driven world does anything, it certainly gives rise to new semiotic domains and transforms old ones at an ever faster rate.

Like the metalanguage of semiospheres, semiotic domains possess a "design grammar" (Gee, p. 30), which have a harmonic quality akin to Derrick de Kerckhove's (1997, p. 154) view of design as being "technology's public relations":

> In a very large sense, design plays a metaphorical role, translating functional benefits into sensory and cognitive modalities. Design finds its shape and its place as a kind of overtone, as an echo of technology. Design often echoes the specific character of technology and corresponds to its basic pulse. Being the visible, audible or textural outer shape of cultural artifacts, design emerges as what can be called the "skin of culture."

Reiterating that writing is a technology, in the case of the cross and circle, the cross is a design reflective of the alphabetic mind, and the circle is in sync with a Native American sense of technology. Native Americans scholars Vine Deloria and John R. Daniel Wildcat (2001, p. 70) submit that:

> two very different understandings of technology are the issue. A deeply seated (metaphysically based) Western view of technology as science applied to industrial (manufacture) and commercial objectives, versus a (metaphysically based) American Indian, or rather indigenous, view of technology as practices and toolmaking to enhance our living in and with nature. The Western conception and practices of technology are bound up in essentially human-centered materialism: the doctrine that

physical well-being and worldly possessions constitute the greatest good and highest value in life. Indigenous conceptions and practices of technology are embedded in a way of living life that is inclusive of spiritual, physical, emotional, and intellectual dimensions emergent in the world or, more accurately, particular places in the world.

If we were to put the Deloria and Wildcat description into graphic form it would be the medicine wheel because its four quadrants cycle through "spiritual, physical, emotional, and intellectual dimensions." Additionally, note how important the sense of place is in their definition, which is an inherent component of their semiotic domain's design grammar because the medicine wheel's four quadrants also represent the cardinal directions.

I now want to add to our theoretical palette Régis Debray's (1996, p. 18) concept of the socio-technological complex that he calls the "mediasphere." Unlike the semiosphere, Debray's idea combines the social, historical, and semiological. He asks three basic questions: "1) the technological question—which machine is at work here? 2) the semantic question—which discourse are we given to understand? and 3) the political question—which power is exerted, how and on whom? Looking not for *that which is behind*, but for *what takes place between*...". We could say that if Lotman was interested in the contents of the sphere and how its boundaries form, Debray is exploring the sphere's shape. What we are looking for is a happy medium between the purely semiological and McLuhan's maxim that the medium is the message. Here, Paolo Carpignano (1999) strikes a balance: "The medium is not a system of transportation, nor a system of representation of a reality that precedes it, but an each time different material mode of perceiving that reality. The medium plays a part, a significant part, in the process of signification, and thus we can see a correlation not just between media forms and ways of communicating, but also between media forms and ways of perceiving reality and ways of thinking" (p. 178). As such, "the experience of mass media is more similar to the experience of architectural forms than of, say, a painting; that is it involves not a critical absorption or appraisal by observer, but the distracted experience of a user, a passer-by" (p. 185). This deviates from a more standard media literacy approach, which focuses primarily on ideology and content. This is not to say that ideology isn't at play, but it's more of a by-product of our cognitive construction of the world. The example of Mexico City's zocalo illustrates this perfectly, because when the Spanish dismantled the Aztec pyramids, they were literally taking apart calculators, calendars and cosmological maps, and reengineering them into the vertical architecture of a Roman Catholic church. Each stone was taken apart and refashioned into bricks, just as the alphabet cannibalizes language by breaking phonemes into discrete units. The construction of the cathedral was also the reconstruction of the cultural mind. One can imagine dazed and perplexed Aztecs when they began traveling through this reconstituted space.

I like to think of semiotic domains as bioregions—ecologies bounded by their watersheds. This allows for scale, because like a bioregion, which can range from a tributary to a major river system, a semiotic domain explains how diverse niches can coexist and interact. And just as Lotman's concept of the semiosphere was inspired by the idea of a biosphere, Debray's mediasphere can be the massive mental biosphere behind the forces of history. Whereas Debray's footprint is huge like that of a satellite beam, Gee takes us to the mountaintop. As we know, mountains vary in size and breadth. The view from Mount Everest is going to be much different than the one from the Sangre de Cristo Mountains outside Santa Fe, New Mexico. Like the Google map navigation tool that allows us to shift scale and the horizon line, our pedagogy needs to be flexible, too. So in an effort to hybridize both ideas, I'd like to propose a mediacological approach called "mediaspheric niches" that preserves Debray's concept of mediation, form and technology with the specific characteristics of localized semiotic domains. This gives us flexibility to maneuver between milieu zones and to recognize the border regions that exist in the diverse design schema of globalized convergence media. This is why the mediacological method of media education is truly multicultural, because it recognizes that any time people interact with media, a number of diverse factors come into play, including cultural frames outside the Western intellectual construct. Thus, climbing to the mountaintop is necessary in order to see beyond our perceptual regions and into new territory. To get there we can trudge through the forest, or cheat by looking at maps. Sometimes it takes a bit of both.

Mapping Mediacological Niches

In 1900–three years before the airplane, nine years before the discovery of the North Pole, eleven years before the discovery of the South Pole, and thirty-five years before radar–world-around geographical information had multiplied to such an extent that the major governments of the Earth agreed to have their geographers hold an omniworld meeting to adopt universal standards of cartography and geography. The world's cartographers agreed to adopt a one-million-to-one scale of producing their master world maps. At that same meeting of world geographers and cartographers it was noted by many of those professionals that the rectilinear, latitude-longitude, geographical coordinate system's angular-direction-and-linearly-measured-distances method of surveying of the world (at that time in universal use) had permitted much large-scale error to creep in. It was proving less and less satisfactory to go on trying to "square" the spherical surface of the Earth.

R. Buckminster Fuller, Critical Path

I oppose the sinister cartography of the New World Order with the conceptual map of the New World Border– a great trans- and intercontinental border zone, a place in which no centers remain. It's all margins, meaning there are no "others" or better said, the only true "others" are those who resist fusion, *mestizaje*, and cross-cultural dialogue. In this utopian cartography, hybridity is the dominant culture; Spanglish, Franglé, and Gringoñol are *linguas francas*; and monoculture is a culture of resistance practiced by a stubborn or scared minority.

Guillermo Gómez-Peña, The New World Border

In the northern hemisphere the sun's shadow follows a right-to-left path; hence our clocks move in the same direction. If mechanical clocks had been invented in the southern hemisphere, our watches would move counterclockwise. Likewise "orient"– as in "orientating" your position on the land– comes from the Latin root for east, which is the location of the rising sun and Jerusalem if you are in Europe (Wood, Kaiser, Abrams 2006, pp. 87-92). If we used a Native American calendar, we'd have 13 lunar months in a year. Instead we have a Roman calendar that imposes an arbitrary construct over natural cycles of time. These are examples of reality frames that result from mediaspheric domains, deeply embedded worldviews that seem natural to us, but are all constructed. As I noted in the introduction, getting oriented, or finding a sense of place, is one of the primary tasks of media literacy. As educators we are really guides, but that can be tricky, as Stephen S. Hall (2004, p. 15) notes, because part of life's pleasures and pains is getting lost and then finding one's way again through the discovery of one's orienteering abilities:

> Orientating begins with geography, but it reflects a need of the conscious, self-aware organism for a kind of transcendent orientation that asks not just where am I, but where do I fit in this landscape? Where have I been? Where shall I go, and what values will I pack for the trip? What culture of knowledge allows me to know what I know, which is often another way of knowing where I am? And what pattern, what grid of wisdom, can I impose on my accumulated, idiosyncratic geographies? The coordinates marking this territory are unique to each individual and lend themselves to a very private kind of cartography.

I'd like to suggest that a good place to start positioning ourselves in the mediacological universe is by returning to the idea of bioregionalism, because the concept can aid us greatly in trying to situate ourselves within our particular mediaspheric niches. Although bioregionalism can be loosely interpreted in the same way that anarchism means lots of things to different people, the general practice is designed to get us to move beyond thinking about geography from the perspective of political map grids and to help us understand how our homes are shaped by the natural contours of the land. Like our embodied mind in the semiosphere, we all live somewhere, and that somewhere needs remediation, protection and a plan for sustainable living. Yet how well do we really know our natural habitat? One exercise can be particularly enlightening. With a digital camera, photograph several common native species of plants or trees and then ask students to identify them by name. Then show cutout letters from corporate logos and ask the students to guess to which companies they belong. You can probably conjecture the results.

Bioregions can range from the area surrounding a small creek tributary to a major river system, but as a rule, they are defined by watersheds, soil and plant types, weather patterns, language, and culture. The natural boundaries of bioregions often cross the arbitrary lines of traditional political borders. The Rio Grande (or Rio Bravo, as it is called in Mexico), for example, is well known as the boundary between Mexico and the United States, yet its watershed starts in Colorado and includes much of New Mexico, Texas and the Mexican states of Chihuahua, Coahuila, Nuevo León and Tamaulipas. At its core, bioregionalism is a cultural idea, one that relies on a mix of hard science and culture to map sustainable futures. Bioregionalists range from indigenous elders to permaculture activists, from writers to acupuncturists, from artists to scientists. Bioregionalism can come across as more cosmological than political. However, it can also be seen as a modern counterpoint to neoliberalism: bioregionalism looks at nature beyond political borders as an integrated part of culture, economic justice, local empowerment, and sustainability. And herein lies the beauty of bioregionalism: to effectively organize an entire watershed, one must start looking beyond legal grids, or borders, by recognizing that nature serves different communities and cultures. Bioregional activists weave cultural and environmental education together and must be at least bilingual to communicate across political and cultural boundaries.

It's not just people who are bound to place; technology also has its geography and constructions of space. Think of Silicon Valley (San Jose, California), Silicon Alley (Manhattan), or Hollywood. These locations were not random creations, but rather came into being as a result of people and the types of places that are suited both in terms of natural resources and to particular social attitudes. For example, it has been shown that the common denominator for the emergence of tech hubs is a community tolerance of homosexuality. Many have argued that California melded psychedelic experimentation with the aerospace and entertainment industry to produce the necessary vision for new technology concepts. New York became a prominent economic powerhouse because it was a manufacturing center at the mouth of the Hudson River, thus enabling goods to be shipped inland and overseas. That Manhattan evolved from manufacturing goods to images has its lineage in the geography of commerce. In New Mexico, the Silicon Mesa (Albuquerque and surrounding area) is a direct result of the Rio Grande being a water resource for chip-making; the Silicon Mesa also exists because of the historical legacy of the atomic bomb project (because of its isolation) that made the area a haven for high-tech research. This is all by way of suggesting that technology is tied directly to land and that it has always had a relationship with how people and geography intersect, including a direct correlation between transportation and media. As Debray (1996, p. 27) illustrates:

> The concordance of the tele-communicative and transportational, which is not only a chronological coincidence, begins with the technological and social use of electric energy (the social break coming between ten and thirty years behind the technological invention). The dates show it: to the electromagnetic telegraph corresponds the railroad, to the telephone the automobile, to radiotelephony the airplane (or, to radio's years the "aircrafts" years), to television the intercontinental missile and space rocket launcher. But before this and for three thousand years, on the ground the saddled horse aligned the speed of circulating messages with that of persons. Travel time for a long while remained stationary, if not unchanging.

We can add to this equation the relationship between satellites and the Internet. As I show in chapter nine, Global Positioning Satellite technology is now reintroducing place into community uses of high technology.

If maps help us understand the geography of space, then the geography of maps can be utilized for understanding mediacological domains. Because maps reflect the mapmaker's inner landscape and cultural subjectivity, a map becomes a worldview, a chart of the cartographer's universe. Maps require "projections," technical jargon for the process of converting geographical data from a three-dimensional sphere to a two-dimensional surface. Ironically "projection" is also the term that Freudian psychology uses to describe the defense mechanism when an individual "projects" his or her undesired feelings about the self onto other people. Mapmakers are not necessarily making psychological projections, but when they are projecting the intentions of their respective mediaspheric domains, are they also inadvertently revealing cultural anxieties and desires to control that which is not controllable?

Maps designed for utility represent a kind of use bias. For example, nautical maps are much different than highway maps, yet the standard Mercator map projection used in most classrooms with the distorted landmass that makes Alaska bigger than Mexico was designed to simplify ship navigation (it delineates with a straight line the most direct route across water). It is the world according to commerce, trade and transportation. As indicated in Jan Vermeer's seventeenth century studio portraits, wall maps emerged as indicators of worldly perspective and control of space at the time when Europe was carving up the world into colonies. The problem, as has become with our GridThink mentality, is that visual representations of the world become distorted reality tunnels. "The map was also a novelty in the sixteenth century, age of Mercator's projection, and was key to the new vision of peripheries of power and wealth. Columbus had been a cartographer before he was a navigator; and the discovery that it was possible to continue in a straight-line course, as if space were uniform and continuous, was a major shift in human awareness in the Renaissance. More important, the map brings forward at once a principal theme of King Lear, mainly the isolation of the visual sense as a kind of theme of blindness" (McLuhan, 2002 [1962], p.11). As if euclidean geometry is being forced into a spherical reality, maps begin to shape reality. Ong (1982, p. 73) notes that HoloGrokers don't necessarily get maps: "For oral cultures, the cosmos is an ongoing event with man at its center ... Only after print and the extensive experience with maps that print implemented would human beings, when the thought about the cosmos or universe or 'world,' think primarily of something laid out before their eyes, as in a modern printed atlas, a vast surface or assemblage of surfaces (vision represents surfaces) ready to be 'explored.' The ancient oral world knew of few 'explorers,' though it did know many itinerants, travelers, voyagers, adventurers, and pilgrims." This quote has been misunderstood, because it implies that oral people are not, or cannot be, explorers. His argument is about how different cultures relate to space and place, and for GridThinkers space is something visually laid out that is moved through a point of view. This contrasts with the notion "being-in-space," a state in which space flows from within a person.

Some maps have been used to change the cultural view of the world, such as Buckminster Fuller's Dymaxion Air-Ocean Map that depicts global land mass as one giant, connected island instead of a collection of nation-states. Such a view would promote his concept of Spaceship Earth. The "South on Top" map that reverses North and South redirects our political orientation highlighting the common Western bias that what is on top is superior (this is a legacy of our body's vertical orientation). By positioning the economically poor regions of the world, which predominantly are in the South, in reverse order, the map forces us to rethink our notion of hierarchy. Or there's the Peters Projection Map depicting true landmass—revealing the geological truth that Africa actually dwarfs Europe.

Earthlings have many concepts of utility. Like the media tools we have discussed, a "projection" is just a medium, so if we were to fault a map, we would have to look at the respective mediaspheric domains of the mapmaker, publisher, and users. This is also an important lesson for media literacy, because the same kind of critical questions we use for a map could be applied to a media sample. These queries include:

1. Does the map show the world whole or does it break it up? In map talk the question is whether the world is displayed as continuous or interrupted.
2. What shape does the projection make the world?
3. How are the continents and oceans arranged?
4. Are the grid lines curved or straight?
5. Do the parallels and meridians cross at right, or at larger or smaller, angles?

(Wood, Kaiser and Abrams, 2006, pp. 37-9)

Obviously these questions don't translate perfectly for media artifacts or works of art, but in general these are good tools to use when considering whether or not a map expresses GridThink or HoloGrok. What we learn from all these maps is that a flat-surface representation of a globe requires distortion. Our eyes are also globes and the various visual technologies developed to reproduce the world, such as linear perspective drawing technique, the camera obscura, and photographic lens cameras conform the world to imitate how the light bends as it passes through the viscous liquid of the eyeball. So even though we say a linear perspective drawing looks "realistic," what we are really saying is that it conforms the world to the way the mind perceives it, remembering that eyes are instruments of the brain. Whenever viewing linear perspective art, the viewer is guided to a single place: the world is set for the eye, not for God. Linear perspective makes the world into a grid, conforming the environment to an objective space in which an autonomous subject can move about:

> Seeing things in perspective means putting everything into its proper place, with its right proportion in your mind. Rationality, from the Latin *ratio*, also implies the sense of proportion. Rationalism is the study of objects, notions and relationships not simply in isolation but with respect to their proportion among other things belonging to the same order. Rationality is part of the alphabetic psychodynamic and is expressed, without doubt, in the perspectivist frame (de Kerckhove, 1997, p.33).

From this many cultural shifts took place. Cartography– the science of mapping– becomes more "accurate," as the world can now become a grid that can be navigated by bodies in space. In the case of the Mercator map, it's ships in space. Land can be "ruled"– measured, defined, exploited. The idea of objectivity becomes a central cultural tenant, which is embodied by painting until the advent of photography.

Maps can be useful for summarizing the difference between GridThink and HoloGrok as is the case with maps by Native Americans. Mark Warhus (1997), a museum curator, researched the world's archives and libraries to dig up an assortment of Native American maps that reflect a different worldview than their European counterparts. "To read these Native American maps it is necessary to suspend Western preconceptions of what makes a map. Unlike Western cartography, where the primary document is the physical map and the conventions of scale, longitude, latitude, direction, and relative location are believed to 'scientifically' depict a static landscape, Native American maps are pictures of experience. They are formed in the human interaction with the land and are a record of the events that give it meaning" (p. 3). The story of how these maps came to be, the context of their creation, and attempts to reconstruct the view of the often anonymous mapmakers is an engrossing tale that parallels the history of European conquest in North America. "Like a double-sided mirror they illuminate the trail of repression, exploitation, violence and death that transformed the face of North America and they hold up this image as a seldom acknowledged aspect of Western historical record. The window these maps open on this other side of the North American history is one of their most important contributions" (p. 4). The irony is that most Native American maps would not exist had they not been made at the request of Europeans. It was the nature of most Native American societies to convey time and space through their oral tradition. Since most bands lived migratory lives, information was communicated through "transitory illustrations" in dirt, snow or ashes. On some occasions, records were left on birch bark, animal skin or rocks. "Many of the maps document this combination of Western media and indigenous graphic technique" (p. 8). Some maps, like the one of time created in stone by the Hopis, delineate prophecy and tribal history.

Native maps lacked "difference between rivers, portages and trails; the map simply represents the route taken as a continuous line. Like the difference between oral and print communications, size was rarely to scale because it lacked the information that needed to be conveyed by the map" (p.11). Distances were communicated in terms of how many days it took to travel to a location. Europeans relied on Native American informants to map unknown regions, define territory for the purpose of treaties, and to establish colonial boundaries. Not surprisingly, more is known about the European who obtained the information and/or made the map than the actual Native American informant. Contrary to popular mythology, explorers like Lewis and Clark could not have achieved their ventures without the information supplied by Native American mapmakers and the Native American intelligence required for charting unknown lands for white explorers. In one case study, a Spanish captive, Miguel, a Native American of unknown tribal origins captured in the Plains, described from memory information from a 42-day trek. He charted land from the Plains, to the Pacific, to Tenochtitlan, now Mexico City. Sadly, this information was obtained through interrogation, as in torture, after he was captured by Spanish troops. Like ghosts from the past, these maps have reentered our collective history, but they're tainted by pain and misery.

The obvious difference between European and Native American maps was the result in their differing views of land usage. For Europeans, land ownership was determined by "right of discovery," which contrasts with the Native American concept of land stewardship. While the colonists engaged in a land grab that required deeds, maps, and written records (as in literacy), Natives relied on their oral tradition to describe social relations combined with the landscape. Land was considered commonly owned, while fishing and hunting grounds and crop fields were assigned to clans or bands. Land use reflected mobile, migratory patterns that changed with the seasons, and sometimes through tribal warfare. That a society would require paper to demarcate land was a totally alien concept to Native Americans, but not to the print-biased mind that equates writing and paper with facts.

Maps are also palimpsests. For example, if you use a common highway map, what may be surprising is that the creation of modern roads often started with animal trails. Susan Calafate Boyle (1997), historian for the National Park Service and author of *Los Capitalistas: Hispano Merchants and the Santa Fe Trade*, a study of merchant activity in Santa Fe during the rise of the Santa Fe Trail, points out that initial Spanish trade routes weren't carved out of a void. "There are certain patterns associated with people moving across the land. For example, routes are selected due to environmental factors. You have to have water, avoid major obstacles like mountains, [travel] where weather is kind to you, and to where passage is easier. For centuries ... these trail routes follow an evolution. Some become highways, some state trails. They all have multiple uses, multiple cultures" (quoted in Lopez, 2000, p. 42). Although the Spanish were able to exploit and develop trade between central Mexico and what is now called the United States Southwest, Boyle sees a larger pattern of trade that existed for centuries with Native Americans. "Some were developed in the nineteenth century, some developed before the Spanish even showed up ... Whenever you see trails, first they are used by wildlife, then by Indians" (Lopez, p. 42). Boyle's work demonstrates that early trade ties between Plains Indians and pre-Columbian Mexicans later became what is now known as the I-25 corridor, a highway that roughly follows the path of the Rio Grande River. This buttresses the importance of bioregionalism as a tool for mapping community because beneath the design of commerce is a natural pattern at play, in this case represented by the Rio Grande watershed.

The relevance here for mediacology is to demonstrate the interplay between mediaspheric domains. Our map projections and depiction of modern trade routes reflect use and purpose, just as the invention of the alphabet evolved from a need to document trade, commercial transactions, and ownership.

CHAPTER FOUR

Reality 2.0

The present age may be the age of space ... We are in an era of the simultaneous, of juxtaposition, of the near and the far, of the side-by-side, of the scattered. We exist at a moment when the world is experiencing, I believe, something less like a great life that would develop through time than like a network that connects points and weaves its skein. Perhaps we may say that some of the ideological conflicts that drive today's polemics are enacted between the devoted descendants of time and the fierce inhabitants of space.

Michel Foucault, "Different Spaces"

Someone once said that war is God's way of teaching geography, but today, apparently war or even the threat of war cannot adequately teach geography... More American young people can tell you where an island that the *Survivor* TV series came from is located than can identify Afghanistan or Iraq. Ironically a TV show seems more real or at least more meaningful interesting or relevant than reality.

John Fahey, president of the National Geographic Society

So far we have discussed the problem that cartographers have translating spherical space into two-dimensional maps, and we also came to understand that Western mapping itself is a kind of mediaspheric domain that biases Cartesian space and GridThink. But how does this all translate in the networked world that transcends traditional notions of time and space in which two-dimensional boundaries are obliterated? By using a media sample as a mediaspheric domain map, one particular advertisement is highly instructive. A recent iPhone print ad featured in *National Geographic* shows a strobed finger navigating a Google map on the phone's touch-sensitive interface. As an unmistakable allusion to Michelangelo's "Creation of Man" that famously depicts a human finger touching God, this could mean three things: either God is the networked universe to which the iPhone is a portal (hence all is God), the iPhone *is* God, or the iPhone is the engineered bridge between the known space of the Cartesian mediaspheric domain to the emergent one of the networked economy. This would complete the circuit started by the Renaissance in which God's love is delivered through the fingertip to humans—but now humans can distribute it equally, and return it.

The other explanations are probably simultaneously true as well, a conundrum for a traditional media literacy reading that solicits one truth. Because the Renaissance began the psychological descent into humanism, which replaced the medieval world emplaced by God with one shaped by human perception, now humanism is being replaced by "cyborgism." I take cyborg to be a neutral term here, simply meaning that we are hybrids with the technology into which our minds and bodies are networked. In this ad fingers touch a screen, drawing us into the in-between-not-here-nor-there acoustic realm of cyberspace. This ad can be a useful ecological metaphor because it visually demonstrates Bateson's (2000) formula that we are human-plus-environment. What he means is that because the environment sustains our bodies, it therefore cannot be excluded from our definition of ourselves. The cyborg is human-plus-electronic environment.

The iPhone ad further composts GridThink by adding one more factor into equation: the strobed, multiple exposure finger that dances on the interface like a Cubist painting. Recall that Cubism was the first Western art movement to incorporate a sense of simultaneity into painting, a reflection of the emerging art form of film and the new theory of relativity:

> Cubism was a singular event in the history of art, you might say the most astounding transformation in the entire history of art. In Cubist painting, solid, apprehensible reality, located in space and fixed in time, crumbled; and, like Humpty Dumpty, its pieces could not be reassembled. Objects fractured into visual fragments then were rearranged so that the viewer would not have to move through space in an allotted period of time in order to view them in sequence. Visual segments of the front, back, top, bottom, and sides of an object jump out and assault the viewer's eye simultaneously (Shlain, 2007, p.189).

This image also instructs us that we can dip our finger into data liquid to connect with our world's vast rhizomatic network graphically represented by a Google map, thus putting the world at our command in the way that maps allow us to master geography. Because this is from *National Geographic*, the ad appeals to the explorer within us all but assures us that wherever we go we will be in control, despite the treachery of nonlinear space. The iPhone also has eliminated the limitations of a hardwired interface; it changes depending on the context of our input choices, revealing an emerging bias of contemporary culture: the tactile is replacing sight as the central sensory experience of our age. This is not to say that sight isn't a kind of "touching," but more and more our bodies are getting involved with new media, whether it is with joysticks, Wii controllers, or cell phones as they increasingly become body appendages. Moreover, if you watch people talk on cell phones you never see them stand still. Often they pace in small circles, demonstrating how much our bodies are in fact engaged with communication. With the iPhone, "I think therefore I am" becomes "I touch therefore I am."

Ironically, the final kicker is that this ad is also a photograph, which represents the most codified product of linear perspective technology: the lens. So in one media sample we see multiple mediaspheric niches remediated by the inclusion of linear perspective, chiaroscuro lighting technique, Renaissance humanist philosophy, Cubism, Cartesian space (in the form of the map), hyperspace, tactile media, and networked communications. Pat yourself on the back, for we have negotiated nearly half a dozen mediaspheric niches and we didn't even begin to explore our own personal domains that would enhance the interpretation even more. The point of this little iPhone excursion is to grapple with our changing conceptions of space that go beyond maps and media objects. To contract a Sun Ra song, "Space is the Place," we could say that much of our new media experience is a hybridized "splace."

Recognizing that something fundamentally had shifted in Western consciousness McLuhan (2002 [1964], p. 12) observed that we had passed a "break barrier": "Just before an airplane breaks the sound barrier, sound waves become visible on the wings of the plane. The sudden visibility of sound just as sound ends is an apt instance of that great pattern of being that reveals new and opposite forms just as the earlier forms reach their peak performance." Was there a point in which our senses began to extend beyond our bodies into mediated realms, as McLuhan suggests? Was it with Socrates, the alphabet, perspective painting technique, the Gutenberg press, electricity, or the telegraph? Pinpointing an exact threshold is difficult, yet Walter Benjamin's (1999) effort to comprehend the milieu of modernity in some respects was trying to do just that. In retrospect, we can say that Benjamin had good instincts. In particular, he was suspicious that something significant had taken place in the nineteenth century, some kind of moment when reality accelerated into the technological media bubble of our times. In the 1939 draft of "Paris, Capital of the Nineteenth Century," he writes:

> What is expressed here is a feeling of vertigo characteristic of the nineteenth century's conception of history. It corresponds to a viewpoint according to which the course of the world is an endless series of facts congealed in the form of things ... Our investigation proposes to show how, as a consequence of this reifying representation of civilization, the new forms of behavior and the new economically and technologically based creations that we owe the nineteenth century enter the universe of phantasmagoria (p. 14).

Others have called this phenomenon a "spectacle" and "simulacra," but the term "phantasmagoria" has a specificity that's indicative of the mindset of both Benjamin and Theodor Adorno when confronted with the phenomenon of commodity capitalism in the nineteenth century. As Adorno's translator for *In Search of Wagner*, Rodney Livingstone (2005, p. 75) notes that phantasmagoria's "negative connotations stem from Marx's use of the word to describe commodity fetishism." Inadvertently, Benjamin challenged Marxist orthodoxy by asserting that the phantasmagoria as dialectic image was an expression, rather than a reflection, of the base. The difference between an ocular metaphor (reflection) and one that signifies a more phenomenological approach (expression) represents an essential split in how reality is viewed in Western intellectual tradition, thereby generating a tension between viewing modern media as illusory (Baudrillard, 1994) versus having physical properties (McLuhan, 2002 [1964]). For Adorno, commodities are hollowed-out containers into which the consumer projects his alienation. For Benjamin, phantasmagoria has physicality, its "expression" being generated from the social.

In Book III of *The Republic* (1964), Socrates holds up a mirror and claims that any common man or wizard can conduct this simple act of simulating the world, but, he says, the mirror world would still only be one of appearances and false consciousness. Hence we reach the core of Platonic thought: that the world is merely a shadow of a greater truth, an ideal that can never be found manifest in our daily reality. Since then we have been ensnarled in an epoch of Greek ocular metaphors, of which we can say Western philosophers have made good careers defending and scorning. After the demonstration with the mirror to the Sophist, Socrates states, "God, whether from choice or from necessity, made one bed in nature and only one. Two or more such ideal beds neither ever have been nor ever will be made of God" (Plato, p. 32). Some art historians claim the Greeks were aware of linear perspectival space as a technique, but rejected it because of its innate distortion of God's natural order (see Pelfrey, 1985). In this respect, the Renaissance and the project of Enlightenment, which conformed the world to the eye and book, would probably have incensed Socrates as a kind of sorcery, for Socrates hated magicians and poets: "I don't mind saying to you, that all poetic imitations are ruinous to the understanding of the hearers, and that the knowledge of their true nature is the only antidote to them." The vitriol continues as he vilifies the Sophist who is a "sort of wizard, an imitator of things" (Plato, 30). Ironically, it was the codification of the alphabet by the Greeks that set our imitative technologies into motion.

Curiously, the debate regarding phantasmagoria's nature is reminiscent of Socrates' distrust of physical appearances. As Jonathan Crary (1999, p. 251) notes (especially as it relates to the quintessential entertainer of the nineteenth century, Richard Wagner), "'phantasmagoric' designates the systemic concealing and mystification of the process of production." Adorno (2005, p. 79) reiterates how concealment is the condition of our age:

> ... the concept of illusion is as the absolute reality of the unreal grows in importance. It sums up the unromantic side of the phantasmagoria: phantasmagoria as the point at which aesthetic appearance becomes a function of the character of the commodity. As a commodity it purveys illusions. The absolute reality of the unreal is nothing but the reality of a phenomenon that not only strives unceasingly to spirit away its origins in human labor, but also, inseparably from the process and in thrall to exchange value, assiduously emphasizes its use value, stressing that this is its authentic reality, that it is "no imitation"—and all this in order to further the cause of exchange value.

As he relates this to the fetish character of music, Adorno (1991, p. 40) is weary of the commodity because, "The works which are the basis of the fetishization and become the cultural goods experience constitutional changes as a result. They become vulgarized. Irrelevant consumption destroys them ... reification affects their internal structure." The commodity is like Plato's bed; it is a mere imitation of a more perfect bed made in a nonexistent worker's utopia.

As we further unpack the term phantasmagoria, we get a clearer understanding of why it was adapted by Marxist thinkers as a primary metaphor for nineteenth century capitalist milieu. The phantasmagoria was an entertainment spectacle that incorporated smoke, mirrors, and projected light to create illusions during live performances. The term itself combines roots for ghost or spirit (phantasm) and gathering place (agora). *Webster's New World Dictionary (Third College Edition)* defines it as,

> (1): an exhibition or display of optical effects and illusions; (2) a: a constantly shifting complex succession of things seen or imagined b: a scene that constantly changes; (3): a bizarre or fantastic combination, collection, or assemblage.

The key words are "exhibition," "illusions," "shifting," and "assemblage," all of which characterize the change that was taking place in the nineteenth century as a result of the rise of mass media, commodities culture and surplus, industrialization, urbanization, and the exponential increase in speed of transportation that was shaping perception. What is particularly interesting about the root "agora" is the sense of an open gathering space of the Greek polis, denoting a collective, public experience later articulated in Jurgen Habermas' public sphere, the phantasmagoria being a shared social experience.

Benjamin explores phantasmagoria as if it were an analyzable dream image produced by society's slumbering body. Quoting Jules Michelet, Benjamin (1999, p. 4) argues that, "Each Epoch dreams the one to follow," through which an ultimate, hidden structural truth of commodity capitalism could explain its emergent dream-like quality. Benjamin's primary theoretical tool, the "dialectic image," was an effort to analyze phantasmagoria through its primary physical locale, the Paris arcades, a place of "ur-phenomena": fetishism, alienation and reification, containing the obvious display of commodities and the shadow side of society all in one place. Roaming this arcade is the flaneur, the "ultimate consumer of the modern city." Much like the "break barrier" concept, "The dialectic image is an image that emerges suddenly, in a flash. What has been is to be held fast—as an image flashing up in the now of its recognizability" (1999 , p. 473). Benjamin notes in the introduction of the same essay (p. 15), "Blanqui's cosmic speculation conveys this lesson: that humanity will be prey to a mythic anguish so long as phantasmagoria occupies a place in it." I think for Benjamin the phantasmagoria is a literal place, like the performance space it takes its name from; and having thus established that, the point of liberation may be that as travelers and inhabitants of that country, we have the potential to alter its course through "awakening" to our condition. This borders on mysticism, for in a sense one wonders if Benjamin is longing for a kind of enlightenment that comes through the revelation of hidden, cosmic truths that are buried within objects not as reification, but as souls (reinforced by his use of the term, "commodity-soul"). This would further explain his optimism concerning media and its ability to bring objects closer to people. At this point, though, I'm not sure why Benjamin continues to use the term phantasmagoria. Given his approach to the commodity as materially constituted by the social, the term no longer seems appropriate because it implies ghostly things and hidden structures. Which brings me back to that dreaded mirror. There is a very telling passage in which Benjamin (1999, p. 542) hints at the realness of the mirror realm:

> A look at the ambiguity of the arcades: their abundance of mirrors, which fabulously amplifies the spaces and makes orientation more difficult. For although this mirror world may have many aspects, indeed infinitely many, it remains ambiguous, double-edged. It blinks: it is always this one—and never nothing—out of which another immediacy arises. The space that transforms itself does so in the bosom of nothingness. In its tarnished, dirty mirrors, things exchange a Kaspar-Hauser-look with the nothing. It is like an equivocal wink coming from nirvana. And here, again, we are brushed with icy breath by the dandyish name of Odilon Redon, who caught, like no one else, how to join with things in the mirror of nothingness, and who understood, like no one else, how to join with things in their collusion with nonbeing. The whispering of gazes fills the arcades. There is no thing here that does not, where one least expects it, open a fugitive eye, blinking it shut again; but if you look more closely, it is gone. To the whispering of these gazes, the space lends its echo. "Now, what," it blinks, "can possibly have come over me?" We stop short in

some surprise. "What, indeed, can possibly have come over you?" Thus we gently bounce the question back to it.

Unlike Socrates' reflected world, here we find the mirror has "immediacy," and even a wink from nirvana. In contrast to Adorno's commodity fetish mediation, here there is some ambiguity, a brief space, albeit just a flash, that allows us to see our nonbeing desiring to join its nothingness, which to me sounds sublime. Whereas one gets the sense that Adorno's invisible fetish character lurking within every object borders on paranoid schizophrenia, I find that at least with Benjamin there is a point of negotiation with the very things that oppress us. This places Benjamin's efforts as novel vis-à-vis the mirror tropes of the past two millennia, making him a troubled but viable guide to the lands beyond phantasmagoria.

But if the phantasmagoria was a kind of break-barrier point for Benjamin, a recent movie concerning the magical arts, *The Prestige*, takes us a little deeper. Be forewarned, though, a movie about magic employs the principal technique of enchantment: misdirection. Thus any film claiming to be about magic has as its subtext the fact of the film itself, which is a carefully constructed illusion, just as any Hollywood motion picture about spectacle is ultimately self-referential (such as *Gladiator*, which was a veiled commentary on the entertainment business and studio system). Curiously, *The Prestige* was released within a year of *The Illusionist*, another film dealing with fabricating reality with its narrative situated in Victorian-era nineteenth century. Both locate themselves at the early stages of media spectacle, a time when phantasmagoria—the predecessor of modern film—was a popular form of pubic performance. That there would be a cultural curiosity about this nascent period of magic, performance, and spectacle is not coincidental. As we are facing ourselves in a fully engaged mirror of mediation, we are innately curious about the origins of our societal identity crises as we encounter our interdependent relationship with media.

Of the two films, *The Prestige* is particularly relevant. The foreground of *The Prestige* is a war between two rival professional magicians. The background is the enmity between two magicians of a different sort: Thomas Edison and Nikola Tesla, the inventors of our modern electrical system. The film's subplot concerning the life and work of Tesla (played by the quintessential space cadet, David Bowie, no less) alludes to the ambivalence the society had with new technology at the advent of electricity. One of the most repressed figures of modern history, Tesla, we may recall, invented/discovered alternating-current (AC) electricity, which competed with direct-current (DC) electricity championed by Edison (see Cheney 1993). As the cliché goes, history is written by its winners, and it's no wonder that Edison, a brazen self-promoter and showman, engaged in a number of public spectacles and dirty tricks to discredit his nemesis, Tesla. Edison publicly electrocuted stray animals to shock people into believing in the dangers of AC (one scene in *The Prestige* alludes to such a public war). Not coincidentally, Edison was one of the earliest innovators and promoter of moving image technology, something that eluded Tesla who preferred to experiment privately with this radical, newly harnessed energy. But even Tesla was known to be a bit of a show-off. When his studio was in New York he was known to entertain celebrity visitors such as Mark Twain and his entourage. He dazzled them by conducting high-voltage electricity through his body that produced an eerie aura and used wireless fluorescent light tubes (one of his many inventions) that were powered as if by magic. Witnesses reported also seeing Tesla hold "balls of lightning."

In a sense we could say that in the nineteenth century our society faced two alternate visions of power: Edison or Tesla, and the one who ultimately was selected by finance has fashioned the world we're in, literally. Among Tesla's many inventions, the one that irked his backers the most was his desire and effort to create free electricity. In a poignant scene during *The Prestige*, Tesla's assistant amazes the magician Rupert Angier (played by Hugh Jackman, better known as the X-Men's Wolverine) when he reveals that the Earth can light bulbs (infused with AC powered by Tesla's Colorado Springs power plant). The film's narrative only references these experiments, but what Tesla went for was developing a system that harnessed the earth and atmosphere as natural conductors of electricity. He dreamed of wireless energy, long before our current age of wireless phones and the Internet (which are still dependent on limited battery life and a physical grid). There remains a debate today as to who discovered radio first, but many claim it was Tesla, not Guglielmo Marconi. Not surprisingly, toward the end of his life, when he was destitute, Tesla worked for the U.S. military designing wireless communication between ships and other projects we still don't know about.

When George Westinghouse learned of Tesla's fundamental designs for free power, he pulled the plug, literally, telling him that he would not finance an operation that would give free power to "Africans." When you look at the history of the "war of currents" between Tesla and Edison, all the early financiers of our electrical system ultimately became the military industrial complex, in particular Westinghouse and General Electric. That these power and technology companies became media corporations as well sums up the situation quite nicely (GE owns NBC and Westinghouse formally owned CBS). Control requires illusion, or misdirection, and it is fitting that the most dominant military contractors, innovators of nuclear weapons, and electrical power, would also be in the business of fantasy, as in magic. Touchstone

Pictures, a subsidiary of Disney, produced *The Prestige*. As a member of the global corporate elite, Disney is one of the few media companies that doesn't also make physical weapons, but as the quintessential trademark of capitalist "magic," its deployment of electrically fueled dreams softens up targets/markets/marks for the inevitable appropriation of energy resources. Our lives are powerfully formed by the convergence of the forces of magic, militarism and the power grid, yet we are rarely conscious of their nexus. Did the filmmakers have this in mind when they conceived *The Prestige*? No matter, they reveal to us the three stages of the magician's performance, and perhaps they can be used as a deconstruction tool: the "pledge" (a declaration of intent to make something vanish), the "turn" (the disappearance), and the "prestige" (the return of that which has disappeared). There is a subtle proposition that the film itself is a trick. Are we paying attention?

These techniques mirror to some extent the three-act play of our civilization since the discovery of the force of electricity. There's quite a bit of academic theory about the psycho-spiritual turn that modern civilization took in the Victorian era. For Benjamin it was symbolized by phantasmagoria, for Adorno it was Wagner's *gesamtkunstwerk*, or "total work of art." For more contemporary scholars, early recording technologies were efforts to capture time, contingency and ultimately catastrophe. It was an unconscious coping mechanism for Western society to contain conditions that were radically destabilizing pre-established notions of the world. Not surprisingly, in the early days of photography and then later with wax cylinder recording and wireless communications, people associated electricity and media with supernatural forces, linking media technology with spiritualism. As people were adjusting to these new technologies, they were unsure of and spooked by their capabilities. We take all of this for granted because they immerse us, but recall that there was a time when electronic media were new and incomprehensible: "What men and women in the late nineteenth century faced with alarm is something we have had over a century to get used to: a superabundance of phantasms of the living appearing in various media" (Peters, 1999, p.141).

In regards to this scenario, McLuhan (2002 [1964]) draws an analogy with the myth of Narcissus. In his version, Narcissus in not enamored with his reflection, but rather is trapped in it. He extends himself into his reflection as we do with our electronic media and then get ensnared by our iteration. Having lost the sensation of ourselves, we amp up the input into the sensory circuit to restimulate ourselves, and the cycle goes on so now it's normal to watch half-second edits on TV and to be assaulted by movie previews that condense films into five-minute roller-coaster rides of nerve stimulation. So like the turn in which the magician makes himself disappear, we are transported into an illusion facilitated by electrically powered media. But the question remains: have we yet to reappear in the final act, the "prestige"? Are we lost somewhere between the trap door in which the magician falls away and his inevitable return from behind the mirror of our fascination? Or maybe it's the case that in our prestige a digital doppelganger is what returns.

Tangentially, Robert Heinlein's novel *Stranger in a Strange Land* (1991) deals with the revolutionary convergence of magic and psychology. The alien-raised human protagonist, Mike, who has an incredible capacity for empathy and psychic prowess, decides to transform human society when he discovers his powers are best understood when combined with magic (and a Bohemian lifestyle that includes free love). People like a good show, and "marks"—as stand-ins for citizens of the rocket age—are in a sense the buying public of the corporate dream world's media torrent. Mike is also the product of a technological magic act. His existence is the result of a birth by humans who disappeared on Mars (because of an accident), and Mike returns to Earth as a reconfigured human—a posthuman whose global perspective and ability to "grok" cannot be contained by the prevailing society, and which ultimately ends with his assassination.

Stranger in a Strange Land does an excellent job of illustrating the particular American skill of combining religion with entertainment, but ultimately for no good. One wonders if the gig is up as transparency ("grokking"?) becomes one of the prevailing characteristics of new media. Without obfuscation, there is no misdirection, no magic. What *The Prestige* illustrates is that we like to be fooled, and though we insist that good magic be illusory, we also want to know that there is a conscious trick. We are ultimately skeptical of miracles. We want to believe that we are partners in the illusion's construction; it gives us a modicum of control. But to know the solution of the trick is also to destroy its allure. Ultimately, maybe it's better to know not God. We want our toys, and to watch TV, but we really don't need to know how they work.

The film asks us, "Are you looking closely?" What *The Prestige* draws our attention to inadvertently is the relationship between entertainment and power (literal and figurative). Do we have the sophistication to see through the film's own misdirection to get to a critique concerning the ideological core of our contemporary nexus between the military, entertainment, and electrical power? I believe anti-television crusader Jerry Mander is correct when we assess the true implications of our electrical power system choice, which incidentally is the number one cause of carbon emissions (see Mander, 1996). Choosing nuclear power or coal means a devil's pact, so to speak, with a highly centralized, bureaucratized, military-industrial complex. A renewable energy system is decentralized and is not dependent on a massive security apparatus or infrastructure delivery system predicated on scarcity. Through his inventions, Tesla proposed an alternative foundation in which power could be obtained freely. The society, or rather, an elite core of financiers also known as robber barons, chose another path. We'll never know if his theories were correct; he wasn't given the chance to implement them. Consequently, it's no coincidence that the twentieth century was the American Century. The core triumvirate of electricity, military and entertainment was consolidated in the United States, funded by pirates of the Industrial Revolution. That power matrix is further fueled by the petrol economy, and ultimately characterizes the prevailing metaleval of the era's mediaspheric niche. What remains to be seen is to what extent we have been altered by the "turn." Fittingly, it's the magic trick, "The Transported Man," that corrupts and destroys the film's protagonists in an era when we began doubling and transporting ourselves into media space. In our "prestige," what will be our ultimate fate?

Like the emergence of conceptual art that dematerialized the art object, the notion of a physical, public space also began to extract itself from geographical space well past the nineteenth century. In 1967, Foucault (1998) gave a lecture in which he observed that people in advanced technological societies were increasingly migrating into an indeterminate space called "heterotopia," which literally means "other place." These realms are both real and imagined, such as the space where a phone call takes place, or within the informational sphere we call "hyperspace" or "cyberspace." Foucault argued that before industrialization, the Western metaleval was characterized by time; that is, we organized ourselves based on how we situated ourselves in relationship to time. Media scholars propose that inventions like the telegraph separated communication from transportation, thereby making information "timeless," because prior to the telegraph, mediated communication was based on the time it took to be delivered. Afterward, it became instantaneous, thus changing our "communication bias," as Harold Innis (1999 [1951]) calls it. Foucault (p. 176) argued, "It should be made clear, however, that the space now appearing on the horizon of our concerns, of our theory, of our systems, is not an innovation. Space itself, in the Western experience, has a history, and one cannot fail to take note of this inevitable interlocking of time with space." Even with the naturalization of telephone's hybrid space, we once knew where people "were" when we spoke to them because at least they were tied to landlines. Now the most common question when we receive a call is not, how are you, but *where* are you?

How are we coping with navigating this new borderless realm that is not bound by geography, but rather is defined by our engagement with hybridized technology? It's undeniable that so-called "reality television" has become the most popular kind of entertainment on television, a phenomenon that is prevalent because it is the one arena that is actually processing how we define ourselves in mediated space (and it's cheap to make). The huge CBS hit show, *Survivor*, exemplifies how reality TV is negotiating our identities as technologically mediated people. The show situates its contestants in a media constructed space with specific rules and parameters. The premise is that these pre-screened contestants are "shipwrecked," but as cultural interpreters, we must ask, from what? Let's suppose that the show's participants are refugees from the mediated world and their job is to sort out the proper roles and behaviors necessary in order to "survive" a life in media space.

Our anxieties concerning this new technological space are justified. Post 9/11 our society has become increasingly one of surveillance. Additionally, more and more people have personal capturing devices, such as cell phones, PDAs and digital cameras that make anyone vulnerable to having their image seized by strangers. As commerce moves more into the Internet, our identities are increasingly tied to our data patterns. The alarm of identity theft perfectly exemplifies this fear that the technological persona is subject to mobility and capture by unknown parties. Add to this mix the glamour our society attaches to the mediated persona. Everyone will be a star, as Andy Warhol predicted. Increasingly people will get their three minutes of MySpace or YouTube fame, especially with the proliferation of reality TV, Web cams and blogs. Given the contradictory attitudes concerning mediated space—we fear identity theft, yet we want to be famous and hence publicly adored—it's no wonder we are confused.

The immense popularity of *Survivor* is due to its ability to situate average Americans in a fishbowl of mediated space in order to gauge and measure their reactions. After all, as Thomas de Zengotita (2005) argues in *Mediated*, negotiating technologically arbitrated space requires that we become performers, or "method actors." What we see in these shows is that people are constantly straddling the line between playing (hence performing) in a game, and believing they are in a real place. There is a constant question of whether or not fellow contestants are truly friends, or are mere allies. In "reality" we have friendships, in a game (or mediated "fake" space) we have associations. And at Wal-Mart, the ultimate of mediated retail spaces, workers are "associates." In all these cases we are alternating between mediaspheric niches.

Reality TV programs and anxiety over the invasive presence of technology also begs the larger question: What is the real geography of our times, if any? *The Matrix* film trilogy grappled with this question; the films' vast popularity has to be at least partially attributed to their discussion of the increasing inability to distinguish between real versus simulated reality, the assumption being that there is a distinction, that there is such a thing as "real." In the SciFi Network's contemporary version of *Battlestar Galactica* the human created Cylons go to war against their creators, nuking the human race and destroying their home worlds. As a consequence, the few human survivors drift in a centerless outer space in search of Earth, that is a future home that will give them a sense of place. Meanwhile, the newest Cylon models are indistinguishable from humans and are attempting to mate with them in order to create hybrids that will fulfill their desire to connect with God, who only exists as an intellectual concept to their computerized minds. Ironically, Cylon-engineered blood is a potent agent that can cure human cancer. The humanoid Cylons have many copies, like the multiple identities we now use in cyberspace; several who have infiltrated the human space colonies are unaware of their robotic origins and only discover their true identity when they spontaneously hum Bob Dylan's "All Along the Watchtower." Popular entertainment clearly reflects our society's ambivalence and anxiety about whether we are living in an authentic world, or one merely mediated by technology. Either way, undeniably we have entered into a new technological sphere that alters our sense of place. For this reason it is good to keep an open mind about popular culture because in many ways it maps our deeper anxieties.

As TV programs cross-migrate into convergence media, we see the traditional mass media model breaking down. Not only are programs mobile between different formats and players, there is also fan interaction via the Web, video games and other interactive features that have made new media more complex and interesting. For media activists, new media challenge our core assumptions about how media function, from the breakdown of the one-to-many communications model to the many-to-many form it is taking, to the disintegration of the world as viewed from print. What we once took for granted—that a book is the basis of truth and perception—is challenged all around us. If print is solid and concrete, new media is liquid. Like it or not, welcome to the Age of Aquarius where knowledge flows like water in and out of a cybernetic jar. With these changes to our spatiotemporal orientation we shouldn't abandon critical engagement, but perhaps we should view the new gods from a more agnostic approach. It may turn out that these new creatures, like the Cylons in *Battlestar Galactica*, are more biological than we suspected. After all, these monsters are our mirrored creations. We just haven't yet figured out how to situate them on a map.

CHAPTER FIVE

Lost in Splace

The speed of transmission of the facts of flight affects the form of the engine, just as the relative wind that arises from the air resistance to an advancing plane did before. We are now witnessing the merger of telematics and aerodynamics, to the point where we could call the plane teledynamic, instead of supersonic or hypersonic, since the speed of information is closer to that of light than that of sound.... Basically, where the televised form-image results from the rapidity of particles that are accelerated by the cathode tube, our perception of the plane is really only a virtual image, a hologram that emerges somewhat from the speed of aerodynamic wind, but more essentially from the excessive dynamic of informatics. This virtual image is the result of a mode of energetic formation that contributes to a transmutation of physical appearances.

Paul Virilio, *Lost Dimension*

While *Survivor* gives us a forum in which to act out our struggles with the new hybrid reality, another show, Disney-ABC's *Lost*, provides a rich scenario in which we can explore the changing mediascape in a new narrative form more closely as a way of summarizing the many concepts with which we have been playing. The pilot episode begins with an extreme close-up of a murky eye pupil whose iris dilates instantaneously like a camera's aperture. We quickly zoom out to a semiconscious, square-jawed man in a burnt Armani suit; he's bewildered, shocked, disoriented. Engulfed by tropical vegetation, the environment is alien, strange, incoherent. A Labrador retriever, even more foreign to this scene, appears, then leads our character out to a clearing, a tropical beach with an unusual feature: a smashed jetliner is in smoke and ruins, and people are wandering around like zombies, crying and wailing. For the next hour our hero, a doctor named Jack, breathlessly dashes from one crash victim to another. He is a healer in the midst of death and destruction, the ruinous remains of civilization where its plane-wrecked survivors are trapped on a remote, liminal island somewhere in the Pacific Ocean. Through Jack, we enter a world of transition/transmission; we enter the world of *Lost*.

   Lost is rich with themes and gestalt that are ripe for our mediacological age. Like *Survivor*, it features castaways in the process of delineating their new reality in an unfamiliar setting. The audience, lost in its own technological milieu, identifies with characters who are saddled with defining their actions within a liminal, fast-changing environment in which we increasingly are searching for our sea legs, so to speak. Media, in the best possible sense, and within the great tradition of storytelling that spans all world cultures and history, sorts out models for survival and morality within its given milieu. In the case of *Lost*, it is a show aired by one of the largest entertainment companies in the world: Disney/ABC. But rather than animated versions of nineteenth-century European folk tales that have been the stock and trade of Disney, what we are offered instead is a stark, mysterious locale out in the ether of media space, a constructed, irreal nexus that reveals the strange, meta-terrestrial world we find ourselves in at the beginning of the twenty-first century.

Lost's premise is fairly simple. Oceanic Airlines Flight 815 in transit from Sydney to Los Angeles soars thousands of miles off course after its communications equipment goes dead. Violent air turbulence causes the plane to split and to crash on a mysterious, uncharted island. Through various backstories and flashbacks, a dozen of the 42 survivors share various synchronistic connections, which reveal themselves over the course of the show's life span. Like players in the video game Myst, *Lost's* characters are quickly immersed into the mysterious presence of seemingly supernatural forces at play on the island and find themselves having to solve puzzles in order to survive the new environment. The island, like cities of noir movies, is a character itself.

Additionally there are inhabitants called "the others," whose existence on the island threatens the safety of the plane crash survivors. The characters draw us in through conventional techniques of dramaturgy: how do they overcome challenges, and how do human emotions persist under such strain? The series contains the core elements of TV drama: man against nature, man against man, but with an added twist—man against unknown. All are elements of classic storytelling and rarely diverge from the formula of the "hero's journey" as articulated by Joseph Campbell. In this sense, we can keep in mind that in the background is a remediation of the hero myth that begins with the "ordinary world" being turned upside down, requiring the hero to enter an "underworld" to retrieve an elixir of power in order to defeat the forces of evil/shadow self. At various points in the journey there are "threshold guardians"—allies, villains, and obstacles that test the protagonists' mettle. The goal of *Lost's* characters is to return to the ordinary world and rebalance the symbolic order. If only life were that simple.

The world of *Lost's* island is a mediasphere with many niches, and it is a prime example of how competing realms run through our lives. Through the process of empathy, we see ourselves enter the universe of *Lost* as a means of searching for harmony in the seemingly chaotic space of virtuality, finding ourselves struggle for identity in a hybridized world that fuses traditional notions of nature and environment with technology and media. "Virtuality," as defined by Pierre Lévy (1998, pp. 29-30), becomes the island's dominant mediasphere:

> When a person, community, act, or piece of information are virtualized, they are "not-there," they deterritorialize themselves. A kind of clutch mechanism detaches them from conventional physical or geographical space and the temporality of the clock or calendar. They are not totally independent of a referential space-time since they must still bond to some physical substrate and become actualized somewhere sooner or later. Yet the process of virtualization has caused them to follow a tangent. They intersect classical space-time intermittently, escaping its "realist" clichés: ubiquity, simultaneity, massively parallel or distributed systems. Virtualization comes as a shock to the traditional narrative, incorporating temporal unity without spatial unity (by means of real-time interactions over electronic networks, live rebroadcasts, telepresence systems), continuity of action coupled with discontinuous time (answering machines and electronic mail, for example). Synchronization replaces spatial unity, interconnectedness is substituted for temporal unity.

Lost is an unselfconscious effort to impose a narrative upon an environment that feels increasingly nonlinear, acoustic and unfamiliar, a hybrid combination of *Survivor* and the *Twilight Zone*. But *Lost*'s production strategy mirrors the disparate and distributed media described by Lévy, which is part of the novel character of the program. Building a storyline for this multisensual, all-at-once reality experience is part of media's function to reframe and adjust to emerging perception, and to train us in developing a strategy for continued existence. As McLuhan (1997, p. 100) notes, "It is important for survival to understand that the simultaneous data of the omnipresent information environment is itself *structurally* acoustic. When people understand this acoustic structure as their new habitat, they will at once recognize the risks for the strange goings-on in the human psyche and in human society in the effort to relate to this new habitat." By studying both the themes and form of *Lost*, we reveal a highly sophisticated, nuanced and complex exposition of our contemporary cosmology manifested in pop culture that maps for us multiple niches of the mediasphere.

The two-hour pilot cost \$12 million (at the time the most expensive in TV history) and was green-lighted within two months without a script, which in terms of normal TV production is highly unusual (see Cotta Vaz, 2005). Moreover, these days a high-budget serial drama on network TV is the exception, not the rule. *Lost*'s success and popularity is contrary to the trend toward low-budget reality-based programs, game shows and talk shows that dominate the major networks. This indicates that for whatever reason, the show strikes a chord deep within the cultural zeitgeist. Like the mediasphere that Debray (1996, p. 33) describes—"The 'sphere' extends the visible system of the medium to the invisible macrosystem that gives it meaning"—there is much more to Lost than its weekly broadcast (an outmoded term, I know). Much of Lost's "meaning" actually takes place outside of its scheduled weekly broadcast. We enter the space of the show through multiple portals: TV, Internet, phones, books, and the iPod. I watched the entire first season on DVD and the second season on my laptop via ABC's Web site and downloaded episodes from iTunes. I also have a hardware/software configuration called EyeTV that records from a cable feed onto my hard drive, so sometimes I watch the show "live" and sometimes I watch it on my own schedule. Moreover, I experience Lost in discussion boards on Web sites and participate in its nonlinear Easter egg hunt throughout the open-ended network that connects to the show. In each instance, I'm extending into my screen, into heterotopic space. As we know from the theory of remediation, what I am viewing combines multiple mediaspheric niches: "As a digital network, cyberspace remediates the electric communications networks of the past 150 years, the telegraph and the telephone; as virtual reality, it remediates the visual space of painting, film, and television; and as a social space, it remediates such historical places as cities and parks and such nonplaces as theme parks and shopping malls. Like other contemporary mediated spaces, cyberspace refashions and extends earlier media, which are themselves embedded in material and social environments" (Bolter and Grusin 1999, p. 183). As a "nonplace," the world of Lost is also real, albeit in a state of ambivalence. As Samuel Weber (1996, p. 125) puts it:

> The reality of television thus no longer follows the traditional logic and criteria of reality. It is no longer a function of identity or of its derived form: opposition. Far and near are no longer mutually exclusive but rather converge and overlap. Such convergence brings a different aspect of reality to the for—the reality of *ambivalence*. For what is ostensibly "set in place" as the television set is also and above all *a movement of displacement, of transmission*.

Keeping in mind the key tenants of remediation—that we experience both immediacy and hypermediacy when encountering any form of media—the dual nature of being invisible and self-referential becomes essential to the whole production of Lost. In particular, since we are dealing with a TV show, it's important to realize that, "Like film, television needs to remediate digital media in order to survive" (Bolter and Grusin, p. 185). The show itself is rather conservative in the formal sense. Episodes are very cinematic in terms of drama, editing, cinematography and the conventions of film structure, although the fact that we will view it on low-resolution surfaces makes it decidedly unfilm-like. The fact that it's a serial and a bit of a soap opera also makes the show predictably televisual. While its broadcast format is fairly immediate, how it ties in with outside weekly transmissions is where it becomes hypermediated. The manner in which *Lost* hybridizes classic mythological themes and new forms of technology is currently unequaled (at least until *Battlestar Galactica* came along). The manner in which Greek mythology is remediated in *Lost* opens up the show's world in a way that allows us to see its vast, rhizomatic presence in the mediasphere.

Throughout the *Lost* universe producers interleave numerous references to the Greek goddess of the underworld, Persephone. How she is inserted into the narrative is through the peripheral backstory that takes place *outside* actual broadcasts. As we learn in the second season, the locale of *Lost*, an unknown island in the Pacific, is occupied by a mysterious group of inhabitants, "the others." Throughout the island there is a network of "hatches" to underground stations that contain clues about the island's other inhabitants. The structures were built by the fictional DHARMA Initiative, a project financed by the Hanso Foundation, led by Dr. Alvar Hanso. Through a series of instructional videos and films found by the plane crash survivors, we learn that Dr. Hanso went from "keeping the world safe through the development of sophisticated weapons systems" to creating "a brighter future for all humanity." We gather from this old footage that participants of the DHARMA Initiative were free thinkers and scientists who came together at this "large-scale communal research compound." One of the stations happens to be the shape of a Fuller Dome (a popular architectural design for the back-to-the-earth communal movement of the 1960s and '70s). We get the sense that this group is a survivalist, quasi-hippie cult not unlike its real life analog, Synergia, which founded Biosphere II, the experimental self-contained, utopian ecosystem created at the University of Arizona between 1987 and 1989. The goal of Biosphere II was to duplicate Earth's varied ecosystems in a single, self-contained structure to be replicated as a space colony facility. It's a subtle echo of a growing cultural trend to position humans as aliens within the space of our mediated environment.

Persephone enters the narrative through a clever tie-in, The LOST Experience. According to its Web site, "The LOST Experience takes LOST fans on an expansive, international easter [sic] egg hunt through websites, commercials, emails, phone numbers, and more, in search of pieces to a larger puzzle, a puzzle which, when solved, will enlighten LOST fans to some of the shows [sic] deepest mysteries!" The online game's narrator is Persephone, whose voice also appears on a toll-free line featured in a TV ad for the fictional

Hanso Foundation at the end of several episodes. The Hanso Foundation, which has its own fictional universe outside the show, warrants its own Wikipedia entry with board-member bios, corporate history and even executive quotes. The Foundation researches "accelerated remote viewing, cryogenics development, electromagnetic research, juxtapositional eugenics/genomic advancement, life extension, mathematical forecasting, mental health appeal, quest for extra-terrestrial intelligence, wellness and prevention development." These are the kinds of topics you find in the world of the fringe science media, such as blogs, online bulletin boards, obscure journals, and zines.

As we know, Persephone, an innocent love child of Zeus and Demeter, was abducted by Hades and taken to his realm. As queen of the underworld, Persephone converted her nymph companions into Sirens. Sirens are famous for calling seamen to their death through their haunting song. By plugging the ears of his crew, only Odysseus on his infamous sea odyssey could survive the Sirens' sweet death call. As Demeter goes on her periodic searches for Persephone, she forgoes her duties as earth goddess, letting the environment go neglected or foul. As a metaphor for media, we could say that Hades is the mediasphere in which we contain death and contingency (as Doane (2002) tells us). In fact, the dead constantly speak to *Lost*'s characters, either appearing in the jungle in broad daylight, or in their dreams giving them instructions on how to solve the island's mysteries. Many of the Internet boards have postulated that the island is actually purgatory; however, in various interviews, the show's producers have discounted this theory. The additional connection to media would be the Sirens, who in a sense are media communicators. Through their voices they call people to their deaths so they can enter the mediated, off-world space of Hades, thereby enclosing death and contingency within a safe container. It could be that the apparitions who constantly draw the crash survivors into the jungle's interior are the island's Sirens, although it's their visuality, and not their voices, that call them (eyes are a constant visual theme throughout the series). The jungle itself is akin to McLuhan's concept of acoustic space: it is a multisensory environment that comes at you from all directions with no sense of perspective, further reinforcing the feeling that the island/Hades is a kind of post-Gutenberg media purgatory.

Lost is also good at remixing genres. The first comes in the form of remediating films about missing, unfamiliar, or strange worlds. The Oceanic Airline flight originates in Australia, whose well-known nickname is "Oz," or the land of "Down Under"—the upside-down world whose time zone exists in tomorrow land (to North Americans at least). There people drive on the opposite side of the road; it is the mirror analog of our world. And as we learn through flashbacks, almost all the passengers are foreigners who had gone to Australia to find personal redemption, to go on "walkabouts," so to speak. It is a decentered zone of transition, one where meaning is already destabilized and malleable. Before even getting on the airplane, the passengers of Flight 815 were all on a global pilgrimage for self-definition, or better yet, identity correction. By the time they define themselves within the community of strangers who have survived the crash, many have become avatars of themselves, idealized projections of who they couldn't be in the normal world, just as in cyberspace.

The flight in transit hits an air turbulence that throws the characters into the alien world, not unlike the tornado that sends Dorothy to the realm of Oz. In *Lost*'s second season, one of "the others" takes on the moniker Henry Gale, also the name of Dorothy's uncle. In *Lost*, Gale's ruse was that he supposedly arrived on the island by balloon (the transportation vehicle that allows the Wizard to leave Oz). *Alice in Wonderland* is also referenced in episode titles and in dialogue between characters. The periodic appearance of apparitions who beckon the characters into the jungle might as well be white rabbits, and the various hatches into which they enter are no doubt bunny holes. Additionally, *Willy Wonka* was referenced in an episode in the form of theater tickets in the plane wreckage. The official literature of the show's producers also cites a dung heap of low-brow American pop culture as primary influences: comics, hard-boiled crime thrillers, '70s disaster films, sci-fi and horror (Cotta Vaz, p.13). The serial format with weekly cliffhangers is also reminiscent of soaps.

As a physical, social space that we share globally, television, and hence the show *Lost* itself, is, "Like ubiquitous computing and the World Wide Web, but unlike film and virtual reality, [it] confronts us with the reality of mediation as it monitors and reforms the world and the lies and practices of its inhabitants. Just as it remediates film or other media, television remediates the real" (Bolter and Grusin, p. 194). As we follow the path of Oceanic Airlines' passengers, we discover that the characters traverse an ambivalent course that very much mimics the complexity of our mediated lives. Sydney's airport in *Lost* is the threshold between the "ordinary world" and the "unknown." The location of the airport set was actually a convention center in Hawaii, itself a constructed artifice for the purpose of being a portal of story information. Like the set, the airport is a nonplace, and like the term we use for such places—terminals—it has the double meaning of an entry point into liminal space, be it of the airplane and international travel, or into heterotopia. "What the individual experiences in these mediated encounters is the hypermediacy of these nonplaces, which are defined not by their associations with local history or even with the ground on which they are built, but primarily by the reality of the media they contain" (Bolter and Grusin, p. 179). Not surprisingly, the nonplace of an airport is not unlike cyberspace: "Cyberspace is not, as some assert, a parallel universe. It is not a place of escape from contemporary society, or indeed from the physical world. It is rather a nonplace, with many of the same characteristics as other highly mediated nonplaces" (p. 179). Like an airport, "cyberspace refashions and extends earlier media, which are themselves embedded in material and social environments" (Bolter and Grusin, p. 183).

According to Virilio (1991), airports are hybrid technological insertion points within contemporary cities, especially characterized by the "metroplex," which represents "sterile zones for departures and nonsterile zones for arrivals" that are "theaters of necessary regulation of exchange and communication" (p. 10). Virilio (p. 11) continues, writing that airport construction explodes the traditional urban grid, introducing a "perspective devoid of horizon" where "continuity is ruptured in time that advanced technologies and industrial redeployment incessantly arrange through a series of interruptions ..." A nonplace like an airport is not one that you necessarily travel to:

> Where once one necessarily entered the city by means of a physical gateway, now one passes through an audiovisual protocol in which the methods of audience and surveillance have transformed even the forms of pubic greeting and daily reception. Within this place of optical illusion, in which the people occupy transportation and transmission time instead of inhabiting space, inertia tends to renovate an old sedentariness, which results in the persistence of urban sites. With the instantaneous communications media, arrival supplants departure: without necessarily leaving, everything arrives (p.14).

Like the porous boundary of a mediaspheric niche, the terminal serves as a threshold on many levels:

> Each surface is an interface between two environments that is ruled by a constant activity in the form of an exchange between the two substances placed in contact with one another.... What used to be the boundary of a material, its "terminus," has become an entryway hidden in the most imperceptible entity. From here on, the appearance of surfaces and superficies conceals a secret transparency, a thickness without thickness, a volume without volume, an imperceptible quantity.... As with live televised events, the places become interchangeable at will (p. 17).

Airport architecture and systems also mimic the increasing complexity of modern society. As air traffic increased, airlines were forced to reconfigure travel patterns from a point-to-point system in which a plane traveled from a place of origin to destination point. Now they are networked as "a switching center within a coordinated 'hub and spokes' system. Hub and spokes refer to a system wherein routes radiate from a centralized airport (the hub) to a number of 'spoke' airports, vastly increasing the connectivity of cities via networks of exchange defined by the infrastructure of linkage" (Govil 2004, p. 235). Much like the transformation of our one-to-many mass media systems, the linkage system of modern airports is akin to the many-to-many system of distribution in the mediasphere, making them an interconnected whole. I'm reminded of McLuhan's comment that airlines are like subways connecting the globe's major cities into one massive megalopolis.

When Virilio quotes Nam Jun Paik, "Video doesn't mean I see; it means I fly," he's pointing at the intimate relationship between media and flight. After all, aviation and cinematography appeared the same year. In many senses airplanes quintessentially intersect media and technology, especially in the context of September 11, 2001. Airplanes are hybrids of machine and information. In a sense, *Lost*'s plane is an interdimensional vehicle that transports passengers between zones of physicality and data. McLuhan (1999, p. 99) identified airplanes as having a particularly contemporary manifestation of our new environment. He tells of a little boy taking his first flight who asks his father, "Daddy, when do we start to get smaller?":

> The little boy's question is rather complex since it is plain that the plane gets smaller, while the cabin does not. The little boy would never have asked such a question in an open cockpit plane, for not only does the plane get smaller, but the occupants also feel increasingly insignificant. However, the enclosed space of the cabin of the plane presents a very special kind of structure, namely, a visual space; that is, a space or *figure* without a *ground*.

The term cybernetics, coined by Norbert Weiner, derives from the Greek word "Kubernetics"—to steer, guide or govern, as in pilot. McLuhan notes that, "On spaceship Earth, there are no passengers, but all crew" (1999, p. 99). In the mediasphere's we are all pilots. The airplane is the actual transportation device that takes us through the liminal space beyond the terminal. Just as Benedict Anderson (1983) demonstrates how our collective imagination creates the nation, so then does airspace become a legal netherworld "through fictions of national jurisdiction, defined in the accounting of flight claims and criminal prosecution of air rage incidents, and invoked by regulatory guidelines on aircraft noise, pollution and waste disposal" (Govil 2004, pp. 234-5).

It appears that whatever enters an airliner is transformed into a meta-national, stateless identity, even media itself. One of the more curious challenges of nationality in modern air travel is the problem of the Balkanized system of coding DVDs for the international market. While the entertainment industry devised a way to encrypt DVDs to play only in specific regions, this became untenable for global airlines as they offered portable DVD players to first-class passengers. The self-contained discs of media needed liberation from geography and being designated a special neutral region, region eight (Govil, p. 234). Even in-flight trackers that chart the flight's travel on cabin monitors avoid geopolitical boundaries (while simultaneously remediating the Mercator map). "Worried about the associations of danger with certain hot-spots of geopolitical strife, most airlines that use moving map IFE [in-flight entertainment] dispense with the country names and borders altogether, while others avoid mentioning particular nations.... If all maps are narrative forms, then the in-flight moving map relates the story of a pastoral topography untouched by the vagaries of geopolitical conflict, industrial waste and environmental blight" (Govil, pp. 246-8); "The complex topography of airline travel, the hybridity of industrial, regulatory and textual practices in the film and in the cabin, generate nodes of intermediary coherence, a lingua franca and inhabited persona for the jet set: background noise for the screen in our new (un)friendly skies" (Govil, p. 249).

The plane, like the space capsule, also reconfigures humans in relationship to the world, because land is viewed from a new perspective. In this sense, the electrical world as an invisible lived environment sets nature into relief; it draws our attention to it more clearly than if we were immersed into it without awareness: "The first satellite ended 'nature' in the old sense. 'Nature' becomes the content of a manmade environment. From that moment, all terrestrial phenomena were to become increasingly programmed artifacts and every facet of human life now comes within the scope of the artistic vision" (McLuhan and Fiore 1968, p.178). When McLuhan says the "end of nature," we should be clear that what he means is the end of nature as a construct.

The original idea behind *Lost* was to create a narrative version of *Survivor* called "Nowhere." As previously stated, the unspoken premise of *Survivor* is that we have a group of "castaways" who vie for survival in an alien environment. The background question that is never asked is: from what are they cast away? The same could be said for the storyline of *Lost*. *Lost's* protagonists survived a plane crash, but plane crashes have specific meaning in our mediated world, especially post-Sept. 11. The plane crash is not the same as a freeway pileup or a tsunami. It always represents a failure of our technological system to keep us safe; it reveals the system's design that should be invisible and seamless. Thus, we must probe deeper into the meaning of why the plane crash figures so importantly into the show's overall mythology.

In yet another example of the extent to which *Lost's* storyline takes place outside the frame of the TV screen, the show's narrative turn takes place before the first episode ever airs (a highly outdated term, I know). The plane crash, which does get revisited periodically through flashbacks, has happened moments before the first shot of the pilot episode. The crash, though, serves as one of the most important tropes in terms of understanding *Lost*'s metaverse. Mary Ann Doane's (1990) essay, "Information, Crisis, Catastrophe," sets the stage for her study of early film and contingency, which establishes that media since at least the inception of photography, has been a conduit through which our society stores death and contingency. Briefly, she outlines how catastrophe is crucial to how media operate. In TV, time is flow, yet through photography it has the capacity to embalm it. "Yet, television deals not with the weight of the dead past but with the potential trauma and explosiveness of the present. The ultimate drama of the instantaneous—catastrophe—constitutes the very limit of its discourse" (p. 222). Doane (pp. 229-30) differentiates between crisis and catastrophe, the former being an evanescent background mediating the flow of human agency, the latter being a rupture, a moment disrupting the ability of media to capture time or contingency:

> ... in its structural emphasis upon discontinuity and rupture, it often seems that television itself is formed on the model of catastrophe.... Catastrophe does, however, always seems to have something to do with technology and its potential collapse. And it is also always tainted by a fascination with death—so that catastrophe might finally be defined as the conjecture of the failure of technology and the resulting confrontation with death. The fragility of technology's control over the forces it strives to contain is manifested most visibly in the accident—the plane crash today being the most prominent example... in the case of the airplane crash, speculation about causes is almost inevitably a speculation about the limits and breaking points of technology.

Catastrophe is a "dystopia" of the idea of progress: "catastrophic time stands still" (p. 231). *Lost*'s plane crash blurs the distinction between pre- and postindustrial accidents because on the one hand, the destructive energy is external (turbulence). But on the other hand, it's internal: the plane couldn't protect its passengers from nature.

Because the staging of this accident is outside mediaspace (we the audience watch it on TV, but the characters in the show are not watching it on TV), the experience for the survivors is not containable and normalized through news coverage. This furthers the notion that the island is a kind of purgatory, not in the sense of a transition zone between life and death, but an actual container of death. For the passengers, television was not there to reedit and contain the disaster as it was during Sept. 11. The constant struggle of the passengers to mediate their experience through the rigging of radios is for naught. The one radio transmission they do capture is a looped distress signal that has been broadcasting since the 1980s. Curiously, the one communications expert on the plane, Sayid (a phonogram of "Said") is an Iraqi war veteran of Saddam Hussein's Republican Guard. Sayid's failure to engineer the equipment parallels the disaster of the Gulf War to stabilize the U.S. Empire. The only mediation that does take place on the island is through archaic technology (such as dead technology) that's already relegated to the island, placed, and used there by "the others." Like the repeating distress signal that never leaves the island, the survivors are stuck in a self-contained feedback loop.

Whereas catastrophe "represents discontinuity in an otherwise continuous system," (Doane, p. 232) *Lost*, through its format as a serial and its ubiquitous presence in the mediasphere, provides continuity to ease our anxiety. Its hero trope in the form of Jack is like the news anchor who comforts and normalizes our experience of catastrophe. In addition, the presence of commercials maintains the security, continuity, and normalcy of what we are experiencing (unless you edited them out with your TiVo). Quoting René Thom, the founder of catastrophe theory, Doane (p. 234) reports that catastrophe theory is like "islands of determinism separated by zones of instability and indeterminacy." In *Lost*, the island itself is a theory of stability, a containable nonplace that's reachable through the unstable zones of the terminal, airplane, and finally the crash. "In this sense, television is a kind of catastrophe machine, continually corroborating its own signifying problematic—a problematic if discontinuity and indeterminacy which strives to mimic the experience of the real, which in turn is guaranteed by the contact with death" (Doane, p.34). As mentioned earlier, the allusion to Hades through the narration of Persephone in the LOST Experience reinforces the notion that *Lost*'s island is indeed a location of death.

But death needn't be an end. The island has a dual nature as a place of healing; however, it also demands sacrifice. Some characters, particularly the ones who exhibit faith, experience miraculous healings. Locke gets back the use of his legs, and Rose is cured of terminal cancer. Both are characters who had sought redemption and healing in Australia but were denied; yet they find it on the island. They are also the characters who most believe in fate. For other characters, though, especially the ones who have a more rationalist take on their condition, when they get close to finding true love, they end up losing their enamored objects to death.

The ultimate challenge comes from "the others" who kidnap and murder the crash survivors; "the others" are particularly interested in kids. In the case of children, one of the most common tropes of our social distrust of new technology comes in the constant refrain that new media facilitates our ultimate nightmare: the abduction of our brood. From the early Gypsy myths of child abduction in silent film to the fear of predation in MySpace, you can always measure the level of discomfort with technology when it threatens our youth—children always being a projection of ourselves as innocent victims of communications technology (while it is simultaneously promoted and idealized by corporations through cell phone and other technology ads). I would further argue that the UFO craze and spate of abduction stories of the past twenty years surrounding aliens manifest the anxiety we feel of being overtaken by hybrid, machinelike creatures, meaning the media. Curiously, the theme is revived by the show, *Invasion*, which followed *Lost* on the same network and night during the second season. Although no aliens have yet to appear in *Lost*, "the others" are as close as we can get, the difference being that they are from the past: they are in possession of obsolete technology, they rule the technological (un)dead.

It is not accidental that Locke shares the name of the Enlightenment philosopher and that another survivor encountered on the island, a French woman who was shipwrecked 16 years before and whose voice was in the looping distress signal, is named Rousseau. Both social contract philosophers are at the root of our system of government: The phrase "Man is born free, but everywhere he is in chains" is the most prominent, but "all men are created equal," is Rousseau's most famous. Given the lack of a social structure among the survivors (in fact the only remnant of civilization that ties them together is language, clothing, weapons, media, plane wreckage, and the hatch system of "the others"), the tenants of Enlightenment—and hence the mediaspheric niche of print literacy— are tested by the island. The immigrant status of the survivors contains precisely the quality of homelessness that enables them to negotiate the new reality of ambivalence.

Time itself is malleable on the island. In one sense, time is suspended from the normal world (that is, within the narrative itself): we travel back and forth between flashbacks and the presentness of the character's subplots, in a sense giving them equal weight. The past is always bearing down on the present. One of the more curious aspects of the storyline is the situation of a mysterious computer terminal in Swan Station, the first hatch to be entered and occupied by the survivors. In Swan Station Jack first encounters an "other," Desmond: someone he actually met before the plane crash, whose past connection is revealed through a flashback. The character is Scottish, someone who was on a round-the-world sailing expedition, but was shipwrecked, abducted, and then forced into having to "monitor" the terminal and enter seemingly random numbers (4, 8, 15, 16, 23, 42) into the computer every 108 minutes (the sum total of the numbers). Failure to do so would supposedly launch something catastrophic, but what exactly is unknown. The sequence is also the winning lottery number of one of the survivors, Hurley, who it turns out was in a mental institution (his love interest on the island, Libby, also was a resident, but he never connects the dots). The winning lottery number ended up destroying Hurley's life, leading him into the asylum and also to his fateful journey to the island. There has been some speculation on the boards that in fact the entire narrative is really Hurley's dream or hallucination, but the presence of dreams and flashback of so many different and disconnected characters has led most to discount this idea. What can be said for sure is that the lottery number from the so-called normal world (where gambling is an accepted social practice and in fact a core component of the economic system as embodied by the stock exchange) intercedes into the island world's mediasphere. The two realms bleed between each other. It challenges the old assumption we normally have that media are simply a representation (or replacement) of the real, and therefore separate. The manner in which the synchronicities of the normal world intersect on the island give the island realm new life, making it not only a place of the dead, but also where the dead can be reborn and reintegrated back into the norm. As Debray notes, "A mediasphere is a mentality's relation to physical space as well as time" (p. 28).

The challenge of entering the numbers every 108 minutes, though, tests the faith of the survivors. They do not know what will happen if they don't enter the numbers; they do it because an instructional 16-mm film made in 1980 found in the hatch says to do so. In other words, an old mediaspheric niche commands them, but they don't know why. Despite skepticism that entering the numbers never really achieves anything other than whether or not they will blindly accept their engagement with archaic technology, the survivors continue to do so. As it turns out, through the discovery of Pearl Station (made possible by a dead African priest who speaks through the dreams of the island's two most faith-obsessed characters, Locke and Mr. Eko), the Swan Station was in fact being monitored as if it were part of a psychological experiment. Pearl Station is full of surveillance monitors that observe the characters who occupy Swan Station, positioning them in an elaborate rat maze. The monitoring of the monitor station recalls both Stanley Cavell's (1986) view that we "monitor" television and also the notion of Foucault's panoptic space. But more importantly the fact that Pearl Station was discovered by Mr. Eko (as in "echo"), returns us to McLuhan's notion of Narcissus: that we extended ourselves into a media space, and now through an endless oscillation between autoamputation and overestimation, we experience iteration gone amok, like guitar feedback, or when two mirrors point at each other (or as in the case of Lost, the monitors monitor the monitors). To reiterate, we extend ourselves into the reflection because we are attempting to numb ourselves, a process McLuhan calls "autoamputation." Echoing Doane, as a kind of catharsis and therapeutic, numbing antidepressant, media become the container in which we transport the suffering caused by the overload of our senses:

> The young man's image is a self-amputation or extension induced by irritating pressures. As counter-irritant, the image produces a generalized numbness or shock that declines recognition. Self-amputation forbids self-recognition.... The principle of self-amputation as an immediate relief of strain on the central nervous system applies very readily to the origins of the media of communication from speech to the computer.... With the arrival of electric technology, man extended, or set outside himself, a live model of the central nervous system itself. To the degree that this is so, it is a development that suggests a desperate and suicidal autoamputation, as if the central nervous system could no longer depend on the physical organs to be protective buffers against the slings and arrows of outrageous mechanism. It could well be that the successive mechanizations of the various physical organs since the invention of printing have made too violent and superstimulated a social experience for the central nervous system to endure (McLuhan 2002 [1964], p. 43).

All this is by way of explaining, to some extent, the root cause of our social anxiety, which is the schizophrenic character of mediated culture that over-stimulates *and* fragments our attention. The danger is that the more we transport ourselves into the mediasphere, we enter a closed system without the negative feedback necessary to regulate itself:

> To listen to radio or to read the printed page is to accept these extensions of ourselves into our personal system and to undergo the "closure" or displacement of perception that follows automatically. It is this continuous embrace of our own technology in daily use that puts us in the Narcissus role of subliminal awareness and numbness in relation to these images of ourselves. By continuously embracing technologies, we relate ourselves to them as servomechanisms. That is why we must, to use them at all, serve these objects, these extensions of ourselves, as god or minor religions. An Indian is a servomechanism of his canoe, as the cowboy of his horse or the executive of his clock.... Physiologically, man in the normal use of technology (or his various extended body) is perpetually modified by it and in turn finds ever new ways of modifying his technology. Man becomes, as it were, the sex organs of the machine world, as the bee of the plant world, enabling it to fecundate and to evolve ever new forms. The machine world reciprocates man's love by expediting his wishes and desires, namely, in providing him with wealth (McLuhan, 2002, p. 46).

That the survivors would be trapped in this liminal space of iteration is the very predicament and test that our society faces today. Given that the logo of the DHARMA Institute, the symbol "bagua," is the wheel of balance used for feng shui (the ancient Chinese art of harmonizing the environment), we can see that the possessors of the archaic and dead media are seeking balance with the island's new inhabitants. Just as McLuhan suggests that we are the servomechanisms of corporate media, perhaps the island's new arrivals are in effect thermostats seeking to balance our hypermediated environment. While the Hero's Journey calls for the protagonist to enter the depths of hell to harmonize a world thrown off balance, maybe *Lost*'s survivors, and hence us as empathetic viewers, enter the hatch to negotiate with "the others"—our dead doppelgangers from technology past—to resolve the social contract we have made with media that began with the alphabet, but accelerated with the advent of electricity, then becoming disembodied by the telegraph and recording technology. It remains to be seen if the conflict is resolved by war or treaty, or some other strategy of hybridization. Something tells me it won't be answered by the end of the series.

Age of Feedback

Anybody who begins to examine the patterns of automation finds that perfecting the individual machine by making it automatic involves "feedback." That means introducing an information loop or circuit, where before there had been merely a one-way flow or mechanical sequence. Feedback is the end of the lineality that came into the Western world with the alphabet and the continuous forms of Euclidian space. Feedback or dialogue between the mechanism and its environment brings a further weaving of individual machines into a galaxy of such machines throughout the entire plant. There follows a still further weaving of individual plants and factories into the entire industrial matrix of materials and services of a culture. Naturally, this last stage encounters the entire world of policy, since to deal with the whole industrial complex as an organic system affects employment, security, education, and politics, demanding full understanding in advance of coming structural change. There is no room for witless assumptions and subliminal factors in such electrical and instant organizations.

Marshall McLuhan, Understanding Media

From the development of phonetic script until the invention of he electric telegraph human technology has tended strongly towards the furtherance of detachment and objectivity, detribalization and individuality. Electric circuitry has quite the contrary effect. It involves depth. It merges the individual and the mass environment. To create anti-environment for such electric technology would seem to require a technological extension of consciousness itself. The awareness and opposition of the individual are in these circumstances as irrelevant as they are futile.

Marshall McLuhan, "The Relation of Environment to Anti-Environment"

Like Benjamin's dialectic image of the Paris arcades, the Electric Age has its own nexus of information, media, culture, and environment. It was at London's Abbey Road Studios on October 6, 1964, when Paul McCartney absentmindedly propped his Hofner "violin" bass against a Vox AC100 bass amp, inadvertently producing feedback between the bass's pickups and the amp's circuitry. The loop produced between the two oscillated into a deep, humming tone that was not human-made, but instead was machine and electricity induced. By learning to control the feedback loop, McCartney harnessed the "mistake" to incorporate it into the chart-topping hit, "I Feel Fine." The rest is recorded history. Feedback became a part of music.

The droning, loopy interaction of guitar, human and the electric grid has become the motif of our age. Looping, remixing and mashing-up existing cultural artifacts is the artistic form of today, the primary mode of artistic expression of the new century. As artists, we have learned to harness and control feedback into art and cultural practice. That we have arrived at this point would not have surprised McLuhan; he anticipated it. It's fitting that *Understanding Media* came out the same year as the Beatles' "I Feel Fine."

Understanding feedback and media is fundamental to creating a sustainable design solution for media education. A loop oscillating out of control without being checked by negative feedback is like being locked in a hall of mirrors with our fragments spinning off into infinity. The deafening screech we hear from a speaker when a microphone is pointed at it is the result of "positive feedback." The same effect is what causes epileptic seizures: the reverberating neuron net fires without being checked by "negative" feedback, a built-in "fatigue" mechanism that causes neurons to rest just enough to stop them from chaotic iteration. Without the split-second pause mechanism, the brain can short-circuit (Johnson 2001, pp.142-3). In a functioning system that achieves homeostasis, such as a simple room with a heater and thermostat, "negative" feedback enters the system to instruct the thermostat to adjust the heater's setting according to a predetermined perimeter, meaning the temperature. As explained in "Reality 2.0," GridThink is in the midst of a reiterating loop out of control. Media literacy should be a kind of negative feedback, or pause mechanism, that regulates our mediated epilepsy.

In order to successfully produce negative feedback, however, it's necessary to understand the circuit. That is the purpose of the mediacological niche and the discussion of symbols. Identifying the foreground/background of a given system enables us to target the area that needs input. Consequently, McLuhan's probe of anti-environment/environment is an essential tool for this purpose. In terms of establishing a framework for sustainability, it's important to first understand how McLuhan views "nature." Traditionally nature is the background, or "negative space" from which we explore media. Because it's a psychological function to tune out the environment (in the same way we are oblivious to our own smell or the sound of our voice), in an "age of accelerated change, the need to perceive the environment becomes urgent" (1997, p.119). In *The Global Village* (1992, p. 130) McLuhan and Powers state explicitly that the primary concern is for readers to understand that they are "not living in a natural environment. If he [the reader] is civilized he's living in

Euclidean space—closed, controlled, linear, static—abstracted from the world around him. Like language, it is an attempt to manipulate as well as interpret the world." The authors (pp. 131-2) then translate the term "nature":

> It is itself an abstraction. We know that literate Greeks had to find a word for their ability to abstract visual order out of the environment which surrounded them. So, having identified a number of balances or cause and effect equilibriums, they called them nature (physis) and everything else was chaos. And you find this idea being adopted right down the time tunnel from Parmenides to Descartes, Galileo, Hobbes, and Locke.... Man's view of his environment was not percept but concept—an almost total extension of one sense, his eye. And a sense keyed to the horizon, to a proportionate sense related to the vanishing point. He has used his eye to create a squared-off, controlled environment, whether he is at home or at work, on the highway, in a train or a plane, and everything outside is "nature"—which by now he has identified with chaos.

The euclidean world is "comfortable," and wilderness is something we "go to." Sadly we can't really experience nature, because our senses are "imbalanced." What throws us out of whack are the mechanical conditions of euclidean space which is characterized by the straight line or plane:

> Yet a continuum does not exist in nature, or better still, the total environment, the material universe. There are no straight lines in space; as Einstein pointed out parallel lines do not meet in infinity. They simply curve back upon themselves. We have invented the straight line to give us a sense of location on the Earth's surface. But Euclidean references will not work in outer space. True nature, as we should understand it, is acoustic. Acoustic space has no center. It consists of countless random resonations. It is the kind of orientation we have when we are swimming or riding a bicycle— multisensuous, full kinetic spaces. Euclidean mathematics has not a real grasp of the acoustic (p. 133).

Having established the natural world as a kind of acoustic, non-euclidean space, as in HoloGrok, it's important to ascertain McLuhan's framework of environment and anti-environment. As explained in the struggle for definition in the border zones of mediacological niches, "Any new technology, any extension or amplification of human faculties when given material embodiment, tends to create a new environment" (1997, p. 110). Content becomes environment, such as the "museum without walls," our collective media unconsciousness (for example, Mona Lisa, brand logos, famous photos). As McLuhan (p. 114) writes, "Paradoxically, it is the antecedent environment that is always being upgraded for our attention. The new environment always uses the old environment as its material"—as in remediation. The repeated media literacy trope that we are like fish who know not the sea is an apt description of our predicament when we are unable to distinguish the background.

The dyad of environment/anti-environment is akin to a painting in which the negative space (environment)/foreground remains unnoticed and is set in relief by the more visible anti-environment, such as the figures of a Renaissance painting. In the case of media literacy, educators push books as a way of displacing electronic media. What may be more effective, though, is the role that art can play in arbitrating the media battles on the mediaspheric fringe:

> In the order of things, ground comes first. The figures arrive later. Coming events cast their shadows before them. The ground of any technology is both the situation that gives rise to it as well as the whole environment (medium) of services and disservices that the technology brings with it. These are the side effects, and they impose themselves haphazardly as a new form of culture. The medium is the message. As an old ground is displaced by the content of the new situation, it becomes available to ordinary attention as figure. At the same time a new nostalgia is born. The business of the artist has been to report on the nature of ground by exploring the forms of sensibility made available by each new ground, or mode of culture, long before the average man suspects that anything has changed (McLuhan and Powers 1989, p. 6).

Further exploring the analogy of Art, McLuhan contrasts the differences between tribal and modern practices. Referencing the Balinese relationship with art— "We have not art— we do everything as well as possible"— McLuhan (1997, pp. 111-12) states:

> In pre-literate society art serves as a means of merging the individual and the environment, not as a means of training perceptions upon the environment. Archaic or primitive art looks to us like a magical control built into the environment. Thus to put the artifacts from such a culture into a museum or anti-environment is an act of nullification rather than revelation.

This is evidenced by the surrealist practice of taking African cultural artifacts and turning them into gallery ready-mades, or Picasso incorporating African masks into his paintings.

When Andy Warhol made everyday commercial objects into art (as in the case of the Campbell's soup can or Brillo Boxes), they become anti-environment, setting into relief the commodity culture to draw our attention to that which has become our ambient surroundings, namely the technological sphere of advanced capitalism: "Pop art serves to remind us, however, that we have fashioned for ourselves a world of artifacts and images that are intended not to train perception of awareness but to insist that we merge with them as the primitive man merges with his environment. The world of modern advertising is a magical environment constructed to produce effects for the total economy but not designed to increase human awareness" (McLuhan 1997, p. 112).

In this sense, the electrical world as an invisible lived environment sets nature into relief; it draws our attention to it more clearly than if we were immersed into it without awareness. Take, for example, the Hummer campaign that refers to the vehicle as extraterrestrial and then ends the ad with a zoom into outer space to reveal a digital composite of Earth as though it were being viewed from a space station: "The first satellite ended 'nature' in the old sense. 'Nature' becomes the content of a manmade environment. From that moment, all terrestrial phenomena were to become increasingly programmed artifacts and every facet of human life now comes within the scope of the artistic vision" (McLuhan and Fiore, 1968, p.178). When he McLuhan says the "end of nature," we should be clear that what he means is the end of nature as a construct. For example, citing *Alice's Adventures in Wonderland*, by Lewis Carroll, "each object creates its own space and conditions. To the visual or Euclidean man, objects do not create time and space. They are merely fitted into time and space. The idea that the world as an environment that is more or less fixed, is very much the product of literacy and visual assumptions" (1997, p. 117). This leads us to a potential double bind: People are still trying to squeeze the current environment into "the old space or environment," when in practice the opposite is true. This is most clearly demonstrated in car ads. As I argued earlier, cars are logical iterations of the print literate mind; yet if you watch car commercials, you see that they often generate their own space, be it animated cities that push up through the earth as they drive through the landscape, or the natural world that comes alive, as when a field of sunflowers follows a speeding SUV. Because cars are so ubiquitous, and hence the "environment," nature becomes necessary to make cars the "anti-environment," as in foreground. This is an example of competing mediaspheric niches. The supreme danger is when a system becomes closed, as is the case of the Hummer, which is like a snake eating its tail: global warming = car = oil consumption = economy = security issue = military = war = propaganda = advertising = fear = buy a Hummer to feel safe.

If schools are anti-environments for print (in order to train us to perceive literacy), McLuhan suggests we have no equivalent for electric circuitry, except in the case of disasters. In the same way that airplane crashes alert us to the invisible design of technology, events like Hurricane Katrina, the 2004 tsunami along the Indian Ocean's coasts, and the 1989 San Francisco Bay Area earthquake represent the few times when human attention is drawn to the natural world. "An environment is naturally of low intensity or low definition. That is why it escapes observation. Anything that raises the environment to high intensity, whether it be a storm in nature or violent change resulting from a new technology, such high intensity turns the environment into an object of attention. When an environment becomes an object of attention it assumes the character of an anti-environment or art object" (1997, p.114). This is perhaps the ultimate lesson of 9/11, because the events that day turned our invisible environment of empire on its head.

I take it as a given that as servomechanisms of the technological realm, we have to collectively choose whether we serve corporations or they serve us. In this sense, I think the Iraq war will become a litmus test, for it is an outward expression of all the contradictions of our system (this should be a self-evident truth for even the most vaguely informed person). At the time of writing, the war remains unresolved and is spinning dangerously out of control. If in our pedagogy we can assist people to become veritable guitarists playing our systems as instruments, we can control the oscillation parameter through the introduction of negative feedback, akin to McLuhan's anti-environment. Systems theorists like Ervin Laszlo (2001) make a strong case for embracing holographic thinking as the primary requirement for developing sustainable consciousness. The acoustic quality of the sensorium interplaying with media and electricity is much closer to holographic, or recursive, modes of perception than the fragmented, alphabetized rationality of literate culture and euclidean space; however, I need to stress my repeated theme that new media remediate old media. One is not entirely exclusive of the other.

Our cultural programming tends to look at things as either good or bad, which makes interpreting our current reality more difficult and less nuanced. We could certainly see a series of break points that would indicate the negative aspect of our technosphere, events like war and terrorism, but one of the barriers of developing solutions is the tendency to dwell on the fearful and negative aspects of our environment. There are optimistic moments in McLuhan (2002 [1964]) that echo some of the proto-New Age thinking about media, in particular Pierre Teilhard de Chardin's "noosphere": "If the work of the city is the remaking of translating of man into a more suitable form than his monadic ancestors achieved, then might not our current translation of our entire lives into the spiritual form of information seem to make of the entire globe, and of the human family, a single consciousness?" (p. 61).

As mentioned, McLuhan (1997, pp. 119-20) values the role of artists for negotiating the interplay between figure and background: "The artist provides us with anti-environments that enable us to see the environment.... New environments reset our sensory thresholds. These in turn, alter our outlook and expectations." The creation of anti-environments is particularly difficult when the media system is so agile in incorporating any kind of opposition (this is where the discussion of autopoiesis in "Mediaspheric Niches" becomes useful). McLuhan proposed employing some kind of social thermostat, which sounds ridiculous, but that's precisely what security states (such as governments dominated by military interests) do: they go to war and engineer fear through such mechanisms as air raid drills or terrorist alerts. Feeding disinformation to the press, propaganda, and advertising are other tools of cultural production that act as a social thermostat. What McLuhan (1997, p.120) advocated was a more enlightened kind of mechanism:

> The need of our time is for the means of measuring sensory thresholds and of discovering exactly what changes occur in these thresholds as a result of the advent of any particular technology. With such knowledge in hand it would be possible to program a reasonable and orderly future for any human community. Such knowledge would be the equivalent of a thermostatic control for room temperatures. It would seem only reasonable to extend such controls to all sensory thresholds of our being. We have no reason to be grateful to those who juggle the thresholds in the name of haphazard innovation.

Ideally schools should serve this thermostat function, but because they are instead designed to replicate the economic system and GridThink, media educators have been trying to play the role of injecting negative feedback into the circuit. The difficulty from a pedagogical view is to know whether or not our practices are actually serving the right kind of feedback function. One cause for optimism is the fact that we have so many readily available examples of feedback in the mediasphere, from hip-hop, to mash-ups, to the Web 2.0, that it's a concept easily grasped by young people because it is their milieu. If we can mindfully engage that which is useful without throwing the baby out with the bathwater, then the Beatles' use of feedback was a prescient omen, and we can take heed John Lennon's song title, "I Feel Fine."

CHAPTER SEVEN

The Meme of Memes:
Information as Objects

The naming of things, of course, is an abstraction of a very high order and of crucial importance. By naming an event and categorizing it as a 'thing,' we create a vivid and more or less permanent map of what the world is like. But it is a curious map indeed. The word *cup*, for example, *does not in fact denote anything that actually exists in the world*. It is a concept, a summary of millions of particular things that have a similar look and function. The word tableware is at a still higher level of abstraction, since it includes not only all the things we normally call cups but also millions of things that look nothing like cups but have a vaguely similar function.

Neil Postman, *The End of Education*

I n the introduction I stated that there is a tension between analysis and design, arguing that most media literacy practitioners adhere to analyzing a world of effects, which leads to solutions based on "fixing" as opposed to solution design. Taking a position against the prevailing view of effects reminds me of the time I was in college working as a dishwasher. My coworker happened to be the chairman of the Young Republicans, and as you can imagine, our hours working together generated "interesting" discussions. Regardless of how many facts I presented concerning the history of U.S. government intervention in Latin America or the number of democracies that the CIA helped overthrow, he'd reply, "It doesn't matter, this administration (it was under Ronald Reagan at the time) is different." We were both long gone by the time the Iran-Contra affair rolled around, but I was left with the understanding that you can argue all you want with someone—but as long as that person holds certain foundational beliefs with different assumptions about reality (such as the president never lies, or that freedom, democracy, and war are compatible), the discussion becomes one of competing monologues, a bit like our current state of media punditry. This is what I think historian Arthur Schlesinger was getting at when he described Marxists as being like Jehovah's Witnesses. I don't mean to single out Marxists, but we should be skeptical of people from all ideological persuasions who claim a monopoly on truth. In this respect, what concerns me are the patterns of actions— not the theories argued in books— of the majority of the media literacy educators with whom I have come into contact. It is my contention that though many media literacy activists pay lip service to the free individual who can shape his or her own opinions given the proper facts, it's not what they really believe. Furthermore, in my view, the effects argument mirrors a Cartesian construction of the world and is not an accurate description of how communications actually take place.

Part of the problem is viewing communications by using the so-called conduit metaphor, which often frames how we think about information. Michael Ready (1993) observed that we use metaphors in everyday speech to convey information and ideas as things, and that thought is a matter of manipulating these objects. Phrases such as, "I grasp that," the "contents of that ad," "that book packed with ideas," "I'm trying to get my ideas across to you," "my message is loud and clear," and "criticism was hurled" convey a sense that information consists of objects that are easily transported or retrievable. The predicament is that we mistake the metaphor for the fact of communication. Neurolinguist George Lakoff (1995, p. 116) suggests that

> One entailment of the conduit metaphor is that the meaning, the ideas, can be extracted and can exist independently of people. Moreover, that in communication, when communication occurs, what happens is that somebody extracts the same object, the same idea, from the language that the speaker put into it. So the conduit metaphor suggests that meaning is a thing and that the hearer pulls out the same meaning from the words and that it can exist independently of beings who understand words.

This leads to the meme trope that nefarious messages delivered by "Big Media," especially in the guise of advertising or structurally biased news organizations, are inserted into the receiver's mind as if being injected. In general, I have observed that many media activists and educators assume the "syringe" model of communication popularized by the Shannon-Weaver Model, which internalizes the conduit metaphor of information. This is echoed in the media activist primer, *Culture Jam*, in which *Adbusters*' founder Kalle Lasn (2000, p. 12) writes,

> Layer upon layer of mediated artifice come between us and the world until we are mummified. The commercial mass media are rearranging our neurons, manipulating our emotions, making powerful new connections between deep immaterial needs and material products. So virtual is the hypodermic needle that we don't feel it. So gradually is the dosage increased that we're not aware of the toxicity.

Lasn recycles a view of media developed during the capital-intensive era of industrial mass media that's represented by the "one-to-many" communications model (as opposed to the "many-to-many" model of the computer network economy), in which the reader exists within a hermetically sealed environment. Justin Lewis (1991, p. 10) basically sums up the attitude of so-called "effects" theories that emerge from this media and communications concept:

> The problem is that the process of meaning construction, for most human beings, embraces almost every aspect of their lives—from their education and social environment to those elusive childhood traumas. For the researcher, it is a veritable nightmare of intervening variable. Locating effects means locating causality, which, in turn, means delving into the murky depths of the history of the human psyche. This is not, to put it mildly, a very straightforward procedure.

As I have been arguing, there are simply too many mediaspheric niches in a person's psyche to come up with any meaningful generalizations about the influence of media on a population. The media impact on a person's life is more context sensitive and on a par with the "it's an art not a science" kind of approach. In this respect, our belief concerning negative media is like how we understand pornography: it's impossible to define, yet we know what it is when we see it. The problem for educators is knowing the difference between our personal opinions about the world and true understanding. Clearly the situation calls for more nuance and flexibility among the media literacy folks railing against the system.

Unfortunately, many well-meaning educators can see themselves as gatekeepers, or "protectionists," representing an "expert paradigm" of mass media spokespeople, a dangerous breed of human that has led us on many misadventures that can end up in some form of censorship or moral dogmatism. Henry Jenkins (2006, p. 284) describes knowledge experts as espousing "a structure of knowledge dependent upon a bounded body of information that can be mastered by an individual and often dependent upon the authorization bestowed on individuals by institutions of higher learning." In other words, it's a hierarchal educational model that promotes a conventional wisdom, such as the Marxist view of the commodity fetish, or the belief that information is a thing. This can lead to a kind of elitism that translates badly when the high-on-horse media critic thinks about "readers," as was the case with film criticism in the 1970s and 1980s:

> Audiences disappeared from the construction of meaning altogether, to be replaced by a witless creature known as the "textual subject." The textual subject, like the unfortunate mouse in the behaviorist's experiment, was manipulated and forced (by the text's structures and strategies) to adopt particular positions. Once in position, the inexorable meaning of the message (produced with consummate wizardry by the analyst) would manifest itself (Lewis, p. 34).

There is a tendency to imagine a character "type" and generate imaginary scenarios based on a hypothetically brainwashed archetype (such as the "American consumer"), when in fact it's usually the critic's projection of GridThink, or more precisely, moral judgment. Sometimes I can't tell the difference between media critics and Victorian-era prohibitionists. I believe it's morally elitist to assume that we know what goes on inside a person's mind, though I will admit that at this moment I am somewhat guilty of this charge because of my generalizations concerning media literacy activists; but I wouldn't be saying any of this if I hadn't seen these attitudes play out over and over again in my field. It is true that some media literacy techniques suggest that readers take into consideration their own values, and some educators are quite good at addressing this. There are many who stress that readers decode according to their understanding of the world, yet in general I find this open-ended approach pretty rare and I don't think this is strongly emphasized in a media literacy pedagogy that results from activist or reformist agendas.

One of the more malleable concepts to infiltrate media activism is the concept of "memes." According to Wikipedia, a meme "comprises a unit of cultural information, cultural evolution or diffusion that propagates from one mind to another analogously to the way in which a gene propagates from one organism to another as a unit of genetic information and of biological evolution." Media critics internalize this concept in the same way that the syringe model of communication presumes that media delivers ideological messages within advertisements and news broadcasts (this differs from the "subjectivity" that media buttress). Consequently there is an epidemiological view emerging that sees corporate media as delivering ideological codes, particularly through symbols. Not all are unhappy about this. Marketers self-consciously boast the latest gimmicks for branding and selling products through "viral" marketing, with Malcolm Gladwell (2002, 2005) being the most recent cheerleader of this view by promoting it in his books, Blink and The Tipping Point. In this case, there is not much difference between media activists and marketers. As Lasn (p. 123) puts it,

> A meme (rhymes with "dream") is a unit of information (a catchphrase, a concept, a tune, a notion of fashion, philosophy or politics) that leaps from brain to brain to brain. Memes compete with one another for replication, and are passed down through a population much the same way genes pass through a species. Potent memes can change minds, alter behavior, catalyze collective mindshifts and transform cultures. Which is why meme warfare has become the geopolitical battle of our information age. Whoever has the memes has the power.

This statement is reminiscent of the earlier Mills quote about how the control of symbols translates as cultural and political control. But is a symbol a static container of ideology? An early version of the meme of memes was articulated in Douglas Rushkoff's (1996, pp. 9-10), *Media Virus!*, which describes emergent themes surrounding the cultural concept of memes:

> Media viruses spread through the datasphere the same way biological ones spread through the body or a community. But instead of traveling along an organic circuitry system, a media virus travels through networks of the mediaspace. The "protein shell" of a media virus might be an event, invention, technology, system of thought, musical riff, visual image, scientific theory, sex scandal, clothing style or even a pop hero—as long as it can catch our attention. Any one of these media virus shells will search out the receptive nooks and crannies in popular culture and stick on anywhere it is noticed. Once attached, the virus injects its more hidden agendas into the datastream in the form of *ideological code*—not genes, but a conceptual equivalent we now call "memes." Like real genetic material, these memes infiltrate the way we do business, educate ourselves, interact with one another—even the way we perceive reality.

Given the divergent views of memes, it's ironic that the concept does not replicate so well. This is the subject of considerable debate among cognitive anthropologists who are looking how culture is distributed in relationship with the biological functions of the mind. On the most basic level memes are spread by imitation. According to Susan Blackmore (1998), "If we define memes as transmitted by imitation then whatever is passed on by this copying process is a meme" (paragraph 37). Contagious behaviors that are innate, she states, like yawing and laughing, are not memes. Also, memes are not "perceptions, emotional states, cognitive maps, experiences in general, or 'anything that can be the subject of an instant experience.'" Finally, imitation is distinguished from contagions. But as Scott Atran (2001, p. 20) remarks, "No replication without imitation; therefore no replication."

The most basic error in the assumptions made by the meme of memes is that the DNA of a cell is the same thing as an idea. DNA can replicate; ideas are messy. Diseases spread by viruses and bacteria, and occasionally they mutate, whereas, "Representations... tend to be transformed each time they are transmitted" (Dan Sperber 1985, p. 75). Also, Susan Blackmore's thesis depends on the assumption that the mind is built for memes as bodies are built for genes. The view of the mind as a computer that simply needs programming may have to do more with the bias of writing technology than with what is actually taking place when information spreads through culture. As Atran (2001, p. 9) suggests,

> Unlike genes, ideas rarely copy with anything close to absolute fidelity. In the overwhelming majority of cases, an idea undergoes some sort of modification during communication. The real mystery is how any group of people manages an affective degree of common understanding given that transformation of ideas during transmission is the rule rather than exception. If transformation (mutation or drift)

affects the information at a greater rate than high-fidelity replication, then a favorable or unfavorable selection bias cannot develop for the replicated (hereditary) information. In such cases, Darwinian selection becomes impossible.

Media activists like Lasn who promote the concept of memes assume that advertisements contain "ideological codes," but Pascal Boyer (1999, p. 883) suggests "...mental representations are never 'downloaded' from one mind to another. Rather, they are built on the basis of cultural input of inferential processes." What is important is not the property of memes but the "properties of memes in interaction with the properties of inferential processes activated about them." Inference is when ideas are associated with other concepts. Reflective beliefs are "interpretations"; they require inference. The underlying quality that makes beliefs reflective is "authority": they are believed if someone such as a parent or a priest says so. This is a primary technique of propaganda, but again, this only works when there is a susceptibility to an idea, such as post-9/11when a desire to "do something" or "punch back" makes messages about going to war with Iraq flow more easily. Clearly, propaganda concepts don't just replicate; otherwise it would be easy to wage wars because all you would have to do is to tell people to go to war. There are other countervailing beliefs that buffer and repel ideological concepts. Shocks like 9/11 are only temporarily effective for creating an environmental niche for fear messages to spread. A system based on fear must generate a perpetual state of warfare, or the threat of war as was the case with the Cold War, in order to keep the sense of threat alive. In this sense I would argue that what we need is not competing memes, as the *Adbusters* folks suggest, but a strong immune system that can withstand guttural propaganda attacks.

The other issue is that even if ads delivered "ideological codes," what would they look like? Would they be statements ("freedom is slavery"), images (skinny women), or sounds (rock music)? How does the mind make sense of any of these units of information, and how would meaning be constructed into cultural concepts? Gladwell's (2002) discussion of *Sesame Street* bears some relevance here. Though he never uses the word meme, he does discuss the delivery of ideas as requiring "stickiness." *Sesame Street*, and its rival show *Blue's Clues*, explicitly designed packages of concepts and information intended to teach literacy to children. These intensely tested programs provide a little window into why some techniques work and others don't. In the end the successful components were storylines, repetition, suspense, puzzle making, interaction, and physical engagement (pp. 89-132). This suggests that children are not passive recipients of media codes, but learn through a process of active engagement. Moreover, as Lawrence Hirschfeld (2005, p. 217) points out regarding race and children, "The race concept is acquired in cultural environments in which race is an ambient belief," meaning it's catchy because a perception of difference exists. This suggests that children who grow up in mediated environments will pick up on the ambient messages that pervade advertising, but how they internalize the information is more complex and environmental than the simple injection of memes. The prevailing culture of the family, religion, community, and society weigh heavily on how the information is processed. This was particularly true of me, because I watched at least four hours of TV a day as a child, I played "Army," made model tanks (and blew them up with firecrackers), listened to misogynistic rock music, and fought other kids in the school yard. Did any of this turn me into a warmongering idiot? I don't believe so. In addition to attending an alternative school, one counter force was the immersion into a contrary set of values promoted by an alien mediacological niche, punk rock. This reinforces my sense that art and countercultural youth practices can be countervailing forces against ideology and commercialism.

So if ads are not delivering memes, what are they doing? Kim Sterelny (2006) argues: "From the meme perspective, it's the properties of technologies or cognoviruses themselves that explain take-off"; properties are only "salient" in particular contexts, and "cognitive biases" work in the context of human environments and psychology. "These biases make some sets of ideas and technologies memorable, salient, easy to acquire and natural to teach." This explains why some things are more attractive than others. Only a limited number of human representations are "sifted and sorted by our innate cognitive structures" (p. 160). It's not the properties of the technology that are appealing but the psychology of the technology users. This moves us closer to an "environmental" explanation of how ideas transfer, the environment being a niche of many components, including cognitive receptivity.

Niches are not without complexity, but Edgar Morin's (1971) exploration of rumor does give us a few tools for describing one aspect of the psychological environment that ads play in—our receptivity to ambient presence of cultural mythology. First of all, let's move beyond the secret ideological code that the meme of memes speaks of. Let's explore what their surface messages are, treating ads collectively as a kind of consumer mythology by employing Morin's (p. 55) definition of myth: "an imaginary narrative, organized consistently within the framework of its own psycho-affective logic, which claims to be rooted in reality and truth." If we were alien anthropologists, what would ads teach us about the stories of late-capitalist society? Reducing the most common message to an "imaginary narrative," it's that commodities have the magical capacity to transform the consumer from an ordinary reality to a magical one. Is this really much different than the one espoused by the priest in a Roman Catholic mass practicing the enchantment of transubstantiation? It may be that the mechanisms that operate in commercials are not that much different than those that propagate religious beliefs.

What I find useful in Morin's work is the potential for ambient motifs to be an aspect of the mediacological niche for concepts to peg on, such as the invocation of World War II (and *not* Vietnam) imagery in military advertising during the Afghan and Iraq war campaigns. Morin's model for the spread of rumor starts with a "germ" that "incubates" in a mythological source and then spreads "virulently" to "metastasis" in the community. Applied to the post-9/11 environment, the germ could be the idea that the United States represents all that is "good" in the world, as in "we are God's nation" and "we promote freedom." It incubates in our institutions, media and schooling, spreading virulently when we are attacked. It metastasizes in war, but collapses when confronted by an "anti-myth," and then regresses into "mini-rumors" until finally "leaving only germs and residual fragments behind" (p. 42), such as was the case with the end of the Vietnam War.

Clearly marketing is a far larger force than a rumor that passes from person to person in a community, though the current trend of peer-to-peer marketing might suggest that sharing information on a personal basis is a far more effective promotional technique than the one utilized in the traditional broadcast model. True enough, marketing is abandoning the industrial one-to-many model for the many-to-many transmission mode of niche marketing through so-called "viral" media and "narrowcasting." But a substantial difference between rumor and advertising and propaganda is that marketing is backed by deliberate and intentional forces that aim to generate sales of their products, develop "mindshare" for their brands (see Klein, 1999), or promote a political agenda. So rather than have a specific, traceable result (we don't know when a person puts money in a soda machine and chooses Pepsi if it is the direct consequence of seeing a specific ad), the theoretical assumption is that patterns of consumption measured in sales, and mindshare measured in stock value, will reflect whether or not a marketing campaign is successful. Value, like the commodity fetish, is an abstract quality and can only be measured in theoretical terms made visible by pattern.

Another helpful concept from Morin's discussion concerns the mechanism of what makes the rumor believable—it's the mythological "germ" that plays on the dynamic relationship between "New Modernity" and "Arkhe," "an imaginary narrative, organized consistently within the framework of its own psycho-affective logic, which claims to be rooted in reality and truth" (p. 55). The "Arkhe is all cluttered about with the realities of news items, bulletins, daily life, ships, the city; and in an amalgam of the real, the plausible, and the fabulous, it has made itself an astonishing and explosive mixture of dream and reality" (p. 54). The Arkhe plays on a kind of cultural "susceptibility." If ads utilize a common trope that commodities transform reality from normal to magical, then they work on an underlying cultural assumption that normal reality is fundamentally unstable and needs to be secured through material means. From Plato's cave allegory to *The Matrix* film series, I believe if there is one common strain in Western civilization, it's the manner in which our intellectual and cultural products consistently view reality as an imitation of a more perfect, intangible world. Western culture has been inherently utopian, always searching for a more perfect reality somewhere in the future. Ironically, this was challenged by Warhol, who embraced advertising by declaring that all images were valid and perfect descriptions of reality. I'd like to suggest that in the context of ad production, the Arkhe that enables ads to make their argument is the belief that a more perfect world exists beyond our daily experience.

But if we were to stick to Morin's model, we'd be in trouble because he argues that countermyths become the manner in which rumors cease spreading. Information is the immune system against the rumor's contagion. If we extended this as an educational strategy to combat advertising's negative messages, then all activist and educators would need to do is supply "good" information. Unfortunately, Morin's model doesn't explain why we are susceptible to beliefs from a biological or systems perspective (his only biological reference is the "condition of being woman" p. 97). This is similar to Johnson's (2005) critique of media literacy: it's not enough to determine what the message is about, but rather, how did it come into existence in the context of environmental factors? Morin repeats a memetic view of information. That is, there is a basic message that is replicated and delivered relatively intact between people within the population. But even in his case study the "anti-myth was itself a myth"; there wasn't objectively "truthful" information that was antidotal; the countermyths also had agendas (p. 87). Contrary to the self-important stance that media activists take against corporate media, they may also be promoting ideas that rely on the same Arkhe that drives ads: reality is not to be trusted; the truth is "out there" (to quote the X-Files). Moreover, as has been demonstrated by the trajectory of marketing, advertising has a remarkable ability to absorb the language of dissent. The current trend of irony as a sales technique, for example, appeals to our sense of distrust by winking at us ("We know that you know that this is all BS, but buy our product anyway"). In the end, truth and counter-truth end up looking like a hall of mirrors.

This is not to say that ads still don't deliver socially harmful messages, but the manner in which they interact with cognition would suggest different educational strategies. Sperber (1996) complains that the "epidemiology of belief" is not a matter of just viewing culture as a system of public representations with public meanings: "Since representations are more or less widely shared, there is no neat boundary between cultural and individual representations" (p. 82). Similar to eating a piece of bread, when does it cease being bread, and when does it become a part of your body? Like the critique of the meme concept, Sperber argues, "... the prevailing view of communication, as a coding process followed by a symmetrical decoding process, implies that replication of the communicator's thoughts in the minds of the audience is the normal outcome of communication." Ultimately, "A process of communication is basically one of transformation." The spectrum is "duplication and total loss of information. Only those representations which are repeatedly communicated and manually transformed in the process will end up belonging to the culture" (p. 83). The saturation of advertising in our lives would meet the final condition. We may not remember the specific message of any given ad, but the accumulated message would be the repeated motif that buying products makes us happy. As media critics often note, the aggregate spiritual message of ads is that we are losers unless we buy into the system.

Television ads are never viewed in an isolated, sense-deprived environment. There is always lots going on all around, such as people making phone calls, people yelling, text messaging, and reading magazines. This point is constantly ignored when media activists cite so-called "effects" studies to prove that videogames cause violence or news channels make wars possible. Unlike the scene in A Clockwork Orange when Alex DeLarge is forced to watch violent media, I don't believe there is a hermetically sealed experiment that can scientifically prove that media specifically change our behavior. Moreover, the model of a one-to-many form of mass communication simply vanishes in the age of Internet, iPod, cell phone cameras, and portable game machines. As Hirschfeld (2002, p. 615) states, "It is now commonplace that cultural environments are manifold: At any given moment the cultural environment which an individual inhabits is fragmented, fluid, noisy, and negotiable—from perspectives of both information and power." What ads do engage are domains of task-specific cognitive mechanisms: "We agree with standard social science that culture is not human psychology writ large and that it would make little sense to seek a psychological reductionist explanation of culture. We believe, however, that psychological factors play an essential role in culture. Among these psychological factors, the modular organization of human cognitive abilities favors the recurrence, cross-cultural variability, and local stability of a wide range of cultural representations" (p. 164, Sperber and Hirschfeld).

From a wide-angle perspective, we can consider corporate media as a distribution mechanism of "representation sets" for the GridThink's mediaspheric niche. Sperber (1985, p. 87) argues,

> Some sets of representations include representations of the way in which the set should be distributed. An institution is the distribution of a set of representations which is governed by representations belonging to the set itself. This is what makes institutions self-perpetuating. Hence to study institutions is to study a particular type of distribution of representations. This study falls squarely within the scope of an epidemiology of representations.

Corporate media distribute representations through advertising in a manner that is cohesive and ideologically consistent. Accordingly, German sociologist Niklas Luhmann (2000, p. 2) defines mass media as "all those institutions of society which make use of copying technology to disseminate communications." What's limiting about Luhmann's argument, and endemic of the other media theorists we've discussed, is this sense that information is autonomous, like the so-called ideological code embedded in media viruses. Boyer (1999, p. 882) suggests that tokens do not "'contain' representations but that they trigger meta-representations. This is the case, for instance, in visual representations." Atran (2001, p. 10), citing Sperber, asserts "cultural representations lies not with their formal (semantic) structure, but with their casual relationships to multimodular minds." In this model, memes would enhance and shape preexisting structures, but would not change the architecture. Ultimately, Atran (p. 20) concludes,

> We are increasingly witness to a rapid and global spread of anonymous electronic messages that many of us would prefer to do without yet cannot seem to avoid. This adds much to the sentiment that these messages are authorless, active, aggressive and alive. I believe this sentiment is an illusion. Ideas do not reproduce or replicate in minds. They do not nest in and colonize minds, they do not generally spread from mind to mind by imitation. It is minds that produce and generate ideas. Minds structure certain communicable aspects of the ideas produced, and these communicable aspects generally trigger or elicit ideas in other minds through inference and not imitation.

Mechanisms of inference are discussed extensively in Sperber's (1985) "epidemiology of representations." He suggests that we have "dispositions" that result from natural selection and have susceptibilities as side effects, as in we have a disposition to eat sweets, but a susceptibility to eat processed sugar (pp. 80-81). As discussed previously, advertisements play on our desire for security. On a basic "biopolitical" (the power to grant and take away life) level, most rhetorical hooks used as persuasion techniques play specifically on procreation (sex) and survival (fear). The sex technique is self-explanatory, usually manifesting in some form of erotic imagery. The fear technique is more subtle. It can range from direct threat messages used in propaganda campaigns ("the enemy will kill us!") to a more tribal appeal to shame the public into believing that by not buying certain products (such as dandruff shampoo), they will be rejected by the group. In terms of modularity and domains, Atran's image of the cognitive "drain basin" (p. 14) serves as a good description of how ads might play upon our minds. Symbols kick in via the physicality and direct stimulus of the senses (light, colors, sounds, shapes), engaging the proprietary database of our mind's perceptual modules.

Television ads use montage as one of the fundamental techniques to construct messages. By juxtaposing disparate images, they implore us to interact with the material to construct meaning. A blonde Shakira in front of a red, white, and blue Pepsi logo, for example, will trigger a number of associations without explicitly stating them, such as "it's good to be blonde" (the Colombian singer is naturally dark-haired), being blonde is American, Pepsi is American, and since Shakira represents Pepsi, drinking Pepsi will transform you into a good American. All these elements were made with dissimilar images that logically have nothing to do with each other. "Broken lines don't make a square. To make a square requires inferences from broken line to pre-existing computational structures. This specific piece of human cognitive architecture selectively reduces the set of all possible relations between stimuli to only those that fit prior determinations of what counts as geometrical well-formedness" (Atran, p. 32), as in memory. Like jumping from one comic book panel to the other, the space between frames is reconstructed by our minds to create cohesion and meaning. As film theorists such as Jean-Louis Baudry (1999) have noted, when we watch movies, we literally "suture" shots together with our minds to construct meaning.

Media work on our "intuitive expectations" (Boyer 1999, p. 879), which are developed through the practice of viewing, not through innate understanding. For example, in terms of how moving images construct reality, I find it interesting that we take it for granted the logical connection between edits when we watch films. The language of films was developed by humans, and is not necessarily inherent. When parallel editing first came into existence in 1913 (the cross-cutting between two scenes such as a man holding up a bank and the police driving to the scene of the crime), it did not necessarily make sense to early viewers. They had to suspend disbelief to understand that these two events were happening at the same time. When modern viewers watch films and see a close-up of a hand, they are able to make a mental adjustment to understand that the hand is not ten feet in diameter. This is not the case with cultures that have no previous experience with film or editing. When they see a close-up of a butterfly, they believe the butterfly is as big as the one depicted on the screen. But somehow we learn very quickly through our "intuitive expectations" about the relationship between edits—from parallel events to the deployment of multiple points of view to create a "seamless" reality. I seriously doubt that a person from 1900 could understand a modern TV commercial or TV show. It would likely come across as a chaotic and random series of sensory stimulus in the form of sight and sound, much like the emergent avant-garde practice of collage of the early century that shocked early viewers. Finally, like religions full of miracle stories, the messages of 99% of all advertising are nonsensical: products are depicted as having magical properties to the extent that they are sentient, and they have the ability to transform our existence from a state of misery to one of ecstatic bliss.

Our ability for forming meta-representations enables us to a) *learn* how these random images form a coherent story, and b) how a series of these mini-stories (such as in the form of TV ads) can be networked together to form an ideology (that is consumer capitalism) and subjectivity. The key here is "learn." We must be trained that these relationships make sense, but we have an innate capacity to make these connections (the modular structure of our cognition to seek out pattern). Recall the advertising maxim that if you place an image in someone's head, you can't take it out. This is the underlying technique of propaganda. All people like Karl Rove care about is that you hear certain phrases over and over again, and that certain images are repeated (meaning the Big Lie propaganda technique). For example, if the intention is to make President Bush a believable patriarch—a strong man at the head of a family (nation) who is there to protect its members (citizens)—then it is necessary to have him repeatedly look "tall," "virile," and "manly," and never to appear vulnerable. The case of the "Mission Accomplished" media event after the U.S. invasion of Iraq and the collapse of its government is an excellent example. Bush is dressed up in a flight suit; he lands on an aircraft carrier; he is surrounded by troops; he is positioned so that every shot of his speech has the banner "Mission Accomplished" behind him. Our capacity for intuitive expectations enables us to relate all the various elements to our social conditioning so that we mentally produce the intended message of the event planners: that Bush is a great military leader who is capable of piloting the nation and its war machine to great victory, and that he can and will protect us.

Because propaganda and advertising work through inference, they do not contain innate facts, just "symbolic" truths. Thus the staged event of "Mission Accomplished" failed because in the end it was a premature statement that did not match the reality of the war's ultimate outcome. The initial believability of the messages is based on environmental factors, such as mainstream media accepting the authority figure of "The President" who makes the information more credible than a counter message from a pacifist hippie. What undermines Bush is negative feedback because it acts as an important constraint on ads or propaganda. Meta-representations are not a given (though our capacity to have them is), and they can change over time as input causes us to constantly reevaluate our assumptions and beliefs (if we have the courage to do so, of course).

We can conclude that various mechanisms contribute to the way meaning is constructed when engaging advertising. Media do contribute to our system of beliefs, but not in a manner described by the syringe model. Media do not inject us with ideological code; our minds are not computers that simply require programming. Media do interact with our cognition and other ambient and environmental factors that enable us to construct beliefs, but I am not convinced that they are nefarious or harmful like a disease as activists often claim. Though I am against pathologizing media, what I do glean from exploring the epidemiology of belief is that building a strong immune system against negative messages typically seen in commercials is still necessary. For me this means that teaching media literacy remains important, but it should be done in the context of other activities. For example, though I watched four hours of TV a day as a kid, I am rather skeptical of the ideologies propagated in commercial media. I attribute this to learning good critical thinking skills in an alternative school, growing up in a family that cares about art and culture, spending time in the natural world, living in a multicultural urban environment (Los Angeles), traveling to foreign countries, playing music, and experiencing many other intangibles that were a part of my learning environment.

I do not doubt the intentions of media activists. Like them I believe that the majority of messages we are exposed to when we experience media ultimately can contribute negatively to the health of the individual, society, and natural world. In a sense we are all trying to "evolve" our society so that we can continue to exist. What the epidemiology of belief teaches us is that taken as a whole, ideas proliferate according to "ecological" factors, that is within complex interactions of differing systems within the brain, nervous system, community, family, and greater culture.

If we accept the meme premise, it leads to its own set of strategies based on effects, not design. One is culture jamming, which is little more than putting graffiti on top of preexisting cultural products. Culture jamming argues that social change comes from "uncooling" brands (such as commercial tobacco) and combating the symbolic order by negating existing symbols: in a sense a style war accompanied by grassroots organizing. The problem of this, Jenkins (p. 248) argues is, "Resistance becomes an end in and of itself rather than a tool to ensure cultural diversity and corporate responsibility." Culture jamming is one of the prevailing legacies of punk, the term being invented by the band Negativland which is famous for pranking, copyright violation, and mastering the aesthetic of cut-and-paste. Culture jamming comes from the concept of radio jamming, which uses competing signals to jam up communications. Before weapons are fired or bombs dropped, there is often electronic warfare going on in the background designed to jam radar signals, or radio frequencies, to prevent ordinance being triggered. Cultural warriors accept the credo that information war is guerrilla war (one of McLuhan's legacies), so the objects of their attack are society's symbols. In order for this to work, though, one must accept Mills' premise that those who control symbols, control the world.

CHAPTER EIGHT

Media Lit's Mediacological Niche

Historically, public education in the United States was a product of the need to distribute the skills and knowledge necessary to train informed citizens. The participation gap becomes much more important as we think about what it would mean to foster the skills and knowledge needed by monitorial citizens: here, the challenge is not simply, being able to read and write, but being able to participate in the deliberations over what issues matter, what knowledge counts, and what ways of knowing command authority and respect. The ideal of the informed citizen is breaking down because there is simply too much for any individual to know. The ideal of monitorial citizenship depends on developing new skills in collaboration and a new ethic of knowledge sharing that will allow us to deliberate together.

Henry Jenkins, *Convergence Culture*

Having explored the rich and diverse metalevels of our contemporary mediasphere and alternative epistemologies, I want to now return to the particular niches held by media literacy and its practices to measure whether or not they are providing the necessary kind of feedback into the mediacological circuit. Like most of my colleagues, I'm motivated by a commitment to the idea of sustainability, peace, and justice, and I believe that media are integral for spreading both positive *and* negative beliefs regarding the environment, self-image, and social structures. From fundamentalist Christians to anarchists, media literacy is a common tool with which to educate about attitudes distributed through commercial media, such as messages about body image, addiction, the petrol economy, war, violence, and misogyny. But can media literacy be an antibody within education and serve as a kind of immune system booster? Are media a kind of disease that requires medical treatment? Again, I am overgeneralizing, but the prescription advocated by most of these arguments is to "reform" media with two common approaches: demonize corporate media and blame advertising for the majority of social problems we face (you can now add video games to this list). But reform is tricky, as some critics have argued, because it is based on an old ideal of mass media that lacks justice for those who historically have been badly represented, such as women, gays, youth, Native Americans,

African-Americans, and Latinos. Critics of this approach ask, what are we "reforming" to? It tends to be some ideal of Jeffersonian democracy flavored by the analytical media model developed during the era of industrialization that looks at mass media from the proverbial "culture industry" critique of Marxists; in particular, it recycles the views shaped by the Frankfurt School. Perhaps the reform argument makes better sense in 1940, but certainly not in the twenty-first century. I want to qualify this by stating that I am not against media industry regulation, but I do not believe it should be the primary task of media education, either.

Books with titles like *The Age of Missing Information* (1992) and *Mediated* (2005) repeat a common view that we are victims of a deluge of harmful ideology delivered through mass media based on consumerism: "electronic media have become an environment of their own—that to the list of neighborhood and region and continent and planet we must now add television as a place where we live. And the problem is that it supplants" (McKibben, p. 53). And then there's Todd Gitlin's *Media Unlimited* (2002, p. 9): "Collectively, the main 'effect' of media saturation is that we live—we have no other choice—in societies whose people while away countless hours watching television, listening to recorded music, playing video games, connecting to the Internet, and so on unto the next wave of technologies." Similar critiques also include books such as *The New Media Monopoly* (2004, p. 9) by Ben Bagdikian that focus on media conglomeration as the cause for democracy's decline: "They do not manufacture nuts and bolts: they manufacture a social and political world"; and Robert McChesney (1999, p. 30), one of the most vociferous critics of Big Media, states, "My argument is institutional.... the problem with the corporate media system is not that the people who own and manage the dominant media firms are bad and immoral people... The owners and managers do what they do because it is the most rational conduct to pursue in the market context they face." What characterizes this deluge of media is the ubiquity of marketing: advertising "is in fact the most important aspect of mass media. It *is* the point" (Kilbourne 1999, p. 34).

I don't doubt the sincerity of any of these critiques, but I concur with Jenkins (p. 247) that the conclusions drawn by these "critical pessimists" hinder our approach to teaching functional media literacy:

> Critical pessimists, such as media critics Mark Crispin Miller, Noam Chomsky, and Robert McChesney, focus primarily on the obstacles to achieving a more democratic society. In the process, they often exaggerate the power of big media in order to frighten readers into taking action. I don't disagree with their concern about media concentration, but the ways they frame the debate is self-defeating insofar as it

disempowers consumers even as it seeks to mobilize them. Far too much media reform rhetoric rests on melodramatic discourse about victimization and vulnerability, seduction and manipulation, "propaganda machines" and "weapons of mass deception." Again and again, this version of the media reform movement has ignored the complexity of the public's relationship to popular culture and sided with those opposed to a more diverse and participatory culture. The politics of critical utopianism is founded on a notion of empowerment; the politics of critical pessimism on a politics of victimization. One focuses on what we are doing with media, and the other on what media is doing to us. As with previous revolutions, the media reform movement is gaining momentum at a time when people are starting to feel more empowered, not when they are at their weakest.

The critical pessimists often assume that media are "dumbing us down," but who are dumber, educators or students? If in most media literacy approaches students are asked only to "read" media, why aren't they asked to make media as a response to what they are studying? Part of this is because of a lack of teacher training or experience. After all, how many adults can shoot video, edit sound, manipulate a Photoshop file and post it to the Web, let alone learn this in teaching college? As the digital media guy at the Native American boarding school where I worked, I frequently got calls from teachers asking how to do simple things like transfer pictures from digital cameras onto their computers so they could put them into e-mails. I don't fault them, nor the school. It tried its best to offer professional development for its staff, but often because of the requirements of the federal law No Child Left Behind, these trainings were de-prioritized for test preparation. Other reasons in no particular order were: a lack of pedagogical imagination, generational hostility to new media uses, bias against media such as television, ignorance, or simply fear of change. Access, I acknowledge, is a fundamental requirement. Many schools, even if they want to utilize new media in their programs, may not have funds or proper access to the tools (hardware and software) and the Net. As such, at a minimum we should advocate that schools have proper equipment and teachers have technological training.

It's my sense that an attachment to literacy practices of the past is the cause of so much distrust of current media practices. That's understandable to a point, because there is a tendency to mine the past for authenticity in order to create a dialogue with the present. But the danger, observes media critic Mark Andrejevic (2004, p. 26), is that, "In short, what emerges in the promise in new media is a tension very similar to that noted by Walter Benjamin in his excavation of the prehistory of consumer capitalism in the nineteenth century: the way in which the promise of the future resonates with the unfulfilled desires of a mythical past—what he referred to as an 'ur-past'... The deployment of the unfulfilled potential of the ur-past may have politically progressive potential, insofar as it offers an alternative to the given state of affairs, but as Benjamin's own analysis suggests, it can also serve as an alibi for the self-proliferation and extension of the logic of the present." I believe the "old school" method evolved from the form of media and education that emerged during the period of modernity; after all, education and economic policy have always worked hand in hand, as the case with Native Americans so clearly illustrates. "Despite minor differences between and within the nations of the global North, it can be argued that the historical emergence of mass compulsory schooling and advertising occurred virtually simultaneously in the last decades of the nineteenth century" (Hoechsmann 2007, p. 654). Perhaps inadvertently, media educators have internalized education practices that reinforce the same system of thought that produces advertising, and the imagined past or glory days of the old media world are too closely emanated.

The presumption of the Read-Text model is that through awareness of media construction techniques, corporate messages can be defused. This is certainly what I believed when I taught it for many years. The method is to take a media sample and "read" it by asking a series of questions, such as who made it, who is the intended audience, what techniques are used, and what values does the media sample represent? The technique also asks students to explore the rhetorical hooks used in its construction, sometimes called "persuasion" techniques. I have discarded the term "persuasion" from my own practice because I find it too pejorative. Good media literacy teachers will emphasize that most communications actually involve some kind of persuasion, and rhetorical practices are necessary to advocate ideas, good and bad. When we demonize media to the average teen we can sound disingenuous because our approach implies that all communication by nature is false.

The root deconstruction technique of the Read-Text approach is reminiscent of the print literacy, in both form and outlook. Accordingly, "What emerged with print literacy... is 'a distinct mode of perception in which the book has become the decisive metaphor through which we conceive of the self and its place'" (Hoechsmann, p. 656). The deconstruction model mirrors common literacy practices in school (partly to meet standards) such as when students read a book and then write a paper about it using the classic "five-paragraph" format (intro, three supporting arguments and conclusion, each paragraph with its topic and concluding sentences). This technique, which is what I learned in high school—and I'm guessing that most who develop educational policy these days went through a similar process— is much like the dualistic scientific model of hypotheses and proof. Furthermore, I'm guessing that many policy wonks were raised on similar archaic technology such as myself (even President Bush admits he doesn't "do" e-mail). Admittedly, I did not use a computer until college. Back then (early 1980s) there were few personal computers, just mainframe terminals in the school library in which I slotted my five-inch floppy and typed DOS commands to access my files. Some education critics have charged that professors from teacher colleges should be forced back into the classroom every four years just so they can stay current with contemporary students.

With the Read-Text model the tendency is to make allegorical conclusions without using a systems approach, such as, "this alcohol ad is misleading, therefore the alcohol industry is immoral." This is probably true, but this approach violates a fundamental ecological principle: you look at the whole system, not just the nodes. In my view, new digital media are more akin to systems thinking discussed in the introduction. At first glance our image-based communication system doesn't easily translate into systems thinking (systems can't be captured by an image because they are distributed and networked). This is a primary criticism of media by critics like Mander (2002 [1978], p. 325) who argue that the nature of the medium will simplify any issue or problem because "Superficiality is easier than depth." But, if you leverage new media practices, they behave more like systems as the discussion of *Lost* indicated. Programs such as *Battlestar Galactica* have taken interactivity to an even deeper level by publishing recordings of its writer "breakouts" (brainstorming sessions) and producers' podcasts that can be downloaded and used as auxiliary narration with the episodes. Fans are also encouraged to upload their retellings of themes and storylines to the show's Web site. Jenkins (p. 259) argues:

> Many media literacy activists still act as if the role of mass media had remained unchanged by the introduction of new media technologies. Media are read primarily as threats rather than as resource. More focus is placed on the dangers of manipulation rather than the possibilities of participation, on restricting access— turning off the television, saying no to Nintendo—rather than in expanding skills at deploying media for one's own ends, rewriting the core stories our culture has given us. One of the ways we can shape the future of media culture is by resisting such disempowering approaches to media literacy education. We need to rethink the goals of media education so that young people can come to think of themselves as cultural producers and participants and not simply as consumers, critical or otherwise. To achieve this goal, we also need media education for adults. Parents, for example, receive plenty of advice on whether they should allow their kids to have a television set in their room or how many hours a week they should allow their kids to consume media. Yet, they receive almost no advice on how they can help their kids build a meaningful relationship with media.

If done with the correct pedagogy, deconstructing media has the potential to teach holistic conceptualization, but it also requires a "reconstruction" component through media making. This holistic approach illuminates how and why a commercial is produced, enabling students to think beyond visual images to connect the ad within a system of production and consumption and to see how that relationship impacts the environment. A more holistic approach scaffolds skills to develop systems thinking by examining mediaspheric niches through semiotics, the language of film, persuasion techniques, and industry practices as a whole, combined with the particular biases that media forms contain. When students work in teams (as is the case with video production), they learn that media are made collaboratively and the individualized knowledge accumulation that evolved from the print media is reconstituted. Finally, through locally relevant media production, a deepened understanding of cognition and local values becomes essential for understanding the impact of how media operate in our lives.

Many of the media activist movement assumptions are based on critiquing an industrial model of media in a communications system that is capital-intensive and thereby dependent on massive infrastructure that coincides with high finance: "The core distinguishing feature of communications, information, and cultural production since the mid-nineteenth century was the effective communication spanning the ever-larger societies and geographies that came to make up the relevant political and economic units of the day required ever larger investments of physical capital" (Benkler, p. 3). Advertising was necessary to cover the cost of such an infrastructure that would tend toward centralization. It's not surprising, then, that the leading industries that fit this model, energy companies, are also the ones that invested heavily in mass media, such as General Electric (parent company of NBC, and Westinghouse, former owner of CBS). In this scheme the subsystem of education would parallel the prevailing economic model of the time:

> If the Church had long played the role of mediating people's relation to everyday life, in providing the moral and intellectual instruction of everyday life, mass compulsory education was instituted to fill this void in the newly industrialized North. The success of advertising converges with the public school's inability to fill this void alone. Where schools held young people captive, training many into blind obedience and mindless vocationalism while only reproducing the cultural capital of those socialized into privilege, advertising captivated the imaginations of young people across class differences. Advertising was able to respond to the needs and desires of a much broader demographic, offering up feel-good aphorisms and promises of material fulfillment o a population affected by the bewildering pace of social and technological change (Hoechsmann, p. 657).

Additionally, the Read-Text model is influenced by propaganda studies. Many persuasion techniques are sampled from classic WWII-era propaganda, such as "The Big Lie" and "Leadership Principle" (see Appendix Worksheet C). The propaganda model is closely aligned with industrial-era advertising and mass media.

I suspect that culture industry critics idealize nineteenth-century print literacy and the public sphere (Adorno certainly was vehemently opposed to recorded music). As Habermas (1989) demonstrated, Western Europe's public sphere was a direct result of the print revolution. But so too was industrialization. According to Ong (1982, p. 119), "The first assembly line, a technique of manufacture which in a series of set steps produces identical complex objects made up of replaceable parts, was not one which produced stoves or shoes or weaponry but one which produced the printed book. In the late 1700s, the industrial revolution applied to other manufacturing the replaceable-part techniques which printers had worked with for three hundred years. Despite the assumptions of many semiotic structuralists, it was print, not writing, that reified the word, and, with it, noetic activity."

In French cafes the "public" read newspapers, discussed the news, and formed opinions in a shared, common space. This evolved into the standard model that looms in the "ur-past" imagination of media critics:

> Mass media structured the public sphere of the twentieth century in all advanced modern societies. They combined a particular technical architecture, a particular economic cost structure, a limited range of organizational forms, two or three primary institutional models, and a set of cultural practices typified by consumption of finished media goods. The structure of the mass media resulted in relatively controlled public sphere—although the degree of control was vastly different depending on whether the institutional model was liberal or authoritarian—with influence over the debate in the public sphere heavily tilted toward those who controlled the means of mass communications. The technical architecture was a one-way, hub-and-spoke structure, with unidirectional links to its ends, running from the center to the periphery. A very small number of production facilities produced large amounts of identical copies of statements or communications, which could then be efficiently sent in identical form to very large numbers of recipients. There was no return loop to send observations or opinions back from the edges to the core of the architecture in the same channel and with similar salience to the communications process, and no means within the mass media architecture for communication among the end points about the content of the exchanges. Communications among the individuals at the ends were shunted to other media-personal communications or telephones which allowed communications among the ends. However, these edge media were either local or one-to-one. Their social reach, and hence potential political efficacy, was many orders of magnitude smaller than that of the mass media (Benkler, pp. 178-9).

These days Starbucks may not count for much in terms of an informed public space, but there is still a prevailing attitude among educated elites (including the blogosphere punditry) that watching the Sunday morning talking heads and/or the evening news is necessary for the survival of democracy. In high school I would go to my U.S. history teacher's house to watch Walter Cronkite every evening because I felt like it was my civic duty as a citizen to be informed of world events. Fox News echoes this sentiment when it advertises, "We report, you decide." Some bloggers have taken this a step further by arguing, "We post, you decide." Such a view believes in an objective world with autonomous informational objects in which— as long as they are known in an unfiltered, non-ideological environment— democracy can properly thrive. Even the popular libertarian rally call of the Internet reflects this attitude with the statement, "Information wants to be free." On the surface these views reflect the conditions of our system to a point. For example, many argue that the Iraq war would never have been started if the public were properly informed by the "right" facts, or shown grizzly images of war. It's impossible to disprove this argument, but I'm a little dubious because media don't exist in isolation of other information sources or learned attitudes, especially attitudes developed within families, churches and insular communities. Moreover, everything from that period has to be viewed in the context of 9/11. I find it interesting that at the time of this writing, even with improved reporting and the known disinformation that led up to the war (and was spread by the media), the political will to stop or defund the war still does not exist.

I noticed in the aftermath of Bush's presidential victory in 2004 that information graphics showed voting patterns falling into two distinct categories: those who voted for Democrats and its vague anti-war platform lived primarily along rivers, lakes and coasts, whereas Republican votes were inland. My guess is that because water facilitates trade and the movement of people, these populations are more flexible, critical, and engaged with alternate views, which has more to do with civic life than media; inland populations, on the other hand, are more isolated and dependent on secondary reporting of world events. So in certain situations media have a greater impact, such as in gated communities where there are fewer mediacological niches to navigate, and will be more successful when the ground is fertile for fear-based messages that tend to proliferate in mainstream media. For ideas and attitudes to "stick" there needs to be receptivity to them. Ideas don't just randomly implant themselves, they need large drainage basins or soil in which to grow.

To summarize: the GridThink mediacological niche draws on the recurrent past where students are encouraged to relate to the world (or not at all) from a nineteenth century perspective shaped by print literacy and the culture industry critique that emerged from a Marxist analysis of mass media. This is a world where students are autonomous learners analyzing informational objects (such as books) in a grid space defined by dualistic thinking that emerged from science and academies in the Western tradition. But this kind of Cartesian thought betrays the ephemerality of the network information economy. What is emerging is a distributed, virtualized public sphere, which is much more of an eclectic ecosystem:

> The Internet allows individuals to abandon the idea of the public sphere as primarily constructed of finished statements uttered by a small set of actors socially understood to be "the media" (whether state owned or commercial) and separated from society, and to move toward a set of social practices that see individuals as participating in a debate. Statements in the public sphere can now be seen as invitations for a conversation, not as finished goods. Individuals can work their way through their lives, collecting observations and forming opinions that they understand to be practically capable of becoming moves in a broader public conversation, rather than merely the grist for private musings (Benkler, p.180).

Media literacy practitioners are diverse, so again I want to emphasize that my intention is to not pave over the difference, but I think it's useful to paint with some broad strokes the movement as I have seen it in action. I believe the field of media literacy breaks down into two broad mediacological niches. The in-the-trenches practitioners of media literacy come in many shapes and hues, from fundamentalist Christians to smash-the-state anarchists. First, there are the capitalist myth-busters who are social, political, and moral activists/educators using media literacy as a device for social change. They are profoundly influenced by the "media pessimists" Jenkins described, who study, critique and write about corporate media and advocate reform. They include public intellectuals such as Noam Chomsky, Ben Bagdigian, Jean Kilbourne, Robert McChesney, and Marc Crispin Miller and journalists such as Naomi Klein and Bill Moyers. Their work has greatly influenced the project of media literacy activists. They prominently focus on media "effects," the social ills perceived to be caused by consolidated corporate media, and the structure of media systems within the context of capitalist economic practices.

The second major group includes those who are concerned with the idea of the literacy of aesthetics, as in how do you understand media as a form of communication and artistic expression? This group is often composed of artists and media producers (documentary, animation, experimental, Web, game developers) who tend to focus on aesthetics and storytelling skills.

Unfortunately, activists and artists often do not get along and frequently advocate educational philosophies based on their respective biases. Not surprisingly, activists focus on the analysis of power and artists tend to advocate production and process. Occasionally the two cross paths, and in a few cases the production process is used to highlight sociopolitical issues, but in general there needs to be more interdisciplinary work.

My observation roughly corresponds with the overview from Douglas Kellner and Jeff Share (2007) in "Critical Media Literacy, Democracy, and the Reconstruction of Education" which defines four groups: "Protectionist Approach," "Media Arts Education," "Media Literacy Movement," and "Cultural Media Literacy." In my view the common denominator of all these groups is that they tend to be oppositional and rely heavily on the deconstruction model that assumes the existence of a hegemonic power structure with clearly defined autonomous subjects consuming coded autonomous information objects. Whether they intend to or not, with the exception of the media arts practitioners, most media literacy advocates have a protectionist intent, whether or not they pay lip service to the concepts of free expression, for the motive is often to reevaluate or contend the myth of capitalism.

I initially was taught the activist camp's methodology and it served me well for several years until I began to reevaluate it within the context of new media practices and working within the context of the epistemology of Native Americans. When I began teaching this method I thought it was a good thing that kids learned that corporations are manipulative, but I was challenged on this point often and found that I was not actually respecting teen uses of media and technology. If you disparage their world without offering alternatives, students can feel disempowered and angered. I don't think it is healthy for kids to learn only that media are trying to control them without showing examples of youth media practices that represent positive examples of engagement and expression. For this I like to expose them to avant-garde art and youth subcultures such as hip-hop and punk. Moreover, unless a production component is included (as it is with classical literacy when we read a book and write a paper), then we are only offering an incomplete approach.

The print literacy bias is ultimately a product of GridThink. As McLuhan and Powers (1989) put it, "The literate Westerner approaches the study of media in terms of linear motion or sequential transportation of images as detached figures (content), while the right-hemisphere approach is via the ground of environmental media effects instead" (p.75); and, "We are all trapped in an assumption about the nature of reality and a manner of thinking that has been the hallmark of Western civilization since before the time of Aristotle; the Shannon-Weaver model of communication is simply an extension of that bias. The model and its derivatives follow the linear pattern of efficient cause. The only sequential form of causality in Western philosophy" (p.77).

There's not much left of the linear world. Benkler (p. 30) observes that the mass media environment is changing drastically, as are the economic models, so we'd better pay attention to the changes that are happening:

> The Internet presents the possibility of a radical reversal of this long trend. It is the first modern communications medium that expands its reach by decentralizing the capital structure of production and distribution of in information, culture, and knowledge. Much of the physical capital that embeds most of the intelligence in the network is widely diffused and owned by end users. Network routers and servers are not qualitatively different from the computers that end users own, unlike broadcast stations or cable systems, which are radically different in economic and technical terms from the televisions that receive their signals. This basic change in the material conditions of information and cultural production and distribution have substantial effects on how we come to know the world we occupy and the alternative courses of action open to us as individuals and as social actors. Through these effects, the emerging networked environment structures how we perceive and pursue core values in modern liberal societies.

Because change is happening so quickly it is difficult to find simple concepts for the extreme complexity of digital multimedia practices, but I have found that the most concise understanding comes from Jenkins, an MIT researcher. I concur with Jenkins that the fundamental media environment of today's students is vastly different than the curriculum they are being taught. We are now experiencing a massive paradigm shift he calls "convergence culture": "the flow of content across multiple media platforms, the cooperation between multiple media industries and the migratory behavior of media audiences who will go almost anywhere in search of the kinds of entertainment experiences they want" (p. 2). This emerging mediascape, he argues, is characterized by collective intelligence, affective economics, transmedia storytelling, and participatory culture. Consequently, Jenkins believes in order to be fully engaged participants of convergence culture, students (and teachers) need:

> the ability to pool knowledge with others in a collaborative enterprise (as in *Survivor* spoiling), the ability to share and compare value systems by evaluating ethical dramas (as occurs in the gossip surrounding reality television), the ability to make connections across scattered pieces of information (as occurs when we consume *The Matrix*, 1999, or *Pokemon*, 1998), the ability to express your interpretations and feelings toward popular fictions through your own folk culture (as occurs in *Star Wars* fan cinema),

and the ability to circulate what you create via the Internet so that it can be shared with others (again as in fan cinema) (p. 176).

The underlying practices are "participatory culture" and "collective intelligence." As such, learners need to work in collaboration with other students and people across various media portals. As Jenkins points out, these activities are generally happening outside classrooms anyway. Schools, he argues, "are still locked into a model of autonomous learning that contrasts sharply with the kinds of learning that are needed as students are entering the new knowledge culture" (p. 183). A reconfigured environment turns normal educational hierarchies on their heads because "we should no longer imagine this as a process where adults teach and children learn. Rather, we should see it as increasingly a space where children teach one another and where, if they would open their eyes, adults could learn a great deal" (p. 205). Additionally, if we add a community context to the mix, we begin to realize that a "glocalized" approach will have a lot more relevance to the needs of learners.

CHAPTER NINE

Community as Text:
Beyond Classrooms

Language is a part of our identity. Deeply embedded in our Native languages are philosophical ideas that skip across centuries to the center of our Native universes. Governments tried to silence us, but still we make our voices heard. Today, we use every means available to pass our languages to the next generation. We can see films made in Seneca, Zaporo, Hopi, and Inupuit check out web sites in Quechua, Aymara, Lakota, and Cherokee; download songs in Cree Shuar, and Hawaiian. Art is a visual language and when contemporary Native artists use the vocabulary of tradition, they, too, are keeping a language alive. When they use that vocabulary in a new way, they show that we can innovate yet remain connected to our Native identity. Embracing change, while holding onto our philosophical center, is survivance.

Jolene Rickard and Gabrielle Tayac, Placard from "Our Lives" exhibition at the
National Museum of the Native American

Community serves as a foregrounding device for the student's divergent mediaspheric niches. This was particularly evident at the Native American boarding school where I worked. Students were closely tied to their reservation geography, their culture and language being aligned with the Northern Rio Grande Valley with the river as its common denominator lifeblood. The kinds of projects and vocabulary that best fit their abilities and understanding of the world were far different than the groups of Afro-Caribbean youth I worked with in Brooklyn. Their mediacological domains were vastly divergent, and it took a radical restructuring of my materials to work within each context. On the other hand, when I traveled around the United States giving workshops and talks on media and health using the conventional media literacy pitch, I was surprised to find that my standard rap that corporate media are manipulative was universally understood and agreed upon, yet no one's philosophy diverged one iota as a result of my talks. This hinted that media literacy has become more of an ideological weapon than a tool, and it reinforced for me the importance of incorporating the local into our pedagogy because when I worked closely with community members to integrate their "life world" into a broader understanding of the mediasphere, the outcomes were vastly different. But this was also the result of media literacy being done in the context of production. We deconstructed, but reconstructed with local materials.

Incorporating community into education is complex, as my experience working at the Native American boarding schools can attest. The school's environment included a curriculum based on government standards and the intrusion of new media and Internet, both serving as contending mediaspheric niches. From observing students in multiple environments—on the Rez and at school where they engaged computers and other media—my sense is that the students are about 25% cybernetic in that there are whole portions of their perception that appear wired into the Net. Media theorist Rushkoff (1999) calls youth the new human prototype, and at the Indian boarding school I felt I was seeing that manifest, for many of the attitudes and beliefs students adapted at school were not coming from the home environment, but rather they clearly were coming through engaging the national pop culture and new media. This is not exclusive to Indian students, but it was made more obvious because of the extreme contrast between the realms they were navigating. I don't deny my own hybridization, but being immersed in my own milieu, it's harder to see objectively. Watching the kids struggle with the various realms helped me appreciate why popular educator Paulo Freire's (1987) concept of reading the world is so crucial—and so contrary to the kind of education that is offered through the system. When he argues that "Reading the world always precedes the word, and reading the word implies continually reading the world" (p.35), I think he's essentially saying that students need to continually skateboard the resonant interval between mediaspheric niches. Consequently, "Now it is no longer possible to have the text without the context" (p.43). As teachers we, too, surfed the edges of these various contexts.

How do we define community? For Okanagan activist Jeannette Armstrong (1996), wisdom entails a heart-mind connection, and from her vantage, the impact of technology (including the technology of writing) has, up to this point, done more to severe this connection than enhance it: "I see the thrust of technology into our daily lives, and I see the ways we subvert emotional ties to people by the use of communications that serve to depersonalize. I see how television, radio, telephone, and how computer networks create ways to promote depersonalized communication" (p. 468). (Warhol would disagree: he said the telephone is one of the most intimate communication tools. I concur.) By contrast, "In a healthy whole community, the people interact with each other in shared emotional response" (p. 469). In order to devise effective approaches for education, we need to be conscious that, "Literacy and education in general are cultural expressions. You cannot conduct literacy work outside the world of culture because education in itself is a dimension of culture" (Freire, p. 53).

Speaking of his home environment as being his first "text," Freire (pp. 30-1) describes his own process of self-awareness through the reading of his childhood memories:

> Truly, that special world presented itself to me as the arena of my perceptual activity and therefore as the world of my first reading. The *texts*, the *words*, the *letters* of that context were incarnated as in a series of things, objects and signs. In perceiving these I experienced myself, and the more I experienced myself, the more my perceptual capacity increased. I learned to understand things, objects, and signs through using them in relationship to my older brothers and sisters and my parents.... Part of the context of my immediate world was also the language universe of my elders, expressing their beliefs, tastes, fears, and values which linked my world to a wider one whose existence I could not even suspect.

I'm moved by this passage because it reminds me of the unique and diverse circumstances my students came from, and how their world is so rich with text. For example, in the school's student population there were two generally dichotomous and culturally distinct groups: urban and reservation, and Diné and Pueblo. Among the Pueblos, there are also differing language groups and a general split between northern and southern tribes. The school itself was run by a conglomeration of nearly two dozen distinct Indian nations. At times, the school's administrative politics seemed more complex than the United Nations General Assembly's debating resolutions. What struck me was that, with the exception of the urban students who were generally acculturated/assimilated into mainstream society (yet they retained many characteristics of regional and Native American identity), students traversed various perceptual realms simultaneously that would be mind-boggling to the average GridThinker. At school students maneuver within a mediated territory fully engaged with technology, the Internet, and the mainstream education system, learning a curriculum necessarily accommodative and constrained by state standards. At home on the Rez, though Internet access is generally limited, students live normal teenage lives, consuming entertainment—including radio, movies and television—like other teens do; yet they are also participants in the ongoing, traditional ceremonial practices of their tribes. It was normal for students to disappear for short periods because of tribal obligations (which were generally kept secret from us teachers). On occasion we'd see them dancing during one of many "feast days" throughout the school year. Such occasions were school events, and staff organized van and bus trips to visit Pueblo celebrations. As teachers we were invited to visit the homes of administrators, staff, students, and friends, eating far too much at every stop.

We would find ourselves gorging on chile stew, Jell-O cake, Diné tacos, Jemez enchiladas, and many other dishes at large tables with the extended network of families and friends. Sometime a face-painted kachari (clown) kachina would enter and spill a dish or insult and harass someone who was misbehaving in the community. Ultimately, these gatherings reminded me of how much the generous and communal spirit of the tribes remains an important aspect of their contemporary cultural life; that's something lost in the greed culture that pervades so much of the GridThink world. Like Freire's own sense of "text," there is the essence of tradition that remains deeply seeded within the Indian students I worked with. Spending time in their homes was critical to my own education and pedagogy. This approach has been noted by other education commentators: "Teachers must become participants in the community; they must observe and ask questions in a way that communicates genuine care and concern. Teachers are learners too, and must let students (and their parents) know this" (Swisher and Deyhle 1992, pp. 86-7).

Freire's connection between "word and world" enables us to foreground the education and media system. Thus we can learn quite a bit from Native American education critics about how to develop a broader mediacological strategy for the general population. In an effort to toward "indigenizing education," Vine Deloria Jr. and Daniel R. Wildcat (2001) propose incorporating two formulas: TC3 (technology, community, communication, and culture) plus P3 (power-and-place-equal-personality). While P3 "makes for a spatial metaphysics of experience," TC3 "is an attempt to identify the natural cultural features of human beingness. P3 and TC3 are not rigorous mathematical expressions; rather, I think of both as symbolic expressions that can serve as mnemonic devices that preclude thinking of technology, or for that matter any of the key features of human culture, as outside of nature" (Deloria and Wildcat, p. 75).

The two keys to this formula are a sense of place and community. Deloria and Wildcat (pp. 31-2) remind us that, "American Indians have a long history of rejecting abstract theologies and metaphysical systems in place of experiential systems properly called indigenous—indigenous in the sense that people historically and culturally connected to places can and do draw on power located in those places. Stated simply, *indigenous* means 'to be of a place' ... To indigenize an action or object is the act of making something of a place." Other Native American education experts echo these concepts: "It is not enough to focus only on students' classroom experiences; expanding the focus is a central component of the change from an Anglo-conformity orientation ... the collective historical experiences of the community must be used as the context for all learning in the school. There are no easy formulas for implementing these changes; patience, ingenuity, and a spirit of committed experimentation are necessary" (Cummins 1992, p. 7).

These approaches complement my argument for a bioregional approach to media education. It's necessary to locate the media "reader" in their lifeworld, and also within the particular niche of their prevailing mediaspheres. This is particularly true of my own experience. As a kid growing up in Southern California, I was heavily influenced by many aspects of the particular environment that made up Los Angeles. From living in a Mexican-American neighborhood, to the skate culture influenced by surfing, to Disneyland and Magic Mountain, to the hard-core punk rock subculture that emerged in Hollywood, to the multicultural environment of my school, the influences were many. The documentary *Dogtown and Z-Boys*, about LA's skate culture in the 1970s, perfectly documented the ambient realm of this childhood space. After watching it I was struck by how so much of my youth was strongly tied to place, even though it was a vast megalopolis containing empty swimming pools drained because of drought instead of fishing holes and concrete passages instead of mountain passes. While it's true that of all world cultures, Americans are particularly migratory, when pressed I think most of us can draw heavily on a sense of some place that impacted us strongly during our lives, simulacra be dammed!

Another obvious reason community context is important can be related to the particular learning style of students, such as whether or not they are right-brain or left-brain oriented:

> In summary, the body of research, although small, on learning styles of American Indian students presents some converging evidence that suggests common patterns of methods in the way these students come to know or understand the world. They approach tasks visually, seem to prefer to learn by careful observation preceding performance, and seem to learn in their natural settings experientially. Research with other students groups has clearly illustrated that differences in learning style (whether they be described as relational/analytical, field dependent/independent, or global/linear) can result in "academic disorientation." While it is not clear where Indian students fit on this continuum, it is clear from the research... that American Indian students come to learn about the world in ways that differ from those of non-Indian students (Swisher and Deyhle 1992, 86-7).

Additionally, "Current theorists and researchers have recognized one difference in thought of oral versus literate people. People from oral traditions contextualize their articulation of thought; they depend on shared knowledge of the people who will be listening to them and do not necessarily articulate what others already know. People from literate traditions tend to decontextualize thought, to add the context that a distant audience will need to make sense of speech or writing" (Cleary and Peacock 1998, p. 188). I found that with the Afro-Caribbean students I worked with in Brooklyn, their artistic expression was highly advanced and rich, something that I think might get ignored or discounted under certain educational contexts, such as when low test scores are recorded.

Local control is not simple in a political environment that is hostile to pedagogical sovereignty. This is particularly starkly true in the situation of Native American schools. At the time of my tenure, my school was funded by the Bureau of Indian Affairs (BIA) but administered under regional tribal supervision. Recently the campus had been designated sovereign status, making it a nation within a nation and requiring its own judicial and security systems so that it could run autonomously from federal and municipal systems. Yet, that was a partial fiction. The school's administrators were constantly under threat by government officials who annually bang a drum to eliminate Native American sovereignty nationally, and ultimately the school is subject to federal and state standards, like all other schools that receive federal funding such as No Child Left Behind (NCLB). So, though the school made special efforts to address the needs of its student community (drawing from more than 25 regional and national tribes), it also was constantly under a federal microscope that some would interpret as harassment. If it's true, as critics contend, that NCLB is an effort to push schools into privatization, this is yet another impending threat to local control of Native American schools (Reyhner and Eder 2004, p. 322).

Since the implementation of NCLB, more often than not I have observed administrators in a general state of crisis that forces them to constantly look over their shoulders. Administrators were simultaneously responding to the needs of the school's greater community, which is diverse and hardly harmonious in its views. In some cases students witnessed what they believed were petty ad hoc policies, such as dress codes banning gothic-style clothing that were instituted to appease the concerns of minority tribes who feared that some youth subcultures threatened the stability of their traditional cultural practices. Among the various tribes you could see that their engagement with mainstream culture was directly related to the tribe's history with colonialism. Those that were heavily Christianized tended to distrust punk, goth and other subcultural youth styles, whereas those that were not seemed more tolerant of student explorations of fashion. Though this might seem trivial in relationship to greater issues of digital literacy, we have to remember that in rural areas where 44% of tribal members live, exposure to subcultures is largely mediated through the Net and other forms of pop culture. Depending on the tribal perspective (and that of individual families as well), the Internet represents either a threat to or opportunity for an already fractured social structure. This is why one-size-fits-all education policies are so counterproductive.

To high-speed techno Westerners such as myself, working through a localized process is terribly time-consuming (I often had to wait weeks to talk to tribal officials just to make appointments to get permission to do projects). Protocol is very important, and little is ever done without the approval or consultation of tribal leadership, an error I made in planning on many occasions. As teachers we negotiated between the concerns of youth and elders, finding that it was not unusual to hear members of one group say they didn't understand the other. No doubt, contrasting experiences, one coming from a reality unmediated by the torrent of mass media, the other from a digitally mediated realm, are bound to crackle against each other. This needn't be the case, though, for there are approaches being made in Native American communities addressing this gap, many of which are promising:

> For example, collaborative research on such topics as local history, geography, flora, fauna, institutions, and people enable students and teachers to interact with community members about issues of mutual interest and relevance. By interviewing community members, discussing their findings with others, relating those findings to correlative materials in books, and then writing about their experiences and publishing the results, students have opportunities to develop their oral and written language abilities in both the native language and English, and to deepen their understanding of themselves and the local natural and social world while learning "new" academic content. Such study also provides a multitude of opportunities to bring parents and elders directly into the classroom as teachers. All this enriches the shared experience of teachers, students, and community members, increases the pool of knowledge to be tapped for future learning, and builds the general climate of support for education (McCarty and Schaffer 1992, pp.123-4).

Another example is the boarding school's community-based model approach in which its interdisciplinary program educates students in an assortment of subjects, including tribal law and technology. The program includes the use of hi-tech gear such as the Global Positioning System (GPS) and Global Information Systems (GIS) mapping, and offers those services to the tribes that are served by the school. The goal is to connect the skills they are learning in school with their communities, for in the past the tendency was that students who learned specialized technology were hired away by companies that did not service their home communities. The program collaborates with communities to best harmonize the learning environment of students in a way that is relevant and beneficial to all parties involved. For example, one of the biggest challenges of Southwestern tribes along the Rio Grande is the remediation of the river forest ecology. As a result, students were asked by several tribes to use GIS to map various stretches of their reservation forests. Back at school students learned how to incorporate the data into maps. On several projects my specific contribution was to assist students in producing digital media documentation of these programs. Here we see a positive convergence of the school working in conjunction with tribal communities to provide technical expertise and training with digital technology, thereby servicing the ecological needs of the tribe and also promoting self-sufficiency by training tribal members to utilize cutting-edge technology. Pedagogically, the application of mapmaking brings students much closer to a perceptual understanding of the spatial thinking required of reading and making maps.

Unfortunately, the trend toward standardized testing promoted by No Child Left Behind is very "review mirror"—it tests rote knowledge, lacks a rubric for other types of learners (such as myself), and threatens these innovative community programs. Native Americans, and minorities in general, tend to score below national averages on these tests, so being subjected to these standards puts them at yet another disadvantage and is a setup for failure. In a detailed study of NCLB, the National Indian Education Association (2005) concluded that:

- The statute is rigid and it tends to leave children behind.
- We need opportunity; we need resources to do that.
- (Any) Success has clearly been at the expense and diminishment of Native language and culture.
- The approach dictated by the law has created serious negative consequences.
- Schools are sending the message that, if our children would just work harder, they would succeed without recognizing their own system failures.
- Indian children are internalizing the (school) systems failures as their personal failure.
- Children have different needs.
- It does not provide for the level funding that we need.
- Music, art, social studies, languages—these areas are totally ignored by the law. (pp. 7-8)

I saw on the ground how one successful Native American program that started out as a way of coping with the new digital media environment was negatively impacted by NCLB. At the Native American boarding school where I worked, Intel financed an eighth-grade computer-building program, based on the company's "Journey Inside" curriculum. Over the course of the school year students assembled and installed PCs, and if they kept up their grades at a certain level, they could take the computers home. For two years I worked with students, going into households and interviewing families who received these computers for a digital video documentary, also financed by Intel. Overall we found that families were grateful for the computers and that multiple people used these systems in their households for a variety of needs. In one case a student's stepfather, a jeweler, used the system to book travel for trade shows. Another family used it for research on water issues. In all cases the computers were intrinsic to the academic achievement of family members (the PCs were shared by multiple users, inside and outside the home). The additional benefit was that students learned technical skills that would contribute to their academic achievement and economic success. Unfortunately, the program was discontinued after NCLB was instituted because science scores were below average for that grade level. The program was ended in order to teach to the standardized test, a cautionary example of an utterly disastrous application of federal education standards.

Digital divide programs are not always the solution for community problems. For example, what is more important to a community: access to the Net or the death of an elder whose knowledge, as the saying goes, is the equivalent of a library? Local knowledge is important. Though a computer can show you the weather, it can't show you how to tell the weather. One is not exclusive of the other, but we have to understand that our cultural priorities need to be viewed within a historical and cultural context. Is the intention of education in the information age, as tends to be the case with the status quo, to homogenize culture and reproduce hegemonic power structures? Is the motivation to provide tools so learners can critically engage the larger discourse of the dominant society? Or is it to empower participants to transcend their current conditions and transform themselves? As Native American filmmaker and educator Jacques La Grange (2006) points out, the presence of new computer technology is

> like a double edge [sic] sword... a sort of damn if we do, damn if we don't. Lets [sic] be honest our children need to know how to use technology. Especially if this is the only way to a better life. But do we give them the keys to the car without first showing them how to drive?... It is difficult enough for Native Americans to have a voice, but even harder for Native American Children to have a voice at all. If we do not nurture their ideas and give them a chance to succeed than it is we who have failed them.

Usually the discussion about technology for underserved communities begins with access, but rarely is it contextualized by wisdom. There are numerous programs by major computer companies that offer technology to reservation schools and after-school programs, but they lack a pedagogy that incorporates art, ecology or community. Part of the problem is that much of digital technology programming draws on conventional thinking about education; moreover, if computers are going to government schools or institutions, their use will be subject to standards and school policies. In the context of Native American communities, it's useful to critique why this is problematic.

In terms of the concept that computers empower individuals, schools have very strict filters on their computer networks, so students are often locked out of many sites, including chat and social networks such as MySpace. Whereas more affluent students in the mainstream have computers at home that give them more unrestricted access, Native American students are constrained by the policies of those who host the computer systems. This is why some of the digital divide remedies—donating computers to schools or after-school programs such as Intel's digital clubhouse at the Boys and Girls Club—don't necessarily empower students individually because institutional filters inhibit them. It takes decisions about access away from the families. Moreover, it is a bit reminiscent of the early days of books when Bibles were chained down in monastery libraries so that they could not be read away from the watchful eyes of proctors. That was done to ensure that the proper interpretation of the text was fully enforced. This goes back to my very strong belief that technology must be accompanied by critical literacy. Students should be allowed to explore the technological world, but also must be trained on how to mindfully engage what they are interacting with within a community context.

Additionally, it's not enough to have a methodology when you are contending with a system that is contrary to your methods. With an increasing emphasis on test standardization, which focuses on the core principles of pre-digital education (the so-called "Three R's"—reading, writing and 'rithmetic), the chances for teaching necessary skills for digital literacy are reduced in U.S. schools and especially in schools that are historically underfunded. As historians of Native American education policy have noted, "The common practice in the United States, Canada, and elsewhere to use teachers and schools to destroy minority cultures and to indoctrinate children in mainstream cultures that continue to maintain ethnocentric and racist attitudes, despite their 'melting pot' philosophies, is a travesty of what education should be" (Reyhner and Eder 2004, p. 326).

Consequently, there have been backdoor efforts by media educators to introduce novel approaches for digital media literacy through a variety of nontraditional education channels. In New Mexico, media literacy units have been inserted into social studies, language arts, and health education curriculum standards, but nationally these requirements are few and far between. Students are more likely to encounter media literacy in after-school or summer programs serviced by nonprofits that are funded by special grants. For example, state tobacco settlement funds have been a boon for media education specialists. In New Mexico, many literacy programs were offered through state settlement grants, administered by the public school system health advocacy organizations or through county and state agencies that value media literacy as an effective public health education tool for prescient issues such as driving under the influence (DUI) prevention.

Native American health advocacy programs have also taken a special interest in media literacy. I have attended numerous commercial tobacco prevention conferences and "wellness" camps led by tribal health agencies to train adults and youth in media literacy strategies in order to produce public service announcements (PSA) for their communities. The workshops are convened with the goal of promoting grassroots, community based media. In my opinion, campaigns that have focused on producing media for insertion into mainstream media have not had nearly as much impact as those programs in which youth- designed and produced PSAs are shown publicly at events that include food and celebration. As youth media producers become peer educators, they inspire the wider community to produce culturally specific and community targeted messages. Unless you are as well funded as the anti-smoking Truth campaign, I liken PSAs in mainstream media to throwing a glass of water into a waterfall. Community events have tremendous power because they incorporate traditional and modern storytelling in a way that brings people together, rather than isolate them. Likewise, when students at the Indian boarding school make PowerPoint presentations to their communities summarizing their fieldwork and findings, these are very important events that dignify and empower the students and their audience. Finally, at the boarding school we started having "film festivals" to motivate students to create work for the school community.

A note of caution, though: media literacy should celebrate the environment that youth occupy, while at the same time offer tools for them to critically engage their digital world. This is the best way to inspire youth to challenge the credibility of media-generated information, because it encourages their natural rebellion and desire to "question authority" (to borrow an old punk and hippie term) as they individuate. But also keep in mind that some tribes do not consider rebelliousness as appropriate behavior, for in some communities individuality is traditionally contrary to community harmony. Ultimately, in my experience, demonizing media backfires because it challenges the veracity of a world that kids find very real. If you focus on the intent of media producers (such as commercial tobacco or alcohol), you get a much better response.

In terms of introducing culturally relevant materials, I have had very mixed results. The first year I worked at the boarding school, I showed students Hopi artist and filmmaker Victor Masayesva, Jr.'s *Imagining Indians*, believing that not only should they see Native-made films, such as *Smoke Signals*, but media that have an "indigenous aesthetic." In retrospect, that assumption produced bad results. In the case of *Smoke Signals*, the students did not identify with the humor or themes related to the Northern tribes that were represented in the movie. When I screened *Imagining Indians*, I figured it would be a slam dunk. Not only was it a documentary on the stereotyping of Native Americans in film, but it was "experimental"; I believed its nonlinear aesthetic was more in keeping with the oral style of communication the Hopi filmmaker was going for. But because the video was outside the narrative structure that the students were used to (as in it did not follow a linear, Hollywood-style plot or editing conventions), the kids failed to grasp it. Indigenous-themed movies like *Whale Rider* and *Rabbit-Proof Fence* were met with greater success because the youth-oriented narratives of each storyline were more within their understanding of standard film language, which ironically was likely acquired by watching Disney films. This doesn't mean students shouldn't be challenged by difficult work, but it needs to be done cautiously through scaffolding.

I had worse luck turning the students on to John Trudell, the spoken word artist who emerged from American Indian Movement activism in the 1970s and whose voice is strong and prescient concerning the plight of Native Americans in the context of mainstream society. The students just didn't like his style or music. I had much better luck with politically conscious hip-hop like KRS-One and Public Enemy, even these artists came across as "tired." It's hard to compete with the deluge of corporate media that dictates taste through its all-encompassing barrage. On rare occasions a student took an interest in experimental art and punk, something I know a lot about, and I happily transmitted my own oral history when asked.

During my first year I was teaching a particularly pesky and cranky group of gifted freshman girls who were fond of harassing an unseasoned gringo teacher such as myself (that is, someone from European descent), but I got from them that my assumptions regarding what they would and wouldn't like based on the ethnicity of the media producers were wrong. Still, I think the spirit of the effort is fair: kids need role models from their communities, but they also gravitate to those who fit into the mold of the youth subcultures they identify with. In a sense they were attracted to particular "brand tribes" as well, and didn't take kindly to some of the culture jams that debunked their favorite fashion lines. Some role models straddle both worlds, such as Indian actor and hip-hop artist Litefoot. When he came to speak at a wellness camp at which I was teaching in Oklahoma, he lit up a room of 100 native teens like no one else I've seen. In this respect, any incorporation of hip-hop cultural production into the education process generally gets student attention. As marginalized youth of color, most Native American kids I've worked with have more in common with hip-hop than anything else, but they also are into heavy metal, country, punk, goth, and reggae. After all, they are kids, and they are American. It's best not to lose sight of this point. Incidentally, whenever we went on field trips, the battle for our driving soundtrack was consistently fierce. The only time all factions could be quieted was when Bob Marley was inserted into the mix. In the end, reggae is an indigenous form of oppositional but celebratory music that wins the hearts and minds of the majority, including that of the teachers! (Peripheral side note: Marley is the only artist I have heard in every country in which I have traveled. It makes me wonder if his musical transmission is more powerful than books, such as the Bible. Just a thought.)

In terms of a community-based model of digital media production and literacy, I'm interested in "internal" forms of production because, though it is important for mainstream society to be familiar with Native American issues (and also to simply have Native Americans as a visible presence that affirms their lively existence in contemporary society), the torrent of commercial media also threatens language, cultural integrity, and mental sovereignty and performs an overall spiritually colonizing effect. The potentially troubling aspect of technological aesthetics and culture is its homogenizing influence, which is duly noted by a group of Native American scholars who examined the subject closely: "Certainly some computer companies and Web sites are pushing the notion of 'one world, one culture' (cyberculture, we suppose!). The idea, however, lacks an understanding that synthetic communication has a push-pull effect that works to push groups apart at the same time as it works to pull them together. We suspect that, with American Indians, it will remain largely the same as it has been, though other more powerful circumstances, especially economic ones, may prevail, and tend to diminish ethnic boundaries" (Zimmerman, Zimmerman and Bruguier 2000, p. 86).

In my view, internal media should have two components: mindful engagement (literacy/deconstruction) and self-empowerment (production/reconstruction). For example, many of the communities that I have worked with are using digital media as an education tool for health issues. In terms of connecting health with digital media, as I noted earlier, the front line of this approach comes from the national media literacy movement of nonprofits, one of the few areas in which tools of critical engagement of media—digital and analog—are actually advocated. When working within Native American communities, I also feel that the content should reflect directly upon their lived experiences and reality. This is a hard task, given that there are so few media samples to work with that reflect contemporary Native American culture. But for every commercial we analyze, we can always lead the discussion to current conditions at home; and in our response, which usually involves producing a PSA, the product becomes a dialogue based on relevant experience. Other kinds of internal media include efforts by some tribes to use digital video to preserve their languages. In Northern New Mexico one group is attempting to have kids interview their elders in their native language on video and then catalog the footage on DVD in the tribal library. In Oklahoma, a high school program is re-creating traditional stories spoken in the indigenous language by using stop-motion Claymation that is then edited on computers.

Because of current funding and standards implementation, there have been backdoor efforts by media educators to introduce novel approaches for digital media literacy through a variety of nontraditional education channels. Though in New Mexico media literacy units have been inserted into social studies, language arts, and health education curriculum standards, these requirements nationally are few and far between. In New Mexico many literacy programs were offered through state settlement grants, administered by the public school system health advocacy organizations or through county and state agencies that value media literacy as an effective public health education tool for prescient issues such as DUI prevention. But here, too, is a cautionary tale of why cultural sensitivity and community context is so important. A lot of anti-tobacco media literacy activists make the mistake of demonizing tobacco and fail to distinguish between the sacred relationship that Native Americans have with the plant and its abuse by commercial enterprises. One well-meaning program was banned from a Native American-run school for this very reason. Without making the distinction between religious and commercial uses, a nonprofit media literacy organization conducted a survey that asked students if they had used tobacco in the previous month. The unusually high percentage who said "yes" were confused because many of the students carry tobacco with them as part of their religious practice. There was also a sense among local administrators that they were being used so that the media literacy organization could generate funding from tobacco settlement grants. In another misstep by a different program, a PSA about DUI depicted Native American students drinking in their cars. Even though the script was written by Native American students, I as the instructor have realized that it's bad to depict the behavior you are supposed to modify; there also is dubious benefit for representing images that are already strongly embedded in the national consciousness, in particular those of Indian alcoholics.

One of the most interesting areas where technological and media literacy have practical applications is through tribal efforts to reclaim tobacco for sacred uses and for promoting smoke-free environments. Media literacy is considered a no-nonsense tool for youth health education, because telling teens to stop doing something because it's bad for them usually produces the opposite result. But if you demonstrate how massive multinational corporations use media to influence their belief systems, then youth relate to health information differently. Here media literacy is not simply an abstract pedagogical tool, but it serves the practical needs of the tribe. After all, if we are dealing with education from a systems view, the prevalence of malnutrition, drug addiction, diabetes, alcohol, abuse, and domestic violence typical of impoverished communities does not induce a positive education environment. As such, media education combined with social justice, especially as it relates to commercial tobacco abuse, is a form of mental decolonization. This directly correlates with history because one of the skills that Indians taught European colonizers was the "culture" of tobacco. That is, by showing them how to grow and cultivate the ceremonial plant, colonists were able to generate great wealth, so much so that tobacco leaves are featured as part of the design of the one-dollar bill. By deconstructing tobacco ads and nefarious marketing practices on the Web and in film, and through the steady effort to both prevent addiction and support abatement, tribes are slowly reclaiming the power of one their most sacred plants and reaffirming its role in their culture and society.

Though it's true that one of the more demeaning stereotypes of Native Americans is that of the "noble savage" and "natural ecologist," of the tribes that I have worked with the most pressing issues for their communities, aside from sovereignty, are ecological or health-related, both of which are intimately linked with poverty and all its attendant social ills. Such a state can be described as a "broken medicine wheel." One way of uniting the circle and the cross and thereby giving new digital media "meaning" is to assure that there is a holistic discussion of technology that incorporates an ecological perspective. Digital technology intrinsically is a feedback system; to not broaden the concept of feedback to the greater system of production and consumption is to look only at the GridThink "angles" of the digital media environment.

One Pueblo elder told me that he believed our culture was doomed when we went to the moon, because it demonstrated an incessant need to probe and touch everything in the universe while disregarding sacred, living domains. This is also why you cannot photograph tribal ceremonies or certain sacred land sites. Trying to capture these places or events for media trivializes them and removes the ultimate power of experiencing them. This view rebukes our ownership society; we take for granted the extent by which we consume and produce media to lay claim to reality and to possess it. For example, think of how when people aim cameras they colonize the space in front of them, prompting us to avoid getting in the way. On many occasions, while working on tribal media projects, we were told never to point our cameras in specific directions or at particular places. For many tribes, people still believe in and respect the limits of digital media's inevitability (such as giving it "rumor" status).

One of the least discussed issues in media is how energy policy and technological research impact Indian reservations. I would be remiss to not reflect on the fact that what we are talking about is encouraging the use of electronic devices that are powered by the consumption of extractive resources, such as coal, fossil fuels, and water. Social justice activists who organize against environmental racism have been pushing for the "precautionary principle" which advocates restricting the implementation of developmental strategies until their full environmental impact can be truly assessed; the burden of proof is on the advocate and not the recipient of any program that has environmental and cultural impact. What I'm suggesting is that as advocates of digital technology we should treat it just as if it were a kind of environmental and ecologically impacting system, such as biotechnology. After all, bioengineered corn could be analogous to corporate media bioengineering beliefs. As one of the most vociferous critics of technology and globalization, Mander (1996, pp. 356-7), observes, "the advance of computers is contributing to a loss of ecological sensitivity and understanding, since the very process of using computers, *particularly educating through computers, effectively excludes an entire set of ideas and experiences that heretofore had been building blocks for developing connection with the earth* ... computers alter the pathways of children's cognition" [emphasis mine].

However, under local control and proper pedagogy, this may be a limited perspective. Take for example the following scenario. Los Alamos National Laboratory (LANL), and other weapons programs across the United States, impacts tribes through the production of toxic waste and its migration onto tribal lands. LANL, in particular, where the first atomic weapons were developed and built, is constructed on the ancestral grounds of a tribe that currently lives in the lab's watershed. The lab itself is surrounded by four tribes, and all of them are affected by the lab's emissions. But because of this, these tribes also receive federal assistance, which ironically is how technological needs are met on some reservations, a bargain not taken lightly.

This relationship produced an interesting program that served both the technological and ecological needs of one tribe I worked for. A reservation bordering the lab was given a FEMA grant because a major fire damaged its lands in 2000; the fire also destroyed a huge part of Los Alamos, New Mexico. The tribe's governor committed a portion of the grant to create a summer youth employment program that was run by tribal employees and teachers from the boarding school where I worked. The nature of our project was twofold. First, generate a baseline study of biological species along the Rio Grande's cottonwood forest that spans tribal lands; next, perform a similar study in a canyon where discharge from the town of White Rock and LANL facilities was being released into the Rio Grande's watershed. The bosque (Spanish colloquial term for woods) study was necessary because of an overgrowth of "introduced" or "invasive" species, such as tamarisks (salt cedar) and Russian olive trees that were salinizing the river's forest ecosystem and crowding out the cottonwoods. The tamarisks were originally planted by the U.S. Army Corps of Engineers to reduce flooding, and had been part of a 50-year project to re-engineer the river's entire system through dams, dredging, and the introduction of exotic plant species. Tribes up and down the river are in the process of remediating the river's ecology through removal of these exotic species and inducing floods to stimulate the growth of new cottonwood trees, without which the vital old-growth tree stands will die out. Our job was to document what was along the river before removal of the exotics commenced, which is a very complex and disruptive process for the river's ecology. It was important to have a baseline study for before and after the procedure to see if the remediation is effective, and also to measure the program's ultimate impact on the river ecosystem and to document in time the natural biodiversity of the local system.

The students, all paid tribal members from the ages of fourteen to nineteen, cordoned off sections of the forest and used GPS, GIS and digital cameras combined with field notes and computers to log and document biological species (animals, plants, and insects). On alternating days we also traveled to a canyon below the labs to test soil for contaminants and to count species. My job was to lead a small crew of students as they recorded video documentation of the program and to later edit a piece for presentation in Washington, D.C.

One of the most telling moments occurred that summer when we were winding up the narrow road that leads up to the sage-covered mesa where Los Alamos and its weapons laboratory reside. We stopped at an overlook from which, across a canyon, you can observe ancient cavates in the cliffs that sheltered the tribe's ancestors. In the shallow valley below, among bark beetle-ravaged pine trees, you can see the outlines of a long-abandoned pueblo that was also once the ancestral home of the tribe we were working with. Lining the mesa ridge above are rows of desert-lawn McMansions that house weapons lab administrators. In one shot we framed a digital photo juxtaposing the ancient and modern lodging for input into a PowerPoint presentation we were to give in D.C. for our state senator and other Washington officials whose departments contributed to our program's funding. A month later, as we prepared the slide show in our D.C. hotel, my colleague Mark Ericson asked the tribal governor what to title the image of the caves and mansions. Without missing a beat, he told us in a deep, grave tone, "Temporary Housing."

The governor's remark demonstrates awareness of the self-destructive logic, and ultimately cyclical nature, of empire and technology. My colleague and I were also conscious of the other subtext of our project: we both recognized that our study of invasive species had greater implications than the biological realm we were cataloging. As educators of European descent, we, too, were an invasive species. Yet we were also bridges; we possessed the technological know-how of GIS, GPS, computers, and media. The tribe's governor reminded the youth at the beginning of the summer program that there was a world beyond the cattle guard at the reservation's edge, and that they would be wise to learn as much as possible about that world to better survive it. It was our job to be guides in that world.

CHAPTER TEN

Traduttore, Traditore—Translator, Traitor

> For to some degree all great texts contain their potential translation between the lines; this is true to the highest degree of sacred writings.
>
> Walter Benjamin, "The Task of the Translator"

Surfing mediaspheric niches can be hindered by the problem of translation. Among professional translators, there's an Italian maxim: *traduttore, traditore* — translator, traitor. It's an acknowledgment that one can never be completely faithful to the original text when transcribing it into another language. Translation is ever precarious and dangerous, yet without it, how could we appreciate the literary arts of other cultures? Rumi, Vallejo and Neruda are all great writers who would be relegated to a homogenous audience had they not been translated. "The translator is always a rewriter," Claire Joysmith once told me in an interview for an article I was writing. A professor at Mexico City's National Autonomous University who researches literary and cultural issues concerning women, ethnicity, borderlands, and U.S.-Mexico relations, she commented, "A translator can never capture the original, therefore one has to find all kinds of strategies to invite the reader to have to deal with a text that belongs to a different culture and language, and therefore is always 'other,' and always different." Thus, interpretation and translation need to be done with respect and healthy skepticism. And because I draw so heavily on Native American epistemology, it is necessary to recognize the problems that this inadvertently incurs, especially considering that I am a non-Native American.

As Laguna Pueblo poet and literary critic Gunn Allen (2003) observes, whites "split-off fragments of the Anglo-European psyche [that] take on an energetic force of their own, appearing to non-Indians as actual people, ideas, systems, attitudes, and values the Western collective mind dubs 'Indian.'" She calls this fragmented projection "white-think," qualifying it as a "mind-set or system of mental processes rather than a racial or genetic term" that's "almost entirely unconscious; nameless, formless, unacknowledged, it exists as a powerful barrier to authentic communication across cultures. While it works for the survival and expansion of white culture, it also results in the spiritual and psychic murder of those who exist outside its projection" (p. 307). While recognizing that Native American and African-American experiences are different, such "psychic murder" is akin to bell hooks' (2001) notion of "eating the other": "Currently the commodification of difference promotes paradigms of consumption wherein whatever difference the Other inhabits is eradicated, via exchange, by a consumer cannibalism that not only displaces the Other but denies the significance of the Other's history through a process of decontextualization" (p. 431). Ultimately, I agree with Gunn Allen's conclusion that, "For the most part, Native American peoples would rather be viewed from their own perspective, a matter of respect certainly, but not easily done when that worldview is so entirely alien to one's own as the Native worldview is to white-think culture" (p. 313). To take the pejorative sting out of Gunn Allen's terminology, I would like to suggest that White-Think is another description of GridThink, since I believe what she talks about is the mechanistic and dualistic mentality of the cross.

Like many societies, Indian Country is very diverse with different languages, views, and cultures and is composed of distinct and separate nations. There is a range of experiences from reservation to urban, from "traditional" to "progressive," from old-timer to young, from open to closed, from East to West, North to South, rich to poor. As such, the mediacological niches are quite varied. The danger remains that we will flatten culture through generalizations. Though McLuhan, who coined the term "global village," was heartened by the retribalizing aspects of new media, I think a global village and tribal village are vastly different concepts, just as a community is not necessarily a demographic, either. Advocates of the "globalized" village, such as free market proponent Thomas Friedman, generally celebrate the homogenizing, or gentrifying if you will, effect of liberalized trade globalization (as opposed to the other global movement thats' composed of peace, justice, and environmental activists). Yes, technology has its equalizing components, but at what cost? So though I think McLuhan was idealizing a bit the potential for global mass media, perhaps the term "global village" should be thought of as this phrase: "it takes a global village." Rather than having a menu of exotic cultures at our disposal to be consumed spectacle style, the words "it takes ..." acknowledge that communities are implicitly knowledge communities and that through collective and shared intelligence problems can be resolved. The complex ceremonial cycles and clan structure of the Hopi are good examples. Every clan has to work together to fulfill its different tasks during the year. This kind of interdependent social structure is not accidental. In a harsh desert environment where resources are precious, each clan needs to be involved in the group program for survival. That involvement enforces diverse participation and integration.

We should avoid the mistake that popular White-Think scholars like Joseph Campbell make in interpreting and pancaking indigenous stories into archetypal monotypes, because ultimately, unless we know the source language and are raised in a particular culture, how can we really know how the "other" really thinks? Not to disparage Campbell, someone I think has done much to enrich our world, but how free was he from his own operating system? The distinguishing characteristic of being displaced and "conquered" (in quotes because this is a transient state) is the spiritual catastrophe that resulted not only from the physical destruction of entire civilizations, but also the mental one that remains continuous. As members of the dominant society, we really have no clue as to what surviving the Conquest really feels like. Part of the reason is because from the onset of relations with European immigrants (a more polite way of saying "invaders"), in the telling of history and their stories, Native Americans have not been self-defined within mainstream education. Rather they have been constructed as a negative in relation to the protagonists of written and mediated history, and in the creation of a national identity in the United States and throughout the Americas. And as an outsider from Indian culture, whether I like it or not, I report from what Edward Said (1997) calls, "community of interpretation." Said warns that much of what we understand about other cultures, such as Arabs (who have been subjected to the same Wild West myths as Native Americans), is through our second-hand worlds that filter and source information from outside our daily experience: "Between consciousness and existence stand meaning and designs and communication which other men have passed on—first, in human speech itself, and later, by the management of symbols. Symbols focus experience; meaning organizes knowledge, guiding the surface perceptions of an instant no less than aspirations of a lifetime" (pp. 46-7). Thus we rely on the cultural apparatus to report and communicate from a distance: "Every man is increasingly dependent upon the observation posts, the interpretation centers, the presentation depots, which in contemporary society are established by means of what I am going to call the cultural apparatus ... Together, this powerful concentration of mass media can be said to constitute a communal core of interpretations providing a certain picture of Islam and, of course, reflecting powerful interests in the society served by the media" (p. 47).

Such a powerful process of interpretation has been particularly harmful to Native Americans, especially in the mythology of the West and all its attendant cultural products such as Wild West shows, dime novels, films, advertising, and TV: "In the building of a new American national mythology, we see this self-identification by a dominant (Euro-American) group emerge as primary in importance, largely because American identity, like all national identities, is determined by its relationships to other cultures. For an immigrant nation where the Euro-American is anything but homogenous the Native becomes a clearly defined Other" (Kilpatrick, xvi). Even more insidious is the dearth of contemporary indigenous peoples in the media (with the exception as props for car commercials). One of the most frustrating things I experience among Native American teens is that they don't see images of themselves in media; their absence is yet another kind of cultural annihilation. So to make up for it, they often project themselves into other youth-of-color subcultures, such as hip-hop. Still, one Native American educator told me that she prefers seeing stereotypical Indians in film rather than not seeing any. I don't know how common this view is, but conditions are changing. As a sign of the positive uses of new media, our exposure to contemporary Native American culture and arts is broadened, and networks enable Native American communities to connect with each other and to share resources. Now there are tremendous Native American-produced resources traditionally unavailable through mass media that guide us through what they have endured and inform about the vibrancy of their contemporary lives:

> Indian people are emerging from the invisibility of a romanticized past and mythological tipi and cowboy-killer culture confined to roaming the short grass prairie and uttering ecological and religious prophesies only. The voice that is emerging is a rich cultural mosaic that invites the listener in and shares a profoundly interesting and surprisingly universal story. Could it be that what it means to be an Indian contemporary society could be so much richer and interesting than all the fantasies non-Natives hoped, even guaranteed, it would be? That the audience would actually prefer stories about real people with whom we can all identify in their quest for meaning in this life? I am reminded of a time when, after reading a screenplay I had written, a non-Native who had never even met an Indian person before me jumped up and gave an impassioned speech about how an elder character would never say a line like "Let us come together and be of one mind." This single phrase is the recognized basis for the formulation of the Iroquois' Great Law of Peace and the resulting foundation of the Iroquois Confederacy, the acknowledged partial blueprint for the United States Constitution. Silence is not golden (Fraher p. 338).

Ultimately, because of the level at which new media are infusing our lives, I don't believe there exists anymore a pure culture in isolation of the global capitalist culture; and the reality on the ground with the kinds of kids I've worked with is that they are living in a hybridized mode of perception. For most people, especially the urbanized, it is not possible to call it living in two worlds, since each world in itself is its own conglomeration of mediaspheric niches. I'm reminded of Néstor García Canclini's (1995) observation, from his vantage of the hybridization of Latin American culture, that all cultures are border cultures. Furthermore, in terms of new media, we are all equal partners when it comes to the threat of mental and technological colonization, although GridThinkers may lack the necessary skills to subsist within it. If one goal of education is to help young people survive the larger mainstream society, then mindful engagement of media is absolutely necessary to enter the Net to enter a deterritorialized zone that transcends traditional boundaries. In my view it is not a world of have and have-nots, as has been the traditional critique of the world, but of the mindful or the mindless.

Could it be that the best way to surf the resonant interval is to explore the space of one's alienation? As a result of being a self-identified "alienated" person from my own knowledge community— punk rock— the problem of "alienation" is one of the chief reasons that media interest me. Moreover, I have traversed cultural milieus my whole life, from being a mixed-blood Latino in an East Los Angeles public high school, to living in the border region of the U.S.-Mexican border, to being a descendant of the Spanish conquerers teaching Native Americans the tools of digital media in New Mexico. To cope with these differing environments, I've had to stretch the capacities of my hemispheric abilities to their limits, a kind of brain yoga that has enriched my life.

I believe alienation can only exist in the context of GridThink, because it is GridThink that leads to disconnection. This is in keeping with Fredric Jameson's (1984) concept of the decentered self, which is so dislocated as a result of our disintegrating postmodern boundaries that one can't even be alienated. One of my earliest senses of this came as an undergrad at UC Berkeley when I took a class on contemporary Native American literature taught by Gunn Allen. The first day she posed a rhetorical question: "What if there were a nuclear war that destroyed your civilization, your family and your culture, and you were one of the few survivors. What would you write about?" The question shook me to the core. It made me deeply respect the manner in which indigenous people from around the world have survived the mind-numbing and soul-destroying project of colonialism. It also reminded me that Native Americans are in some sense canaries in our "global coal mind." Their catastrophe is our catastrophe. The struggle for survival remains, but I'm constantly reminded over and over of the clever strategies that human societies have developed in order to deal with adversity. In Gunn Allen's class we read numerous novels by Native American authors from the past 100 years. Consider that they were writing in a foreign tongue and alien mindset— alphabetic literacy— yet they incorporated many aspects of their cultural heritage, in particular storytelling, to struggle with and redefine their fast-changing reality. It goes to show that even though a communication system such as literacy may be strongly biased toward a specific way of perceiving and thinking, it can be effectively maneuvered.

Gunn Allen's course was similar to another literature class I took, "East vs. West," that was taught by an East Indian professor. The syllabus consisted of two halves, the first featuring books by Europeans in colonial territories, and the featuring those written by the colonized in Europe. (One that really sticks out is the farce *Bozambo's Revenge*, by an African author who imagined a Europe colonized by Africans where the main protagonist, a white man, struggles for survival in his occupied lands.) What I concluded was that for so-called Third World writers grappling with their marginalized identities, without a home or land to connect to and the false masks of the oppressors as a poor substitute for a true self, literature allowed writers to turn inward and to use a floating nonidentity nested in the workings of the human mind as a means of survival. I noted that in many ways their approaches to literature were similar to those of the beatniks, who warped and disfigured classical notions of writing to create literary jazz in the same way that the descendants of slaves transformed European instruments to play some of the greatest and most influential music ever created. I was coming to understand that oppressors produce artistic innovation within their ranks because there are always disenfranchised people who oppose the dominant mentality, regardless of skin color, who are able to tweak that which would control them. As a punk, I was one of them, and through participating in a self-organized community of cultural rebellion I felt that we had developed our own innovative survival strategies. We, too, became adept at using the oppressor's language—in our case mass media—to critique and maneuver in order to redefine ourselves and the world around us. To quote William Barrett's *Irrational Man* (p. 36), "... man's feeling of homelessness, of alienation has been intensified in the midst of a bureaucratized, impersonal mass society. He has come to feel himself an outsider even within his own human society. He is terribly alienated, a stranger to God, to nature, and to the gigantic social apparatus that supplies his material wants." In punk, we, too, were attempting to find a sense of place.

For my final project in Gunn Allen's class I contrasted Albert Camus's *The Stranger* (1946) —apparently one of the few books to make George W. Bush's limited reading list ... hmmm— and Blackfoot author James Welch's *The Death of Jim Loney* (1979). I was interested in comparing both books because they were grappling with the problems of colonization and alienation. I didn't have a way of articulating it at the time, but what I was aiming at was understanding how GridThink and HoloGrok articulated themselves in respective literature. *The Stranger's* central character, Meursault, is a French bureaucrat administrating in the colonial territory of Algeria. He kills an Arab (remember the Cure song?) and at the book's conclusion faces his death in classic existential fashion by musing: "As if that blind rage had washed me clean, rid me of hope; for the first time, in that night alive with signs and stars, I opened myself to the gentle indifference of the world. Finding it so much like myself — so like a brother, really — I felt that I had been happy and that I was happy again. For everything to be consummated, for me to feel less alone, I had only to wish that there be a large crowd of spectators the day of my execution and that they greet me with cries of hate" (Camus, p. 154).

The Death of Jim Loney's character is a half-breed, at war with his worlds. He ends up going on the lam and during the book's climax, runs into Mission Canyon as police hunt him down. There in the wilderness he finds solace, knowing that he will die in his "home." The difference between his perspective and that of the character in Camus's book is one of a fundamental paradigm that differentiates the cultural perspective on dislocation. For the "stranger," recognition of his spiritual poverty was enough. It is a highly individualistic solution, because it implicitly recognizes the Western axiom: I think, therefore I am. Camus is concerned with how the individual can construct, psychologically, a reality that validates the place of the Individual in an indifferent universe. Welch, on the other hand, rejects this resolution for a more cosmological solution. The powers in the universe become the transforming properties in Jim Loney. He resolves his alienation by going back to the land and by coming to terms with his vision quest. It is as if "I think, therefore I am" is transformed to "it all thinks, therefore I am." The latter concept, oddly enough, is now being confirmed by the most current scientific models of the holographic universe. Welch appropriately made Jim Loney a "breed" (half white, half Indian), which makes *The Death of Jim Loney* not a white or Indian novel, but an American novel. This is an important distinction because, as Barrett (p. 10) notes, "The American has not yet assimilated psychologically the disappearance of his own geographical frontier, his spiritual horizon is still the limitless play of human possibilities, and as yet he has not lived through the crucial experience of human finitude." Jim Loney is an American, and his experience is our experience because, although whites have not suffered the devastation that Indians have, the potential for a great ecological disaster is out there—and unless we develop practical tools to get a handle on our place in the universe, we may not survive.

Mending the Media Wheel

Standardizing written form by the pixel and instant optical recognition, turning all graphic signs into equivalent visual contrasts, serves Asia more than the West. Japan, which places a premium on digitization, has as well become the best if not the only producers of cameras, photocopiers, and scanners. The switching places of the planet's center and peripheries, a cruel trick of the larger historical development of things, is vouched for by the humble history of reprography.

Régis Debray, *Media Manifestos*

Brian Eno once famously remarked that the problem with computers is that there isn't enough Africa in them. I kind of think it's the opposite: they're bringing the ideals of Africa. After all, computers are about connectivity, shareware, a sense of global discussion about topics and issues, the relentless density of info overload, and above all the willingness to engage and discuss it all— that's something you could find on any street corner in Africa.

DJ Spooky

Native Americans have demonstrated time and time again a mastery of the rhetoric techniques that presumably would be used to oppress them; sometimes I wonder whether GridThinkers could survive if they were subjected to the same treatment. From creating internal media (as in radio, newspapers, film, and Web sites directed toward their own communities), to external media that communicate to other cultures' points of view, stories, concepts, and information, Native Americans have used ingenious survival skills to enable them to withstand Gunn Allen's metaphor that the Conquest was the destructive equivalent of nuclear annihilation. Consequently, whenever I get pessimistic about the state of the world, I reflect upon one of the more powerful experiences I had while working with a group of tribal youth in the Northwest when these communications technology tools were reappropriated for healing. The group was part of a summer employment program designed to create health- related messages for its community. I met the project coordinator at a Native American commercial tobacco prevention conference. She was a theater instructor by trade and we had a similar approach of combining art and social change through performance and media production. By the standards of mainstream society, it was as if her group of kids had been through war. But for life on the reservation, these kids were not atypical. Some were orphans, others had parents in prison, almost all were touched by the suicide of a family member, many struggled with addiction, and some were homeless. All acted and spoke as if the undead were present. Yet the spark of creativity and desire for change was very alive; they hungered to tap into the creative and participatory matrix that our media project created in order to envision a healthier future. As usual, in the beginning, our group dynamic struggled for equilibrium. Kids on the edge tend to act up out of the simple desire for attention and love. But as the workshop progressed, we slowly harmonized and built a group synergy that was unlike anything I have experienced. As we brainstormed our project goals, the kids defined their most pressing problem by using the metaphor of the broken medicine wheel. In our production process, we created a video that depicted mindful choices that would reconnect with life and community, and hence mend the broken wheel.

After we completed shooting, we approached the edge of a small inlet bay that's part of the Puget Sound. The calm, glassy water gloriously reflected the deep, blue light of a bright summer afternoon. A day earlier at this same spot one of the project mentors caught and smoked a salmon for us to snack on. Here the youths took turns fanning each other with feathers and sage smoke. Finally we held hands in a circle while the kids spoke of restoring the medicine wheel through art. One of the most troubled teens apologized to the group for initially acting up and being a disruptive presence. He said the experience of working in a group toward a common goal had helped him understand his own power to change his relationship with his agitated mental state. With heads dropped solemnly toward the fresh grass, I could hear sniffles emanating from the circle.

Such experiences remind me of a prescient remark by National Geographic Society explorer-in-residence Wade Davis (2004, p. 216), who has been traveling around the world to document so-called "vanishing" cultures: "There is a misconception that ... indigenous cultures ... are somehow fragile and delicate, destined to fade away as if by some natural law. Nothing could be further from the truth. In every instance these are dynamic, living cultures and languages being driven out of existence by identifiable external threats... [Indigenous] cultures are being overwhelmed by powerful external forces. This observation is discouraging, for obvious reasons, but also encouraging, for it implies that if humans are the agents of cultural destruction, we can also be facilitators of cultural survival." Gerald Vizenor (2000, p. 15) argues "survivance, in the sense of native survivance, is more than survival, more than endurance or mere response; the stories of survivance are an active presence."

Survivance is a concept that appears often in new literature about the contemporary state of Native America. It adds a dimension of resistance to the mere concept of survival and "victimry"; it affirms that Native Americans are rather ingenious in their ability to respond to the dominant culture. Their ability to transform the tools of mental colonization and oppression into empowering acts of literature and art is distinctive, demonstrating "the truism that in situations of extreme oppression, the oppressed of necessity know more about the oppressors' ways than the oppressors understand the ways of those whom they oppress" (Stromberg 2006, p. 6). In this respect, Native American people should not be regarded as has-been detritus hindering global progress, but as our greatest teachers on how to survive GridThink's "invader dreaming."

As has been demonstrated by the resourceful harnessing of media by Australian Aborigines, communications technology should ultimately be in the service of self-determination, sovereignty, and empowerment. Anthropologist and indigenous media scholar Faye Ginsburg (1994, p. 378) concludes from her work in Australia, "that the social relations built out of indigenous media practices are helping to develop support and sensibilities of indigenous actions for self-determination. Self-representation in media is seen as a crucial part of this process. Indigenous media productions and the activities around them are rendering visible indigenous cultural and historical realities to themselves and the broader societies that have stereotyped or denied them. The transitional social relations built out of these media practices are creating new arenas of cooperation, locally, nationally, and internationally."

Consequently, HoloGrokers may actually be poised to take great advantage of new communications technologies. Of all the cultural groups I've worked with across the United States, I've noticed that Native Americans get digital media literacy in ways that I believe is unique to their history and culture. It is my sense that because Native Americans are generationally closer to an oral tradition, and because they have been less conditioned by print literacy than European societies have, that they have the potential to leapfrog us in terms of harnessing digital media. It is increasingly clear from studies of knowledge work that the beneficiaries of new modes of engagement will be those who are most adept at "symbol management." I am assuming the mentality best suited for this activity belongs to the right-brainers who are spatial thinkers; it's possible that border jumpers the world over will fare better as future operators of new media systems than those conditioned by print. "This provides us with the intriguing but perhaps no longer so unusual situation of a people's moving rapidly from 'oral' to electronic society, but bypassing print literacy. Attention to the particulars of both the traditional system and accommodation to the imposed one offers insights into the limitations of our unexamined theories of unilineal media evolution" (Michaels 1994, p. 84). The emergent potential of the social Web (Web 2.0) based on communities and relationships could represent the most positive development of new digital technology for HoloGrokers and the greater society, enabling a process of organic, self-organizing affinities to develop beyond the traditional power structure: "Internet, with its particular reliance on visual imagery to be effective, is such that it is not so far removed from traditional forms of Indigenous communication—the sense of community is immediate, given without interpretation by non-Indigenous peoples, except as technicians and facilitators where needed. This may well be one of its main strengths, and the imperative to communicate, grounded in traditions of oral and visual forms of communication may, in fact, be one thing underlying the rapidity with which Indigenous peoples in First World nations have adopted the new technologies" (Smith, Burke and Ward 2000, p. 18).

If we look at brain functions we can also understand how these different perceptual modes operate. But I would like to take the discussion beyond culture, because I'm assuming that we all have similar brain structures that were developed in the context of a biological wilderness. That some cultures choose to emphasize different functions or biases of the brain is now a matter of choice because unlike past societies, we actually have the understanding and historical perspectives of different societies and systems to inform our path forward. We are at a great vantage point because we can learn and evolve very rapidly, but it's a matter of will and self-awareness. Without stepping outside our prevailing mediaspheric niche, it is unlikely that as a whole we will solve the crises facing humanity today.

If we were to extend the analogy of the circle as having an oral quality, and the cross as being an extension of the mental traits of alphabetic literacy and Cartesian thought, then new media have the potential of bringing the cross and circle together, since digital media have a hybrid quality of different thought systems and hemispheric biases of the brain. The bridge between them is like the "resonating interval" that connects the hemispheres' divergent functions. As McLuhan observes, the brain hemisphere that deals with the visual has dominated the other for thousands of years: "The isolation and amplification of one sense, the visual, is no longer enough to deal with the acoustic conditions above and below the surface of the planet.... The resonant interval may be considered an invisible borderline between visual and acoustic space ... Whenever two cultures, or two events, or two ideas are set in proximity to one another, an interplay takes place, a sort of magical change.

The more unlikely the interface, the greater the tension of the interchange" (McLuhan and Powers 1989, p. 4). In the best of possible educational settings, one would learn as completely as possible both the productive and perceptual characteristics of media. Thus, we should highlight, leverage, and foreground those cultural practices that are harmonious and circular: the circle reintroduces the circuit, feedback systems, ecological principles, and cybernetics into the GridThink realm.

The world of symbols that Mills writes about is opaque with hidden meanings and agendas. No doubt there are those in power grasping to control strategies, but they are increasingly weaker as the world, ironically aided by new communication networks funded by military research, is becoming more transparent, an example being the efforts of the U.S. government to unsuccessfully suppress documentation of its torture tactics; this is something unprecedented, given that 20 years ago these practices were known to researchers and human rights groups yet they would get scant coverage in the mainstream media (see Solnit 2004). Cry all we want about the power of propaganda, but it is still not nearly as powerful as the force of amateur photography as the case of Abu Ghraib demonstrates. The ubiquitous presence of surveillance is accompanied by its doppelganger of ubiquitous cell phone and digital cameras. "They" watch us while we simultaneously watch them. Our dirty little secrets are now broadcast across multiple channels around the world. This is not a force that can easily be dammed; the proverbial genie can't be put back into the circuit board.

The greatest benefit of our media, and it is a huge one, is that it externalizes human tendencies that historically have been suppressed and thus becomes a mirror, however distorted we may think. Yes, it means that often we are looking at our shadow, but it is a great teacher in the same way that our enemies can instruct us so much about ourselves. To think we are holier than the things we are against is a fallacy; I can assure you that some of our greatest media critics are not the most beautiful people in private (trust the art, not the artist, a friend once told me). We engage in our own forms of mental violence and addiction like anyone else; to pretend otherwise is to be like the people we claim to oppose. Media should be a tool to help uplift our society and enable us to become better people. As we are traversing media forms, languages, cultures, perceptions, nationalities, and hemispheric niches, we also need a sense of place and an ability to communicate across boundaries, meaning to be bilingual. We have to center ourselves within some kind of resonant interval, despite what Jameson says about the decentered self. It is only decentered if it is oriented to GridThink. The Mediacologist is bilingual, but in the perceptual sense: one must know how to operate with both sides of the brain in harmony.

In the Aztec (Mexica) pantheon, there were twin gods known as Quetzalcoatl and Tezcatlipoca. Like our experience within the postmodern world, their identities and forms were fluid. These gods existed within a cyclical calendar, one that assumes the sun rises and sets, along with the moon, no matter who rules the land. Twins are mirror images of each other, and in the case of these brothers, one represented light and unity (Quetzalcoatl, which is "Feathered Serpent," the linking of the earth and sky) and the other war and sorcery (Tezcatlipoca, better known as "Smoking Mirror"). With a mirror at the back of his head and one replacing his mangled foot, Smoking Mirror represented the earthly power of men. The Aztecs had their suspicions concerning the world of appearances, given Smoking Mirror's abilities to monitor the world via a mirror; likewise, if humans wished to see him, they, too, could access him through specular devices. The obsidian mirror enabled him to rule the universe, and its power lay in the ability to reflect back at someone's true nature. But as a remedy for the activities of humans, which invariably spiral to war and illusion, the Aztec poets responded with "flor y canto," flower and song. Moreover, by acknowledging that Quetzalcoatl and Tezcatlipoca were twins— one does not exist without the other— evil was just an illusion. When the Aztecs tell us that a pure heart will cast no likeness in the smoking mirror, they may be suggesting that GridThink's world of mediation may not be the appropriate place to search for tools of heart. The split between the left and right brains is a bit like the difference between love and fear. Love can encompass fear, but the opposite is not true.

Many years ago in Kentucky I was working with the mountain people typically labeled derogatorily as "hillbillies." Though they are not indigenous, I think they experienced something that Native Americans often have had to endure from mainstream society. The Appalachian term for do-gooders is "brain eaters"—the social workers, sociologists, and outsiders who are engaged in the social engineering that began with Lyndon Johnson's Great Society program that was designed to lift people out of poverty, but was also very paternalistic. The potential threat of the greater social agenda of digital media education is to produce yet another set of "brain eaters" without being sensitive to the very real needs of young people who are confronting thousands of years of psychic and mental colonialism. By taking a cue from the Hopis' insight about the use of cultural symbols, we could learn to draw a circle around our cultural cross and learn from the HoloGrokers of the world who have had to compost GridThink to survive. It's best that GridThinkers study fast, for we would be remiss to not learn the valuable insight that technological pedagogy without holism has disastrous consequences.

Incidentally, it's no accident that the astronomical symbol for planet Earth is a circle enclosed by a cross. For a harmonious world, that is the only way.

Redesiging Media Literacy

So how do we redesign media literacy to make it functional in the new, networked HoloGroking mediasphere that is emerging? Postman (1995, p. 175) felt that educators had too much power with which to manufacture conclusions judging by how they used language and framed questions: "Definitions, questions, metaphors—these are three of the most potent elements with which human language constructs a worldview. And in urging, as I do, that the study of these elements be given the highest priority in school, I am suggesting that world making through language is a narrative of power, durability, and inspiration. It is the story of how we make the world known to ourselves, and how we make ourselves known to the world." This aligns with Thomas S. Kuhn's criticism that scientific research produces answers that are predetermined to be correct.

McLuhan also emphasized the importance of framing questions. He was skeptical of Ivan Illich's radical assertion that if students are learning more information from outside school about how to survive, then schools should be closed. McLuhan (1997, p.108) responded by stressing: "What Illich fails to see is that when the answers are outside, the time has come to put the question inside the school, rather than the answers. In other words, it is now possible to make schools not the place for packaged information, but a place for dialogue and discovery." Postman would concur: "Whether it be molecule, fact, law, art, wealth, genes, or whatever, it is essential that students understand that definitions are instruments designed to achieve certain purposes, that the fundamental question to ask of them is not, Is this the real definition? or Is this the correct definition? but What purpose does the definition serve? That is, Who made it up and why?" (p. 183); and, "The idea is for students to learn that the terminology of a question determines the terminology of its answer; that a question cannot be answered unless there are procedures by which reliable answers can be obtained; and that the value of a question is determined not only by the specificity and richness of the answers it produces but also by the quantity and quality of the new questions it raises" (pp. 186-7).

Science journalist Steven Johnson (2005, p. 203) argues that media analysis tends to be about "appreciation," not "explanation." He contends, "The question is not: 'What are the creators of *Grand Theft Auto* trying to say?' The question is: 'How did *Grand Theft Auto* come to exist in the first place? And what effects does it have on the people who play it?'" Curiously, this little gem of an insight would have been completely missed if we had only listened to the "media pessimists," for this book was heavily derided and attacked because it argues that new media—and television— make us smarter. I don't know if I agree with that sentiment, because intelligence and "smart," if you have been following my argument closely, are the wrong things to measure because they are culturally relative concepts that measure particular types of thinking. I can say this, though: I am convinced that media do not make us "dumber." The Pew surveys may show that people who watch specific networks, such as Fox, are less *informed*, but they are not "dumber."

Johnson is promoting a design solution by asking the right question about media, because we change our emphasis from analyzing objects to understanding and designing systemic responses. When we ask, "what does the text say?" the question leads to a dead end, because it limits us to the content of the ad by presuming that it's a conduit of information objects. If it "says" something, then we presume the ad is telling us something rather than being in conversation within an overall system's design, including our paradigm filters that determine how we perceive and think with our given mediacological niches. Part of that process is gaining a deeper understanding of how our minds process information patterns, and which forms of media interact with the different brain hemispheres. Recalling Orr's comments, we are not simply trying to find a better analysis tool; we are designing minds for human survival.

Deconstruction Grid

To reiterate, the problem is that when information is treated as an isolated object it gets reified, the very problem that media critics claim to contend with, as in the complaint that capitalism "thingifies" human emotions, desires, and aspirations. The situation is that information does not replicate well in the mind of the viewer (for example, how many know the Ten Commandments word for word and agree with what they mean?). Media pedagogy operates in an old paradigm that isolates parts, dissects them, and claims to understand their inner workings in isolation of other systemic conditions (such as personal life experience, cognitive functions, environmental factors, community context, and education). It's a mechanical model of the world that does not reflect a more creative systems approach in which students are not just autonomous subjects learning about autonomous objects. By teaching information as objects rather than as "events" or relationships, we replicate the old system's "thought process" without fundamentally exploring its paradigm. For example, the Read-Text approach of media literacy (see *Figure 1*, page 11) is parallel to the newspaper model for objective reporting, which we know is greatly flawed because "objectivity" is a value and not the natural state of the world. This is a different issue than "fairness," which means you are open about your bias but also graciously explore differing views or approaches to a particular topic.

The Read-Text model is obviously more complex than the "Who, What, Where, When, Why, How" model of journalism, but the intent is the same: to find some kind of truthful, objective meaning within the media sample. Typically media activists use this deconstruction model to ask students to decode "what" the ad means. The following questions are part of the standard technique, with their updated versions to reflect a mediacological approach to the right:

- Who paid for the media?
- Who is being targeted?
- Why is the storyteller presenting this message?
- What kind of lifestyle is presented?
- What does the story say, and what does it mean?
- How is the story constructed?
- What is not being told in the story?
- Is the story accurate, fair, truthful, and complete?

Sometimes the above list also includes "What values/beliefs do you bring to the process?" and "What is the context?"

As you can see, this approach has a linear trajectory, and therefore only works on the level of object-based analysis. In the accompanying graph I deliberately laid out the Five-W Read-Text model into a cross-shaped grid. We descend from the top to bottom in a linear series of questions. In the middle we intersect with a horizontal line to represent rhetorical techniques (see Appendix Worksheet C). The power of suggestion, of course, is that I am symbolically demonstrating my belief that this approach is a GridThink way of responding to media. However, I think the linear deconstruction method is useful under two conditions: (1) it is done in the context of other approaches using the Media Wheel (see *Figure 2*, page 16), and (2) the questions changes from *what* to *how* so that we move away from the analysis of objects to one of design (see below). In the context of the Media Wheel we can better understand the underlying design of mediacological niches. The grid helps us with the analytical aspects of media, and is still useful to evaluate news reports, propaganda messages, health messages, and environmental messages. But if we continue to evaluate these atomized media artifacts without a systems approach, we won't achieve a deeper understanding necessary to transcend our dualistic predicament. By leveraging the HoloGrok characteristics of new media, we are introducing negative feedback into the system.

The alternative set of questions make up the Deconstruction Grid:

- How do your values influence your attitude or understanding of the media sample?
- How does the context influence the media example?
- How is the media example paid for? Who benefits from the business relationship (if any)?
- How does this ad address its audience? How is the audience constructed?
- How does the story reflect the storyteller's intention?
- How does the lifestyle reinforce the storyteller's intention?
- How does the story's text differ from its intention?
- How is the story designed? How does the storyteller use symbols to make the story's argument/point? How does it remediate other media?
- How is the storyteller framing the story? What is missing from outside the frame? What information or counter messages are deliberately ignored?
- Is the story accurate, fair, truthful, and complete? In what ways is this a healthy and/or unhealthy example of media?

Media Wheel

Unfortunately, the common media literacy approach to "deconstruct" is a form of Cartesian dissection. Like peeling the skin of a frog, we approach advertising as if it possesses finite working parts that, once known, can be fully explained and understood, and therefore controlled. This is true to a point, but as long as we maintain the dualistic approach that ignores the environmental, mental, and personal factors that contribute to a broader understanding of media, we will never transcend the very thing that traps us: our false belief that GridThink allows us to control our world. What is required is that we switch from a mentality of independence to one of interdependence. To do so we have to change how we do deconstruction.

Typically the Read-Text technique is done in isolation of other activities. In the mediacological approach, I introduce three other processes, all of which combine into the Media Wheel. In the Media Wheel graphic I break down four major components for exploring our mediacological niches: "Mind/Body," "Environment/Community," "Content," and "Medium." From this holistic approach we should be able to extrapolate the major concerns of critical media pedagogy: "Applying concepts of semiotics, feminism, multiculturalism, and postmodernism, a dialectical understanding of political economy, textual analysis, and audience theory has evolved in which media culture can be analyzed as dynamic discourses that reproduce dominant ideologies as well as entertain, educate, and offer the possibilities for counter hegemonic alternatives" (Kellner and Share 2007, p. 11). Because it is circular, there is no linear direction that is necessarily appropriate. You can cross different quadrants or choose to work in a clockwise or counterclockwise direction. In this construction, each sector is given equal weight. The Deconstruction Grid is placed within the "content" quadrant.

Mind/Body — As explained in the discussion of memes, the mind processes information in a nonlinear, holographic pattern-seeking approach that uses both sides of the brain. Additionally, the body is part of the equation, considering that media are experienced via the senses. Media are "tactile"; they touch our nerves. One can do a "sense ratio" exercise which involves making a chart of what senses are targeted by different media; for example, one might draw heavily on a particular sense (such as music and the ear), and one might eliminate another (such as sight). You could take an outline drawing of a person and assign a colored pen or pencil for each sense; then, for each media sample, color in areas according to input and sensation. The same exercise could also be done with an outline drawing of the brain hemispheres. Assuming that students understand the different functions of the brain hemispheres (as outlined in chapter one), the pens could also chart the mind with colors by representing different functions (such as language, symbols, type, and sound). Other techniques are to watch video with no sound, or to close your eyes while a video plays.

Environment/Community — This follows the path of the "community as text" discussion. This is where values, cultural bias, ideological context, and history are discussed. Exploring this area is far more investigative and nuanced. This is where mapping exercises would be very useful, from students making personal symbol maps, to mapping their communities based on different concepts (such as the locations of liquor ads in their neighborhood). Students could also make bioregional maps that help them locate where they live in the context of their natural surroundings. Also, recall from the discussion of mediaspheric niches that one way to tell what is predominant in a cultural landscape is to identify what symbols stick out in the cultural production of their home community. This would involve comparing a homegrown piece of media against one from the dominant mediasphere. If no local media exists, ancestral examples could be used, such Native American pottery designs or African weaving patters. Finally, remember the TC3 (technology, community, communication, and culture) plus P3 (power-and-place-equal-personality) formula. What variables could be added from this department? Another project could include an automatic writing exercise that begins with the line, "Where I come from ..."

Content — See the "Deconstruction Grid" discussion. This is the area where traditional media literacy is practiced (with the question changed from "what" to "why", and where symbols coding and decoding takes place).

Medium — This is perhaps the most holistic of all the quadrants because media forms incorporate the senses, the media itself, and the environment that they come from. One of the most critical aspects of this would be the discussion of space (as in the production of space) and energy consumption. For example, one of the key components of television is electricity and heterotopic space. This means it is a networked structure (as in it comes into existence from many different components and inputs), not just an object. What other nested forms are there in the media, such as lenses and photography? Or text? As an exercise it would be interesting to do a comparison of media using something like Franz Kafka's *Metamorphosis* in which students compared adaptations by reading the short story, a graphic novel version, listening to it read out loud, watching a filmed version, posting intertextual commentary on the Web, and then creating their own version or commentary using a medium of choice.

Worksheet A–Media Deconstruction Key

A note on technique: To turn this into a group exercise you may break students into smaller groups (of three or four) and distribute laminated magazine ads. The ads may feature topics according to the workshop's theme, such as tobacco, alcohol, cars, or political ads. I instruct students to work together to come up with some kind of understanding of the ad's meaning. The danger of the "what" approach is that they will respond robotically, that is, go down the list of questions and supply the "facts," such as, "This is a magazine ad paid for by Tobacco Giant International. It uses beautiful young people of color and is directed at urban youth. It shows that cigarettes are fun, and does not show any negative health consequences." Frankly, given the sophistication that young people have regarding media, the average student will already see this interpretation as being quite self-evident. Rather than have students read off a list of answers according to the grid's structure, ask that they create a presentation in a manner of their choosing that tells a story about the media they are examining; the story should be told from a broad perspective that underscores the design behind the overall production scheme, not as in "visual design," but as in system design. As you will see, if they approach it from the alternate set of questions that ask "how," they should come up with a deeper understanding of the media they are examining.

Normally the deconstruction technique is applied to a specific media object, such as a magazine or television ad. It can be applied to other media, but in short workshops I find it is simplest to stick to an ad. If you are working with students for an extended period, I suggest applying the model to increasingly more complicated forms of media to the point where the model breaks down (as in the case of nonlinear, collaborative media) to show the limits of the approach.

This deconstruction model is geared toward building an awareness of systems by asking "how" rather than "what." Use questions with "*" for shorter sessions or when working with younger students. You can also start the session by asking how symbols are used.

Take a media sample and answer the following questions in order:

- *How do the values you bring to the process affect your understanding?* Your knowledge, life experience, and biases are important to note before you start the process. These things are both assets and hindrances, but self-awareness is crucial. Start with your intuitive response, becoming aware of such things as shapes, colors, symbols, contrast, and sounds. What is your gut reaction? There is no right or wrong answer. Refer to "Worksheet B" for activities to generate an intuitive, aesthetic response.

- *How does the context influence the media example?* What outlet/venue does the media example come from? What kind of magazine or what channel did the sample appear in?

- *How is the media example paid for?** Who paid for it, and who profits from the business relationship (if any)?

- *Why is the storyteller presenting this message?** What messages and values are being expressed?

- *Who is being targeted?** Who is the story being told to? Who are the consumers of the message? Who are the readers of the media?

- *How is the portrayed lifestyle reinforcing the message?** Is it glamorized? How?

- *How is the story constructed?** What techniques does the storyteller use? What technological tools or attention hooks are used? Refer to "Worksheet C."

- *How does the story's text differ from what it means?** What is the surface text of the message? Is there a subtext?

- *How is the story framing the information? What is missing from outside the frame?** What information or counter messages does the media maker not want you to think about?

Worksheet B–Reading Aesthetics

Media are constructed by any combination of sound, moving images, and visuals. From a purely aesthetic view, TV ads are a kind of sequential art. When analyzing media, the following are aesthetic considerations:

What is your intuitive response? Do a free write (automatic writing exercise) to generate an unedited response to the media sample. This means continuously writing and keeping your pen or pencil moving for either a set amount of time or pages. The only rule in automatic writing is to never stop the hand from moving and to not edit, delete, or backtrack anything written down. Spur students by asking: Do any particular words come to mind when you look at this sample?

Consider the following:

Picture:

- How would you describe it to a person who cannot see?
- What are the shapes?
- What are the colors like? Do they have a mood?
- How is it spatially? Is it crowded or airy?
- What's the contrast between lights and darks?
- If it's a moving image sample (TV, film, animation), what is the style of editing? Is it fast or slow? A mix? How is the pacing?

Sound:

- How would you describe it to a person who cannot hear?
- What do you hear?
- Is it loud or quiet?
- Is there music? What kind? Is it something you know (pop), or is it ambient (background)? What is the style of music, who would it appeal to?

Intention:

- What was the media producer intending? How successful is the attempt?

Worksheet C–Hooks and Symbols

The most deceptive aspect of media is their very existence. Just by combining images, sound and text, and putting them in the context of other media, immediately legitimizes them as authentic descriptions of reality. Media also deploy specific techniques to construct believable stories. They hook our attention through psychological devices and technical tools. The techniques are vast and many, but some common ones are easily recognizable and are identified here. Remember, media producers will use many techniques not listed. Add to this list as needed.

Technical Tools:

- The mise-en-scène (set and setting inside the camera frame) creates a cultural and ideological structure. Is the set a concert, a mansion, a shopping mall? How glamorous is it?
- Camera angles enhance perspective, such as low angles that can give the subject power, or high angles that make the figure small.
- Close-ups provide emphasis.
- Sound effects animate products, giving them emotion.
- Accessories enhance the product. What's being associated with the product, such as clothes, props, and models?
- Lighting is used to draw your eye to certain details.
- Happy and attractive people are made-up and constructed to enhance the message. What kinds of people are in the ad?
- Music, popular songs, and jingles create mnemonic devices to program or trigger your memory (some songs are used for nostalgic reasons, while others are used to cross- promote products, such as cars and Moby's latest album).
- Products are sold by drawing from three main areas: fear, sex, and humor. (See below for more examples). Ads appeal to our emotions through "emotional transfer" and are rarely dependent on intellectual analysis.
- Special effects bring inanimate things to life and make them exciting. This is especially true with children-targeted ads.
- Editing is used to pace and generate excitement. Notice how military and video game ads have very fast cuts, usually a scene change every second.

Common Attention-Getting Hooks:

- *Emotional Transfer* is the process of generating emotions in order to transfer them to a product. For example, a Coke ad shows happy, beautiful people but tells us nothing about the product. The point is to make you feel good and to transfer that feeling to the brand or product. This is the number one and most important process of media manipulation.

- *Sex* sells, without exception.

- *Fear* messages are directed at our insecurities, such as "no one will like you if you have dandruff," or "bald people are losers." This is a very common technique, and extra attention is required to resist these messages.

- *Symbols* are easily recognized elements from our culture that generate powerful emotions, such as flags and crosses.

- *Humor* is often used because it makes us feel good and is more memorable. Notice how the majority of Super Bowl commercials are funny.

- *Hype*, don't believe it. Be skeptical of exaggerated claims, such as "America's favorite burger." Statements like these sound good but are meaningless and vague.

- *Fitting In* is a very common technique that tries to influence us by stating that if everyone else is buying the product, so should you. This is often seen in beer commercials, which promote a "big lie" that everyone drinks (alcoholics are the main consumers of alcohol).

- *Wink-Wink*: Media consumers have become so sophisticated and skeptical, that advertisers often self-reference their own techniques, even making fun of the fact that they are marketing to us. They "wink" at us to let us know that they are in on the joke.

- *Cute*. Children and animals always steal the show. "Family" and "girl next door" also fit this category.

- *Fetish* is typically used in car commercials. It deifies and anthropomorphizes inanimate objects in order to make them into living, vital things of desire.

- *Vague Promises* like "might," "maybe," and "could" are red herrings that divert our attention. "Super Glue may heal cuts better than Band-Aids" sounds absurd, but you will often hear claims as preposterous as this and it would still be true (because it can't be disproved).

- *Testimonials* are statements by people explaining why certain products are great. Famous, plain folk, or actors can do them. It's more powerful when someone we really like or respect endorses a product (such as Tiger Woods or Michael Jordan).

- *"Beautiful"* people are usually used to glamorize merchandise, especially unhealthy products such as alcohol, tobacco, and junk food. Models and actors generally have rare body types and don't represent average people; instead, they represent idealized notions of beauty that are constantly changing (compare, for example, Marilyn Monroe's body to a contemporary actress or model).

- *Famous People* such as Jordan make products appealing and attractive through association.

- *Ordinary People* are people that might be like you or me. This is common in ads, such as from Wal-Mart, that stress community or family.

- *It's Easy.* Simple solutions are often used to convince us that a product will solve our problems, such as "bald spot hair spray will get you a date," or "doorknob disinfectant wipes keep us healthy." Larger ideological messages are common as well, such as "cars conquer nature."

- *Macho* is generally used to appeal to males, but not exclusively. It demonstrates masculinity and male stereotypes; these are common in military and tobacco (print) ads.

- *Femininity* is another gender stereotype used in a variety of ads, from teen make-up commercials to alcohol ads.

- *Repetition* is done to reiterate a sales pitch over and over again, like the phone ads that repeatedly display and annunciate the phone number to access a company's service (for example the Carrot Top AT&T ads).

- *Big Lies* are exaggerated promises that are impossible to deliver, such as, "This is America's best all-weather vehicle" (also see hype). More subtle examples include "eating Sugar Corn Flakes will make you as strong as an Olympian." In propaganda studies the Big Lie represents a false statement that is repeated over and over, such as "Saddam Hussein possesses weapons of mass destruction."

- *Exotic.* This is the appeal of the "other"; it could be a beach location, tribal person, something strange or unknown. This is often meant to hook you through presenting something that is out of the ordinary or beyond our everyday experience.

- *Flattery* (see *wink-wink*) is used to make you feel good about being a consumer and to convince you that you are making the right choice when choosing a product." Smart people like you always buy premium aquariums when purchasing exotic fish ..."

- *Social Outcasts* generally represent a put-down or demeaning comment about a competing product or cultural group. This is not limited to ads, but is common in propaganda as well (such as "they don't believe in God").
- *Free Lunch* offers you something in addition to the product such as "buy one, get one free" or tax cuts. Freebies constantly hook us, but there are always hidden costs. Rarely is a thing truly free.
- *Surrealism.* Commercial media companies employ some of the brightest minds of the media world and often require cutting-edge artists to keep their material fresh (for example, MTV). Often, as a reflection of how unreal the fantasy world of media is, you will see juxtapositions and dream-like imagery that make no sense because the advertiser is trying to get your attention by presenting something strange and different.
- *The Good Old Days.* Images, fashion, film effects, and music depicting specific eras or subcultures are meant to appeal directly to the demographic represented in the ad (for example, a Volkswagen bus, classic rock music, and sepia tone effects).
- *Culture.* Niche marketing is more common as advertisers hone their messages for specific cultural groups. Latino-targeted ads, for instance, might have family scenes or specific uses of language.

Bibliography

Adorno, T. W. and J. M. Bernstein 1991. *The Culture Industry: Selected Essays on Mass Culture.* London, Routledge.

Anderson, B. R. O. G. 1983. *Imagined Communities: Reflections on the Origin and Spread of Nationalism.* London, Verso.

Andrejevic, M. 2004. *Reality TV: The Work of Being Watched.* Lanham, Md., Rowman & Littlefield Publishers.

Anonymous. "Fleeting Life." From http://www.geocities.com/katacha/aztec.html.

Armstrong, J. 1996. "Sharing One Skin": Okanagan Community. *The Case Against the Global Economy: And For a turn Toward the Local.* J. Mander and E. Goldsmith. San Francisco, Sierra Club Books: 460-70.

Atran, S. 2001. "The Trouble with Memes: Inference Versus Imitation in Cultural Creation." Human Nature 12(45): 331-81.

Bagdikian, B. H. and B. H. Bagdikian. 2004. *The New Media Monopoly.* Boston, Beacon Press.

Barrett, W. 1962 [1958]. *Irrational Man: A Study in Existential Philosophy.* New York, Doubleday.

Bateson, G. 2000. *Steps to an Ecology of Mind.* Chicago, University of Chicago Press.

Baudrillard, J. 1994. *Simulacra and Simulation.* Ann Arbor, University of Michigan Press.

Baudry, J. L. 1999. "Ideological Effects of the Basic Cinematographic Apparatus." *Film Theory and Criticism: Introductory Readings.* L. Braudy and M. Cohen. New York, Oxford University Press: 345-55.

Benjamin, W. and R. Tiedemann. 1999. *The Arcades Project.* Cambridge, Mass., Belknap Press.

Benkler, Y. 2006. *The Wealth of Networks: How Social Production Transforms Markets and Freedom.* New Haven, Conn., Yale University Press.

Berge, K. O. 1989. The Information Ecosystem, Putting the promise of the Information Age into Perspective. IN CONTEXT 12.

Berry, W. 2005. "Solving for Pattern." *Ecological Literacy: Educating Our Children for a Sustainable World.* M. K. Stone and Z. Barlow. San Francisco; Berkeley, Sierra Club Books: 30-40.

Blackmore, S. 1998. "Imitation and the Definition of a Meme." *Journal of Memetics* 2(2).

Bolter, J. D. and R. Grusin 1999. *Remediation: Understanding New Media.* Cambridge, Mass., MIT Press.

Boyer, P. 1999. "Cognitive Tracks of Cultural Inheritance: How Evolved Intuitive Ontology Governs Cultural Transmission." *American Anthropologist* 100(4): 876-89.

Boyer, P. and C. Ramble 2001. "Cognitive Templates for Religious Concepts: Cross-Cultural Evidence for Recall of Counter-Intuitive Representations." *Cognitive Science* 25: 535-64.

Boyle, S. C. 1997. *Los Capitalistas: Hispano Merchants and the Santa Fe Trade.* Albuquerque,

University of New Mexico Press.

Briggs, M. (2005). "Rethinking School Lunch." *Ecological Literacy: Educating Our Children for a Sustainable World*. M. K. Stone and Z. Barlow. San Francisco; Berkeley, Sierra Club Books: 241-49.

Camus, A. and S. Gilbert 1946. *The Stranger*. New York, A. A. Knopf.

Capra, F. 1983. *The Turning Point: Science, Society, and the Rising Culture*. Toronto, Bantam Books.

Carpignano, P. 1999. "The Shape of the Sphere: The Public Sphere and the Materiality of Communication." *Constellations* 6(2): 177-89.

Cavell, S. 1986. "The Fact of Television." *Video Culture: A Critical Investigation*. J. G. Hanhardt. Layton, Utah, G.M. Smith, Peregrine Smith Books, in association with Visual Studies Workshop Press: 192-218.

Center for Media Literacy "Five Core Concepts." Retrieved August 12, 2007, from http://www.medialit.org/pdf/mlk/14A_CCKQposter.pdf

Cheney, M. 1993. *Tesla: Man Out of Time*. New York, Barnes & Noble Books.

Cleary, L. M. and T. D. Peacock 1998. *Collected Wisdom: American Indian Education*. Boston, Allyn & Bacon.

Cotta Vaz, M. 2005. *The Lost Chronicles*. New York, Hyperion.

Couldry, N. and A. McCarthy 2004. *MediaSpace: Place, Scale and Culture in a Media Age*. London; New York, Routledge.

Crary, J. 1999. *Suspensions of Perception: Attention, Spectacle, and Modern Culture*. Cambridge, Mass., MIT Press.

Cubitt, S. 2005. *EcoMedia*. Amsterdam; New York, Rodopi.

Cummins, J. 1992. "The Empowerment of Indian Students." *Teaching American Indian Students*. J. A. Reyhner. Norman, University of Oklahoma Press: 3-12.

Davis, W. 2004. "A World Made of Stories: Saving the Web of Cultural Life." *Nature's Operating Instructions: The True Biotechnologies*. K. Ausubel and J. P. Harpignies. San Francisco, Sierra Club Books: 214-226.

De Bono, E. 1991. *I Am Right, You Are Wrong: From this to the New Renaissance: From Rock Logic to Water Logic*. New York, N.Y., U.S.A., Penguin Books.

De Kerckhove, D. and C. Dewdney (1997). *The Skin of Culture: Investigating the New Electronic Reality*. London, Kogan Page.

De Landa, M. 1997. *A Thousand Years of Nonlinear History*. New York, Zone Books.

de Zengotita, T. 2005. *Mediated: How the Media Shapes Your World and the Way You Live in it*. New York, Bloomsbury.

Debray, R. 1996. *Media Manifestos: On the Technological Transmission of Cultural Forms*. London; New York, Verso.

Deloria, V. and D. Wildcat 2001. *Power and Place: Indian Education in America*. Golden, Colo., Fulcrum Publishing.

Diamond, J. M. 1999. *Guns, Germs, and Steel: The Fates of Human Societies*. New York, Norton.

Dick, P. K. 1991. *Valis*. New York, Vintage Books.

Doane, M. A. 1990. "Information, Crisis, Catastrophe." *Logics of Television: Essays in Cultural Criticism*. P. Mellencamp. Bloomington, Indiana University Press: 222-229.

Doane, M. A. 2002. *The Emergence of Cinematic Time: Modernity, Contingency, the Archive*.

Cambridge, Mass., Harvard University Press.

Fixico, D. L. 2003. *The American Indian Mind in a Linear World: American Indian Studies and Traditional Knowledge.* New York, Routledge.

Foucault, M. (1998). "Different Spaces." *Aesthetics, Method, and Epistemology.* J. D. Faubion. New York, New Press: 175-85.

Fraher, D. (2003). "About Native American Artists, Inc." *Genocide of the Mind: New Native American Writing.* M. Moore. New York, Thunder's Mouth Press/Nation Books: 337-339.

Freire, P. and D. P. Macedo 1987. *Literacy: Reading the Word and the World.* South Hadley, Mass., Bergin & Garvey Publishers.

Garcia Canclini, N. 1995. *Hybrid Cultures: Strategies for Entering and Leaving Modernity.* Minneapolis, University of Minnesota Press.

Garcia, R. L. G. and J. G. Ahler 1992. "Indian Education: Assumptions, Ideologies, Strategies." *Teaching American Indian Students.* J. A. Reyhner. Norman, University of Oklahoma Press: 13-32.

Gatto, J. T. 1992. *Dumbing Us Down: The Hidden Curriculum of Compulsory Schooling.* Philadelphia, New Society Publishers.

Gee, J. P. 2003. *What Video Games Have to Teach Us About Learning and Lteracy.* New York, Palgrave Macmillan.

Gibson, W. 2003, December 4. "Books of the Year 2003." Retrieved September 18, 2007, from http://www.economist.com/books/displaystory.cfm?story_id=E1_NNGVRJV.

Ginsburg, F. 1994. "Embedded Aesthetics: Creating a Discursive Space for Indigenous Media." *Cultural Anthropology* 9(3): 365-82.

Gitlin, T. 2002. *Media Unlimited: How the Torrent of Images and Sounds Overwhelms Our Lives.* New York, Owl Books.

Gladwell, M. 2002. *The Tipping Point: How Little Things Can Make a Big Difference.* Boston, Back Bay Books.

Gladwell, M. 2005. *Blink: The Power of Thinking Without Thinking.* New York, Little, Brown and Company.

Gómez-Peña, G. 1996. *The New World Border: Prophecies, Poems, & Loqueras for the End of the Century.* San Francisco, City Lights.

Goody, J. 1995 (1977). *The Domestication of the Savage Mind.* Cambridge (UK); New York, Cambridge University Press.

Govil, N. (2004). "Something Spatial in the Air: In-Flight Entertainment and the Topographies of Modern Air Travel." *Mediaspace: Place, Scale and Culture in a Media Age.* N. Couldry and A. McCarthy. New York, Routledge: 48-54.

Gunn Allen, P. (2003). "'Indians,' Solipsisms, and Archetypal Holocausts." *Genocide of the Mind: New Native American Writing.* M. Moore. New York, Thunder's Mouth Press/Nation Books: 305-15.

Habermas, J. 1989. *The Structural Transformation of the Public Sphere: An Inquiry into a Category of Bourgeois Society.* Cambridge, Mass., MIT Press.

Hacking, I. 1998. *Mad Travelers: Reflections on the Reality of Transient Mental Illnesses.* Charlottesville, Va., University Press of Virginia.

Hall, S. S. 2004. "I, Mercator." *You Are Here: Personal Geographies and Other Maps of the Imagination.* K. Harmon. New York, Princeton Architectural Press: 15-9.

Heinlein, R. A. 1991. *Stranger in a Strange Land.* New York, Putnam.

Hirschfeld, L. 2002. "Why Don't Anthropologists Like Children?" *American Anthropologist* 104(2): 611-27.

Hirschfeld, L. 2005. "Children's Understanding of Racial Groups." *Children's Understanding of Society.* M. Barrett and E. Buchanan-Barrow. New York, Psychology Press.

Hoechsmann, M. 2007. "Advertising Pedagogy: Teaching and Learning Consumption." *Media literacy: A reader.* D. P. Macedo and S. R. Steinberg. New York, Peter Lang: 653-66.

Holmgren, D. 2002. *Permaculture: Principles and Pathways Beyond Sustainability.* Hepburn, Victoria, Holmgren Design Services.

hooks, b. 2001. "Eating the Other: Desire and Resistance." *Media and Culture Studies: KeyWorks.* M. G. Durham and D. M. Kellner. Malden, Mass., Blackwell Publishers.

Hyer, S. 1990. *One House, One Voice, One Heart: Native American Education at the Santa Fe Indian School.* Santa Fe, N.M., Museum of New Mexico Press.

Illich, I. 1971. *Deschooling Society.* New York, Harper & Row.

Innis, H. A. 1999 [1951]. *The Bias of Communication.* Toronto, University of Toronto Press.

Jameson, F. 1984. "Postmodernism, or the Cultural Logic of Late Capitalism." New Left Review (146).

Jenkins, H. 2006. *Convergence Culture: Where Old and New Media Collide.* New York, New York University Press.

Johnson, S. 2001. *Emergence: The Connected Lives of Ants, Brains, Cities, and Software.* New York, Scribner.

Johnson, S. 2005. *Everything Bad Is Good for You: How Today's Popular culture is Actually Making Us Smarter.* New York, Riverhead Books.

Kanwisher, N. 2000. "Domain Specificity in Face Perception." *Nature Neuroscience* 3(8): 759-763.

Kellner, D. M. and J. Share (2007). "Critical Media Literacy, Democracy, and the Reconstruction of Education." *Media literacy: A Reader.* D. P. Macedo and S. R. Steinberg. New York, Peter Lang: 3-23.

Kilbourne, J. 1999. *Can't Buy My Love: How Advertising Changes the Way We Think and Feel.* New York, Touchstone.

Kilpatrick, J. 1999. *Celluloid Indians: Native Americans and Film.* Lincoln, University of Nebraska Press.

Kist, W. 2005. *New Literacies in Action: Teaching and Learning in Multiple Media.* New York, Teachers College Press.

Klein, N. 1999. *No Logo: Taking Aim at the Brand Bullies.* New York, Picador.

Klein, N. 2007. *The Shock Doctrine: The Rise of Disaster Capitalism.* New York, Metropolitan Books/Henry Holt.

Korten, D. C. 2006. *The Great Turning: From Empire to Earth Community.* San Francisco, Bloomfield, Ct.; Berrett-Koehler, Kumarian Press.

Kuhn, T. S. 1996. *The Structure of Scientific Revolutions.* Chicago, University of Chicago Press.

La Grange, J. 2006. "50 - RE: Do we need to be concerned about how young people encounter and interact with race and ethnicity issues online and in other digital media technologies? And what do our histories teach us?" Retrieved October 26, 2006, from http://community.macfound.org/openforum.

LaDuke, W. 2005. *Recovering the Sacred: The Power of Naming and Claiming.* Cambridge, Mass., South End Press.

Lakoff, G. 1995. "Body, Brain, and Communication." *Resisting the Virtual Life: the Culture and Politics of Information.* J. Brook and I. A. Boal. San Francisco, City Lights 115-29.

Lasn, K. 2000. *Culture Jam: How to Reverse America's Suicidal Consumer Binge—and Why We Must.* New York, Quill.

Laszlo, E. and Club of Budapest. 2001. *Macroshift: Navigating the Transformation to a Sustainable World.* San Francisco, Berrett-Koehler Publishers.

Lévy, P. 1998. *Becoming Virtual: Reality in the Digital Age.* New York, Plenum Trade.

Lewis, J. 1991. *The Ideological Octopus: An Exploration of Television and its Audience.* New York, Routledge.

Liu, A. 2004. *The Laws of Cool: Knowledge Work and the Culture of Information.* Chicago, University of Chicago Press.

Livingstone, R. trans. 2005. *In Search of Wagner*, by T. W. Adorno. London; New York, Verso.

López, A. 2000, July. "Journey of Riches." *Santa Fean Magazine.*

Lotman, Y. M. 2001. *Universe of the Mind: A Semiotic Theory of Culture.* New York; London, I.B. Taurus.

Lovink, G. 2002. *Dark Fiber: Tracking Critical Internet Culture.* Cambridge, Mass., MIT Press.

Luhmann, N. 2000. *The Reality of the Mass Media.* Stanford, Calif., Stanford University Press.

Mander, J. 1996. "Technologies of Globalization." *The Case Against the Global Economy: And for a Turn Toward the Local.* J. Mander and E. Goldsmith. San Francisco, Sierra Club Books: 460-70.

Mander, J. 2002 [1978]. *Four Arguments for the Elimination of Television.* New York, Perennial.

Masayesva Jr., V. 2006, October 26. "50 - RE: Do we need to be concerned about how young people encounter and interact with race and ethnicity issues online and in other digital media technologies? And what do our histories teach us?" Retrieved October 26, 2006, from http://community.macfound.org/openforum.

Mau, B., J. Leonard, et al. 2004. *Massive Change the Institute Without Boundaries.* London; New York, Phaidon.

McCarty, T. L. and R. Schaffer 1992. "Language and Literacy Development." *Teaching American Indian Students.* J. A. Reyhner. Norman, University of Oklahoma Press: 115-131.

McChesney, R. W. 1999. *Rich Media, Poor Democracy: Communication Politics in Dubious Times.* Urbana, University of Illinois Press.

McKibben, B. 1992. *The Age of Missing Information.* New York, Random House.

McLuhan, M. 2002 [1962]. *The Gutenberg Galaxy: The Making of Typographic Man.* Toronto, University of Toronto Press.

McLuhan, M. 2002 [1964]. *Understanding Media: The Extensions of Man.* Cambridge, Mass., MIT Press.

McLuhan, M. and Q. Fiore 1968. *War and Peace in the Global Village: An Inventory of Some of the Current Spastic Situations That Could be Eliminated by More Feedforward.* New York, McGraw-Hill.

McLuhan, M. and M. A. Moos 1997. *Media Research: Technology, Art, Communication.* Amsterdam, G&B Arts International.

McLuhan, M. and B. R. Powers 1989. *The Global Village: Transformations in World Life and Media in the 21ˢᵗ Century.* New York, Oxford University Press.

Menchú, R. and E. Burgos-Debray (1984). *I, Rigoberta Menchú: An Indian Woman in Guatemala.* London, Verso.

Michaels, E. 1994. *Bad Aboriginal Art: Tradition, Media, and Technological Horizons.* Minneapolis, University of Minnesota Press.

Mills, C. W. 1963. "The Cultural Apparatus." *Power and Politics.* Ed. I.L. Horowitz New York, Oxford University Press.

Morin, E. 1971. *Rumour in Orleans.* New York, Pantheon Books.

National Indian Education Association and Center for Indian Education 2005. *Preliminary Report on No Child Left Behind in Indian Country.* http://niea.org/sa/uploads/policyissues/29.23.NIEANCLBreport_final2.pdf.

Nhat Hanh, Thich 1988. *The Heart of Understanding: Commentaries on the Prajñaparamita Heart Sutra.* Berkeley, Parallax Press.

Ong, W. J. 1982. *Orality and Literacy: The Technologizing of the Word.* London; New York, Methuen.

Orr, D. W. 1994. *Earth in Mind: On Education, Environment, and the Human Prospect.* Washington, D.C., Island Press.

Parks, L. 2004. "Kinetic Screens: Epistemologies of Movement at the Interface." *Mediaspace: Place, Scale and Culture in a Media Age.* N. Couldry and A. McCarthy. New York, Routledge: 48-54.

Pelfrey, R. H. and M. Hall-Pelfrey (1985). *Art and Mass Media.* New York, Harper & Row.

Peters, J. D. 1999. *Speaking into the Air: A History of the Idea of Communication.* Chicago, University of Chicago Press.

Plato 1964. "Book III The Republic." *Philosophies of Art and Beauty: Selected Readings in Aesthetics from Plato to Heidegger.* A. Hofstadter and R. F. Kuhns. New York, Modern Library: 8-51.

Postman, N. "What Is Media Ecology?" Retrieved July 12, 2007, from http://www.media-ecology.org/media_ecology/

Postman, N. 1993. *Technopoly: The Surrender of Culture to Technology.* New York, Vintage Books.

Postman, N. 1995. *The End of Education: Redefining the Value of School.* New York, Knopf.

Pungente, J. "Media Literacy Key Concepts." Retrieved August 12, 2007, from http://www.media-awareness.ca/english/teachers/media_literacy/key_concept.cfm

Reddy, M. 1993. "The Conduit Metaphor: A Case of Frame Conflict in Our Language About Language." *Metaphor and Thought.* A. Ortony. Cambridge [UK]; New York, Cambridge University Press: xvi, 678 p.

Redfield, K.A. 2006. "Inside the Circle, Outside the Circle." *American Indian Rhetorics of Survivance: Word Medicine, Word Magic.* E. Stromberg. Pittsburgh, University of Pittsburgh Press: 149-164.

Reyhner, J. A. and J. M. O. Eder 2004. *American Indian Education: A History.* Norman, University of Oklahoma Press.

Rushkoff, D. 1996. *Media Virus!: Hidden Agendas in Popular Culture.* New York, Ballantine Books.

Rushkoff, D. 1999. *Playing the Future: What We Can Learn from Digital Kids.* New York, Riverhead Books.

Said, E. W. 1997. *Covering Islam: How the Media and the Experts Determine How We See the Rest of the World.* New York, Vintage Books.

Shlain, L. 2007. *Art & Physics: Parallel Visions in Space, Time, and Light.* New York, Harper Perennial.

Silverblatt, A. 2001. *Media Literacy: Keys to Interpreting Media Messages.* Westport, Conn., Praeger.

Smith, C., H. Burke, et al. 2000. "Globalization and Indigenous Peoples: Threat or Empowerment?" *Indigenous Cultures in an Interconnected World.* C. Smith and G. K. Ward. Vancouver, UBC Press: 1-24.

Soleri, P. 1973. *The Bridge Between Matter & Spirit is Matter becoming Spirit: The Arcology of Paolo Soleri.* Garden City, N.Y., Anchor Books.

Solnit, R. 2004. *Hope in the Dark: Untold Histories, Wild Possibilities.* New York, Nation Books.

Sperber, D. 1985. "Anthropology and Psychology: Towards an Epidemiology of Representations (The Malinowski Memorial Lecture 1984)." Man (N.S.) 20: 73-89.

Sperber, D. 1996. *Explaining Culture: A Naturalistic Approach.* Oxford, UK; Cambridge, Mass., Blackwell.

Sperber, D. and L. Hirschfeld 2006. "Culture and Modularity." *The Innate Mind: Culture and Cognition.* T. Simpson, P. Carruthers, S. Laurence and S. Stich. New York, Oxford University Press.

Sterelny, K. 2006. "Memes Revisited." *British Journal for the Philosophy of Science* 57: 145-165.

Stromberg, E. 2006. "Rhetoric and American Indians." *American Indian Rhetorics of Survivance: Word Medicine, Word Magic.* E. Stromberg. Pittsburgh, University of Pittsburgh Press: 1-11.

Swisher, K. and D. Deyhle 1992. "Adapting Instruction to Culture." *Teaching American Indian Students.* J. A. Reyhner. Norman, University of Oklahoma Press: xiii, 328 p.

Teish, L. 2004. "Planet 'Hood: Making the World Our Home." *Nature's Operating Instructions: The True Biotechnologies.* K. Ausubel and J. P. Harpignies. San Francisco, Sierra Club Books: 211-213.

Twitchell, J. B. 1996. *Adcult USA: The Triumph of Advertising in American Culture.* New York, Columbia University Press.

Tyner, K. R. 1998. *Literacy in a Digital World: Teaching and Learning in the Age of Information.* Mahwah, N.J., Erlbaum.

Virilio, P. 1991. *Lost Dimension.* New York, Semiotext(e).

Vizenor, G. 2000. *Fugitive Poses: Native American Indian Scenes of Absence and Presence.* Lincoln, University of Nebraska Press.

Walker, J. A. 1994. *Art in the Age of Mass Media.* Boulder, Colo., Westview Press.

Warhus, M. 1997. *Another America: Native American Maps and the History of Our Land.* New York, St. Martin's Press.

Waters, F. 1975. *Mexico Mystique: The Coming Sixth World of Consciousness.* Chicago, Sage Books.

Weber, S. and A. Cholodenko 1996. *Mass Mediauras: Form, Technics, Media.* Stanford, Calif., Stanford University Press.

Weinberger, D. 2007. *Everything Is Miscellaneous: The Power of the New Digital Disorder.* New York, Times Books.

Welch, J. 1979. *The Death of Jim Loney.* New York, Harper & Row.

Wilson, R. A. 1986. *The New Inquisition: Irrational Rationalism and the Citadel of Science.* Phoenix,

Ariz., Falcon Press.

Wood, D., W. L. Kaiser and B. Abrams 2006. *"Seeing Through Maps: Many Ways to See the World."* Amherst, Mass., ODT, Incorporated.

Wright, R. 1992. *Stolen Continents: The Americas Through Indian Eyes Since 1492.* Boston, Houghton Mifflin.

Zimmerman, L. J., K. P. Zimmerman, et al. 2000. "Cyberspace Smoke Signals: New Technologies and Native American Ethnicity." *Indigenous Cultures in an Interconnected World.* C. Smith and G. K. Ward. Vancouver, UBC Press: 69-86.

Studies in the Postmodern Theory of Education

General Editors
Joe L. Kincheloe & Shirley R. Steinberg

Counterpoints publishes the most compelling and imaginative books being written in education today. Grounded on the theoretical advances in criticalism, feminism, and postmodernism in the last two decades of the twentieth century, Counterpoints engages the meaning of these innovations in various forms of educational expression. Committed to the proposition that theoretical literature should be accessible to a variety of audiences, the series insists that its authors avoid esoteric and jargonistic languages that transform educational scholarship into an elite discourse for the initiated. Scholarly work matters only to the degree it affects consciousness and practice at multiple sites. Counterpoints' editorial policy is based on these principles and the ability of scholars to break new ground, to open new conversations, to go where educators have never gone before.

For additional information about this series or for the submission of manuscripts, please contact:

Joe L. Kincheloe & Shirley R. Steinberg
c/o Peter Lang Publishing, Inc.
29 Broadway, 18th floor
New York, New York 10006

To order other books in this series, please contact our Customer Service Department:

(800) 770-LANG (within the U.S.)
(212) 647-7706 (outside the U.S.)
(212) 647-7707 FAX

Or browse online by series:
www.peterlang.com